P9-DIY-892

# The Good Girl's Guide
# to Getting Lost

# The Good Girl's Guide
# to Getting Lost

*A Memoir of Three Continents,*

*Two Friends, and One Unexpected Adventure*

## Rachel Friedman

Bantam Books Trade Paperbacks ❦ New York

*The Good Girl's Guide to Getting Lost* is a work of nonfiction.
Some names and identifying details have been changed.

A Bantam Books Trade Paperback Original

Copyright © 2011 by Rachel Friedman

All rights reserved.

Published in the United States by Bantam Books,
an imprint of The Random House Publishing Group,
a division of Random House, Inc., New York.

BANTAM BOOKS and the rooster colophon are
registered trademarks of Random House, Inc.

"The Suicide Song," lyrics and music composed by Michal Imielski.
Produced by Michal Imielski.

Photographs are from the author's collection.

LIBRARY OF CONGRESS CATALOGING-IN-PUBLICATION DATA

Friedman, Rachel.
The good girl's guide to getting lost : a memoir of three continents, two
friends, and one unexpected adventure / Rachel Friedman.
p. cm.
ISBN 978-0-385-34337-4
ebook ISBN 978-0-553-90820-6
1. Friedman, Rachel. 2. Women travelers—Biography. 3. Voyages and
travels. I. Title.
G226.F75A3 2011
910.4—dc22 2010052236

Printed in the United States of America

www.bantamdell.com

4 6 8 9 7 5 3

Book design by Virginia Norey

For my parents, my support
For Carly, my guide
For Martyn, my home

*How do we go about turning into
the people we are meant to become?*

—LUCY GREALY,
*Autobiography of a Face*

# Contents

# Contents

[4]  *Our heroine takes up residence with three strangers of various and unaccountable natures, one of whom is an entirely different kind of girl species indeed.*  34

[5]  *Our heroine considers some advice from her unnervingly wild new friend. She finds steady employment and an even steadier drinking habit, though it is not her intention to imply that the fine country of Ireland is in any way responsible for such youthful debauchery, other than to note that it does have a very high number of excellent bars in conjunction with an overabundance of rainy days. Our heroine might choose church, another fine, dry place in which to ponder life's questions, but alas, she is Jewish.*  50

[6]  *Our heroine returns to her former life as a student, where she normally would be comforted by books and the lofty ideas contained therein, but finds herself unable to muster the necessary enthusiasm for anything but list making and bellyaching. Somehow she finds the will to both graduate and entertain her relatives. An unexpected call answered.*  62

## Part Two: Australia

[7]  *Our heroine alights on Australia, a faraway land she has only read about, and not much at that, and is ferried to the exotic suburbs of Sydney by her native friend and guide. Though she is much jet-lagged and rather perplexed by her host's progenitor—a skilled caller of birds—she nevertheless finds herself quickly and comfortably ensconced in her welcoming new abode.*  75

[8]  *Our heroine embarks on a brief journey to the Outback, wherein she meets a rock of indecent proportions and heat of insulting voracity. Locates gainful employment of coffee and curry, philosophizes and questions—questions and philosophizes.*  87

## Part Three: South America

# Contents

## Author's Note

I've made every effort to relate my experiences accurately and to ensure that those represented still speak to me after reading this book. Some names have been changed, for privacy's sake, and some time collapsed, for narrative's. I relentlessly hounded my Australian travel companion to corroborate my memories; still, some of them are fuzzy around the edges. But all of this happened—and much more, too.

# Part One

---

## Ireland

# [ 1 ]

*Our heroine, verily drowning in self-pity at the tender age of twenty, embarks on a grand adventure that is not yet either grand or an adventure but, rather, a hastily concocted plan to escape the confines of her current existence and the quotidian yet oppressive pressures contained therein.*

The plane descends through a thick belt of clouds into blinding light. I haven't fully registered the transition from night to day until sun pours through the oblong windows, jarring me out of semi-consciousness. For the past eight hours, ever since I waved goodbye to my father at the airport and marched myself onto a plane bound for Dublin, I've been wondering if I was in some altered state when I planned this trip, because the reality of it feels distinctly like a bad hangover. Being bathed in golden light only adds to my surreal arrival. Isn't it supposed to be raining in Ireland?

We thud against the tarmac, and my fellow passengers shuffle to life, folding in half to gather their belongings from beneath the seats. Eager to depart, the frizzy-haired girl in the row ahead of me springs up like a jack-in-the-box as soon as the seat-belt light clicks off for the last time. I remain belted in, doing my best deer-in-headlights impression. I might just stay on this plane all day, ride it round-trip like I did once when I was little and too frightened to get off the revolving ski lift at the top of the mountain. The elderly woman sitting next to me, a tiny person with papery hands and merlot-stained lips, leans over and taps the book sitting in my lap: *Angela's Ashes.*

"Oh, that poor Angela," she sighs in one of those lilting Irish accents that make a grocery list sound like a Yeats poem. "Heaven knows she did the best for those boys, then Frank comes along and airs their business to the whole bloody world." Her tone is heavy with disdain, as if the author sold naked photos of his mother to the tabloids, not penned a Pulitzer Prize winner about his Irish childhood. Coming from the land of "all publicity is good publicity," I'd just assumed McCourt's native country embraced his memoir, proudly adding him to their long list (suspiciously long, really, considering Ireland's size) of distinguished writers. But like I was wrong about the weather, it seems I am mistaken about this, too.

Here are the facts of the present moment. It's 2002. I'm twenty years old. I've just embarked on four months in a foreign country alone. I'm carrying six hundred dollars in traveler's checks, money saved up from waitressing last semester. I booked two nights in a Dublin hostel before I left. Other than that, I've got no plan. And this greatly confounds me because I *always* have a plan. At least I used to be the kind of girl who always has a plan.

In a few months, I'll be a college senior. School has been the organizing principle of my existence for as long as I can remember, and I have no idea what comes after that. My academic parents raised me to be ambitious and goal-oriented. In particular, my father, a film professor, molded me into a second-wave feminist whose duty it was to burst forth into the world and crush the male competition. He used to routinely deconstruct the PG films we watched together to comment on the functioning of the male gaze, say, or to illustrate how gender is performative. I still remember his lecture on *The Little Mermaid:* "It's just not equi-table. Ariel has to give up everything for this guy—first her voice, then her home. On a very real level, Rachel, she has to give up who she is. What are we to make of this?"

"Jesus, Lester," my mother would sigh.

I was eight.

But I listened. I always listened.

I was a scholarship kid at a small, eccentric college-preparatory high school, the kind of place where you juggled two dozen AP classes at once. Much of my teenage world revolved around studying, carefully calibrated extracurricular activities, and end-less rounds of practice SATs.

There was never a question of whether I would attend college— only where. And I was desperate to go, both because my parents' divorce when I was fifteen had left me without a place I truly identified as "home" and because I genuinely loved school, where the formula for success was straightforward. Study and you get good grades. Simple, safe. But no class has prepared me for the post-student leap I am facing now, and being an eternal over-achiever who bases her self-worth on her GPA, I am woefully ill-equipped to take on the unpredictable, unscheduled life awaiting me after college graduation. I am terrified of this unknown.

In the Dublin airport, confident, purposeful travelers swirl around me, off to meetings and reunions and homes. All of them seem to know exactly where they are headed—except me. For a few moments, I am frozen and directionless, lost amid the drift-ing crowds. My brain works in slow motion, registering my tasks: pick up suitcase, exchange money, find hostel.

I've never been to a foreign country alone, though I've been abroad a few times, starting with Germany when I was ten. My brother Dan was stationed there, and I flew over with my par-ents to visit him. We rented a car and dashed all over Europe. Ten days in at least as many cities, pausing just long enough to snap photos. It was exhausting, and I'm told I didn't appreciate much of it. Every few years, my brother reminds me, shaking his head with renewed disgust, that I slept (slept!) through the pristine Alps.

After my sophomore year of high school, my parents discharged me to Israel with a temple youth group, even though I had recently articulated that I was "so over Judaism." But it was difficult to stay pissed off for an entire summer, especially on a bus with twenty-five other teenagers and Yamud, our gigantic, hairy Israeli graduate-student guide who insisted on blasting "We Built This City on Rock and Roll" on his boom box every morning at six A.M. as we boarded the bus, still bleary-eyed. If you were drooping sleepily into the aisle, one of his enormous flailing wrists would smack you in the head. You might slip quietly into a window seat in the back and shut your eyes only to find his meaty fingers jabbing them open.

Each of us was assigned an identifying number and forced to shout it out (in order) at least twelve times a day, making our trip resemble one long *Sesame Street* episode. Peter, an unruly Canadian, insisted on substituting his name for his number. He was Rastafarian and claimed he was simply "too burned out to remember my number, brotha." We found this, along with the dreadlock wig he wore over his shaved head and the fact that he smoked an invisible joint for hours at a time, across-the-board hilarious. Our Israeli guides, so unlike our regimented parents back home, just smirked and checked him off the list. They told the bus driver—a skinny man with the same real cigarette burning out of the corner of his mouth, seemingly for days, as if fueled by miracle menorah oil—that we were all accounted for and ready to go.

My souvenir from this first semi-independent trip to a faraway land was a small tattoo. I acquired it in a dingy corner of

Jerusalem from one of those muscly guys who have inked every available nook of their flesh canvas. The tattoo is a simple quarter-sized blue flower on the lower-right side of my back: five blue petals with a hint of purple at the base, outlined in black ink. Tiny tendrils poke out like rays of sunlight. I arrived at the tattoo parlor with two quivering guy friends who insisted I go first. I smiled reassuringly up at their worried faces as the needle scratched into my bare flesh. I felt incredibly wild.

But this trip to Ireland is my first time alone in a foreign country: no family, no friends, no crazy Yamud making sure number twenty-eight is on the bus. I have only myself to rely on—which is precisely what worries me. My friends' and families' collective concerns echo in my brain: *Where will you live? How will you find work? Won't you be lonely?* I don't know. I don't know. I don't know. All I knew was that I needed to get away. I hadn't actually pictured myself on the other side of that conviction.

"You're so brave to go off on your own," my best college friend, Erica, told me a week ago, bestowing "brave" upon me with the distinct tone usually reserved for the word "insane." Erica is interning at an art gallery in New York City this summer. It's the kind of thing I think I should be doing, trying out my career instead of skipping town for no discernible reason.

I can barely heave my massive red suitcase off the conveyor belt. It feels twice as heavy as when my father and I launched it into the trunk of his Hyundai before heading off to the airport. I'm here for just over four months (an impossibly long time, now that I think about it) and have, I think, packed accordingly. Several outfits for day or night, flats for walking, sandals for warm days, sneakers for running, boots for trekking (will I be trekking anywhere? I don't trek back home), two pairs of pretty heels for nights out, though, of course, I don't know anyone in Ireland to go out with. I've packed toiletries, twelve books, twenty pairs of underwear, ten pairs of socks, three sweaters, two jackets, three swimsuits, enough vitamin C to turn me into an orange, and two fluffy bath towels.

A guy with greasy blond hair and Atlantic-blue eyes hoists a backpack onto his shoulders. He snaps it around his waist. It's half the size of his body, and I could fit four of them inside Big Red. Surely, with such modest gear, he must be traveling only for a week or two. And he must be moving around a lot. I plan on staying right here in Dublin. My instinct, as always, is to settle down, dig my heels in, and work hard at something, even if that something is only waiting tables. But it will be waitressing in a foreign country, far away from home. The backpacker strides swiftly out the door, looking carefree and unencumbered, leaving me with the exhausting thought of maneuvering my monstrous luggage through an unfamiliar city.

Why Ireland? Well, for starters, four hundred dollars (my parents' generous, hesitant contribution) is enough to purchase a student work visa, something available in only a handful of countries, two of them—Australia and New Zealand—instantly ruled out because they are too far to find cheap airfare. Also, the rainy Irish weather appeals to me. If I am going to be miserable, I want the skies to match my mood. Last fall I took a course on Joyce, and I've been conjuring up long, dreary days wandering like Ulysses, rainy nights in cafés punishing myself with *Finnegans Wake*. This portrait appeals to my romanticized notion of melancholy, the kind I plan to undertake in Ireland, not at all like my current depressive state of pondering my postgraduate future, which consists of numbly attending lectures, sleeping twelve hours a day, and when I'm feeling really ambitious, staring blankly at the wall. Most of all, I just want to be somewhere else. When it comes to Ireland, it's not so much a matter of *Why here?* as *Will it be far enough?*

It is not solely the post-graduation unknown that has unhinged me recently. It is also the fact that I was not expecting to be facing the abyss at all because I've had a very specific plan for my life since fourth grade. Up until recently, I fully expected to transition smoothly into the "real world," riding into the gloriousness of my adulthood on the coattails of my one true calling: music. Viola, to be specific, the instrument I devoted myself to since I was eight. I even spent my freshman year of college studying with the principal of the Boston Symphony. But somehow, everything fell apart that year, and I was no longer on my way toward being a professional musician.

One might assume that this is an exciting turn of events. A serious child who, from an early age, dedicated herself with rather extreme discipline to one thing, is now liberated. While all the other kids were able to acquire and discard hobbies, figuring out their likes and dislikes, merrily wandering the aimless path of youth, this poor dear was stuck practicing and practicing and practicing. And now she's free! The possibilities are endless!

Oh, the possibilities are *endless*. They weigh me down, tramp around my brain in their muddy boots. I was happy along my determined, orderly path. I don't want options. I don't want to explore. My future used to be a straight, sturdy line, but now it's all blurry, as if I'm under anesthesia.

On the plane, I diligently studied my guidebook's entry on the hostel where I'm staying, but I have no clue how to actually get there. A new surge of confident travelers envelops me, and when the wave subsides, I have been spat out on the other side, face-to-face with two angular women behind an information kiosk.

"Hi? I'm trying to get to my hostel?"

The one not texting whips open a map and expertly traces my route. "Right, you're after the Airlink bus, which is outside now. Take it to the civic offices. Walk up Fishamble Street onto Lord

Edward Street. Your hostel is on the corner." She circles the spot twice with her pen, then pushes the map toward me and flashes an obligatory smile.

"Thanks," I mumble. Forward motion, I think. Just keep moving.

I will myself through a revolving door and out into Ireland, where my bus is sunning itself. Three massive steps lead up into it, though there might as well be one hundred.

"You're grand," says the driver encouragingly, but I cannot see any graceful way to get myself plus Big Red inside.

I briefly consider splurging on a taxi, but it seems like an unnecessary indulgence when the bus is right here. It's cheap—and it's waiting. Okay, I tell myself. You may very well be about to make a complete ass of yourself, but no one knows you. Come on. Get on the bus. Get. On. The. Bus. I put two feet on the first step and then turn back around to face my engorged red opponent. Twisting the suitcase sideways, I drag it awkwardly up onto the step with me. Only half of its girth makes it; for a moment we are in a perfect precarious balance of bag and girl. Just as I am about to lose the battle to the overhanging weight, two steroidal angels reach down, and my suitcase floats the rest of the way in. We shove it into the space designated for luggage, leaving enough room for someone else's small purse or perhaps a wallet.

I did it. I'm on a bus alone in a foreign country. For a fleeting second, I feel something surprising alongside the familiar emotions of confusion, doubt, and apprehension. Later, I'll look back and recognize this rush of excitement as my first glimpse of what exactly it means to travel alone in a faraway land: I can go anywhere. I can do anything. And the all-important: I can be anyone. Soon enough I'll come to crave this feeling, seek it out and cultivate it, but right now it's an indecipherable sensation, quite possibly, I consider, indigestion.

# [ 2 ]

*Our heroine discovers a strange tribe of people with no steady residence or employment, among them one of her neighbors to the north, a riddling Italian, three fearsome giants, and a confounding native who speaks a strange repetitious tongue. She bravely orders a meal to be eaten all alone while pondering the age-old question: Is one really the loneliest number?*

I've never stayed in a hostel. I didn't even know what a hostel *was* until I opened my *Let's Go Ireland 2002* to a helpful explanatory entry: "Hostels are generally laid-out dorm-style, often with large single-sex rooms and bunk beds, although some offer private rooms for families and couples. They sometimes have kitchens and utensils for your use, bike or moped rentals, storage areas, and laundry facilities. The Internet is becoming an increasingly common hostel amenity, though Web access is often via mind-numbingly slow connections." It sounds kind of like sleepaway camp. And it's by far the cheapest accommodation going, which means it's for me.

Besides being at the top of an unforgivingly steep cobblestone hill, my hostel, Kinlay House, is fitted with a seemingly impenetrable door. After I'm buzzed in, I manage to pull the handle at the exact wrong moment, getting nothing but an unsatisfied click as it relocks. After three tries, I finally get the timing right and find myself red-faced but inside. An unimpressed blonde slouches behind a counter, her Rapunzel hair twisted into a thick braid that hangs drowsily over one shoulder. Her green corduroy dress has patches for pockets. Like the girls in the airport, she is surrounded by maps and pamphlets advertising attractions and tours. Here, however, there seems to be no organizing order to the papers, which are fanned out on the counter and stuffed into hanging racks behind her. She's tracing her middle finger on one for Dublin historic walking tours.

"How many nights are you staying?" she asks in an accent I can't quite place—Russian, maybe.

When I tell her two, she glances at her computer but doesn't ask if I have a reservation. Since it doesn't seem like a piece of information that would strike her as particularly interesting, I keep it to myself.

She eyes my massive suitcase before informing me with a smirk that my room is on the third floor. I hand over forty euros.

"There's an elevator, but you won't be able to fit inside," she tells me with unchecked glee. "The stairs are right behind you."

Freshly polished, slippery-looking oak steps spiral high into the air. But I have made it this far, and the thought of collapsing onto a bed fuels my determination. I twist. I pull. I curse. I am breathless when I finally reach the third floor; I lean against the railing, panting. My gaze follows drifting smoke to a room down the hall where three pairs of bare feet stretch out toward a blaring television.

A dripping male body in a discolored towel and flip-flops emerges from the door across from me. A high-pitched, virginal "Oh!" slips out of my mouth before I can stop it. In my college dorm, half-naked guys strolled through the halls at all hours, but I'm caught off guard now. Since there was a check-in area, I've revised my notion of hostels from a summer camp to some place more like a cheap hotel, where people typically remain fully clothed in the common areas. Shower dude ignores my prudish exclamation and continues down the corridor, trailing squishy wet footsteps.

My room is the farthest one from the stairs. The hobbit-sized door rests askew on its hinges, forcing me to lean both down and slightly to the right in order to enter. A guy my age with shaggy blond hair and the shadow of a light beard is propped up on one of the beds, reading a guidebook.

"Oh!" I respond stupidly for the second time in three minutes. I knew this hostel was co-ed, but I didn't realize that meant there would be boys in the *same room.*

"Hey," he says. It's an infinitely more articulate greeting than anything I've offered so far.

The room's furnishings are minimal. A low table accompanies each bed. All four mattresses sport matching maroon sheets with colorful quilts neatly folded atop. I survey the church steeple and small swath of Dublin rooftops through the triangular window above my bed. The sun is lost behind clouds that have descended rapidly upon the city in the last ten minutes. A mass of cranes pierce the gray sky. I saw them on the way in from the airport, too. The whole city seems to be in a state of renovation. New buildings shoot up higher and higher next to structures that look as old as time.

"Are you headed out?" the stranger inquires. He looks up at me. No, I'm not headed out, I think. Headed out where? All I want is to sleep, to just close my eyes and start over again tomorrow, when I'm less overwhelmed.

But I nod because it seems, from the way he asked the question, that I should be headed out, that heading out is the thing you do once you arrive in a new city alone with no idea what you're doing there.

"Want some company?"

"Sure," I say. I gingerly tear the Dublin section out of my Ireland guidebook, and then there is nothing left to do but leave the room with this stranger, still grimy after my long flight.

Matt is Canadian. He's been in Dublin for a few days, waiting for his brother to turn up. They're backpacking for eight weeks through Europe; the next stop is Germany.

"What are your plans for the summer?" he asks me.

"Well, I might...I'll probably just...I'm not sure, I guess," I stammer.

"If you have time, you should go to Galway. Try living out there for a few weeks and see how you like it."

Of course I do have time. Time is all I have, stretching out like a waking dog, but go live somewhere I've never heard of?

"It's great crack," he declares.

Here we go. Here's where things with your new drug-dealer buddy get weird, I think. Matt must notice me flinch, because he rushes to explain. "*Craic*—that's the Irish term for a good time. You know, good drinks, good company, good music."

"Of course," I bluff unconvincingly.

"Where to?" Matt asks.

When I shrug, attempting to convey that I'm easygoing as opposed to completely disoriented, he tells me that if we take a left, we'll hit Trinity College. Now, Trinity I know. All the best universities, whatever nation, have been drilled into me by my father. McGill is the Harvard of Canada, St. Andrews the McGill of Scotland, Oxford and Cambridge a debatable tie for most prestigious in England. Every time my dad lectures somewhere elite, he procures for me a souvenir sweatshirt from the campus store, the way some people collect stamps or magnets from different cities.

Trinity is a fortress. Spiky wrought-iron gates surround the massive stone structures. An enormous wooden door serves as the main entrance, though people move only through a small aperture cut into it, no wider than to allow two at a time. A constant glut of tourists and students dribble through it.

Inside, the sounds of the city are muted. We traverse the cobblestones, pass the rows of bicycles lining every path and the looming arch where tourists listen attentively to guides, and head to the Book of Kells exhibition, where ornate Latin manuscripts transcribed by Celtic monks are housed. In those days, a young monk entered the monastery at fifteen or sixteen years old. He received a tonsure, a shaved head, the mark of a slave. He also accepted a new name. Then he undertook a life devoted to the study of God's word, fasts, and manual work. It is a sign of my somewhat disturbed state of mind that I'm jealous of this imagined monk who, day after day, transcribed minute letters by hand with a creaky calligraphy pen (and it's not like they had Wite-Out back then). I'm jealous because he knew his exact purpose in life.

It's nearly six P.M. when we emerge, and the narrow streets are buzzing with Dubliners returning home, their heads bent against the rain. The air suddenly feels cold and lonely. I move closer to Matt without realizing it, awkwardly bumping into him. I'm apologizing when I glance into a brightly lit pub where the customers are glowing like an altogether different species from the rush-hour traffic. I'm delighted by this timely reminder that I am spending the summer before my twenty-first birthday in a country where the legal drinking age is eighteen.

"Let's get a beer," I say conspiratorially.

"After you." Matt bows chivalrously as he opens the door for me.

We order Guinness, since that seems like the Irish thing to do, though I notice only two elderly men nursing the same thick concoction. All the younger patrons are sipping fruit-accessorized cocktails. The bartender tips my pint glass to one side. He pours it nearly full with creamy brown liquid before setting it atop a sticky bar mat. The beer trickles down like sediment, light, foggy brown giving way to deeper colors. A minute later, he returns, holds the glass directly under the tap this time, and places a small spoon upside down over the rim, the hump extending up toward the ceiling. This time he pushes the handle away from him, letting the beer cascade over the spoon and become a half inch of dense white foam. It's not sweet—not by a long shot—but the bitterness is more subdued than when I tried it back home, and it goes down smoothly. We order a second one, then a third.

I know absolutely no one in Ireland other than this stranger I have just spent the afternoon with. I imagine my lawyer mom finishing up the day's client meetings, my professor father being greeted by students' groans as he distributes a pop quiz. Erica is back in Connecticut, maybe unpacking the contents of her dorm room, unloading clothes into her childhood dresser or shopping for a new skirt to wear the first day of her internship.

I imagine the people whose lives are most intertwined with mine, and I realize life has gone on without me. The planet has not imploded because I, the girl who has always done what is expected of her, decided not to, just this once. As centuries of inebriated Irish before me have surely found strange wisdom at the bottom of their Guinness glasses, so too do I as I polish off my third one: apparently, I am not the center of the universe, and the earth will continue to revolve around the sun whether or not I decide to spend a purposeless summer in Ireland. This is the kind of revelation that is liberating when you are drunk, and rather depressing when you are sober, but luckily, at the moment I am the former.

Back at the hostel, the last thing I mumble to Matt before drifting into a deep, drooly sleep is "see you tomorrow," but in the morning he and his bags have disappeared. He is replaced by three massive Dutchmen who make my oversize suitcase look like doll furniture. They appear as I am exiting the room, and naturally "Oh!" is all I can think to gasp at the disconcerting sight of them.

"Uh," one of them replies in a cross between a greeting and a grunt. He steps aside to let me pass. Each guy is bigger than the next, like a matryoshka set. All top six feet and are thick as tree trunks.

"Hello!" says the last of the threesome cheerily. He offers me his baseball mitt of a hand. "We are from the Netherlands."

This cannot be happening. Staying with Matt was one thing, but bunking with three Brobdingnagians is another thing altogether. As I hurry downstairs, I think that the Dutchmen are probably at this very moment sweating and farting and lying around the room in their gigantic underwear. But none of this is as worrisome as the fact that I have to sleep in there with them. As if this is even an option; whoever put those three hulks in a room with a five-six American girl who has never set foot on foreign soil on her own is seriously deranged. I'll bet it was that snarky blonde at the front desk.

I hear my mother's voice. If I'm uncomfortable, I need to be an adult (I *am* an adult, after all) and let the person in charge know. After all, I doubt my parents will be too thrilled when their youngest daughter is molested and mutilated, her lifeless body thrown into the River Liffey in the dead of night. Right? Right, I tell myself as I screw up my courage and walk determinedly down the last few steps only to realize that the blonde has been replaced by a stubbly-bearded guy rolling a cigarette. He looks how I imagine *National Geographic* writers look: rugged, self-reliant, and unimpressed with squeamish little girls who request a room change.

Shit, shit, shit. I backtrack from the group of travelers milling around the desk examining street maps and strapping on well-used backpacks. *National Geographic* notices my presence and gives me a questioning look. I'm frozen close enough to the counter to seem like I need something but just far enough away that, since I'm not actually saying anything, I must appear a smidge nuts. The seconds tick by in slow motion. Sunlight streams through the windows, and the fear I felt in the enclosed space of my room drains from my body as if I'm waking from a bad dream; a dark blush blooms on my cheeks. You're being ridiculous, I admonish myself, and scurry toward the scent of breakfast.

The kitchen is bursting with activity. Tables are painted bright summer greens, blues, and oranges. The chairs are all different shapes and sizes and look as though they have been gathered at yard sales. Now *this* is more like summer camp. People still wearing pajama pants rub their eyes. More disciplined groups pore over guidebooks and journals. Couples gaze at each other across their cereal. Tea and coffee steam from mismatched mugs, while various shades of bread pop nonstop out of an overworked toaster. It's as if I've arrived late at a party where everyone has already been introduced. I sit down at the edge of a long table, and a short, dark-haired guy plops down across from me.

"Hello to you!" he says joyously, as though we are old friends, then he immediately launches a litany of questions at me.

"What's your name?"

"Where are you from?"

"How long have you been here?"

"Where are you going?"

"What have you seen?"

"Do you know when the next bus to Limerick is?"

Pedro, a Spaniard living in Italy who is traveling around Europe for a few months, tells me all about Ireland—where I should go and the names of several restaurants where I should eat if I make it up to Belfast or down to Cork. Later, I will pull out my guidebook so I can circle his suggestions, but I'll find none of them in there.

"Where will you go next?" he asks excitedly.

"Maybe Galway," I say, surprising myself by considering Matt's advice.

"*Che bella!*" he shouts with embarrassing enthusiasm. "The food is shit," he announces next without warning, and I don't know whether he means Dublin, Galway, or the hostel. "I am headed to Galway in two weeks. I will give you my phone." He pulls out a pen and a small cloth-covered book bound with a piece of fraying string. He throws a ripped piece of paper with a number scrawled on it in my direction. "*Ciao!*" he yells, already out the door.

People seem to be moving at warp speed in this hostel, while I feel like I have barely managed to catch my breath.

Eventually, I have to eat. Yesterday I got by on the sandwich I bought in the Dublin airport, but today I've awakened to grumbling insides. The free toast distracts my stomach for a few hours before I'm forced to locate some real food. But how to do it? Do I walk into a restaurant and say, "Table for one"? Should I strike up a conversation with someone here at the hostel, then, like Matt did when I arrived, ask if they want some company? Only when I am dizzy with hunger do I finally succumb to entering a pub a few doors down from the hostel. I sidle up to the bar and request a pint of Guinness (nearly a meal itself, I've already been told several times). I ask the bartender for one of the bags of potato chips clipped to the wall beside the cash register.

"Crisps," he corrects me with a smile.

You have to be able to sit quietly in your own skin in order to eat alone, and that's something I've never been very good at. I'm great at being by myself with a task, but I've always been too self-conscious to be alone in public without at least the company of a book to bury myself in. But I feel okay after that Guinness. So I order a turkey sandwich and another beer to wash it down. Usually, these days, my brain races around, filing mental lists of anxieties, goals, and questions. But right now my thoughts are focused on my new environment. I take in the pub, the gleaming oak bar against the dull, scuffed stools, a handful of Irish guys to my right debating something to do with "the footie." I consider the little differences I've come across so far, like the fact that Irish garbage cans are all labeled with the Gaelic word *bruscar* and that they are called "bins" here. Soothing differences because they are distracting ones. I might just be fine here all on my own.

Or... maybe not. When I return to my room around eleven P.M., the Dutchmen are gone. Their packs are open, the various contents splayed across their beds, waiting for their owners' return. I lie waiting, too. Three drunken Hercules banging into the room is not something you want to catch you off guard. At two A.M. they finally stumble in, consecutively knocking some part of their head or shoulders against the crooked doorframe. When they collapse on their beds, the mattress springs squeal in protest against their bulk, and they are snoring into oblivion before their beds even quiet beneath them. Once again, I feel stupid for worrying, for not knowing the rules of my new surroundings.

Around four A.M., I think I have drifted off to sleep when a drunken Irish stranger bursts through the door. He shakes my shoulders, and I leap out my bed as if it's on fire.

" 'Ello! 'Ello! 'Ello!" he greets me with feverish insistence.

Backed up against the wall, I attempt my own echoing introduction. "Hello. Hello. Hello."

This only serves to confuse and agitate him. I expect the giants to come to my rescue at any moment, but they continue slumbering obliviously, hard-liquor breath curling out through their nostrils. The Irishman and I face off silently for a few more seconds before a lightbulb appears above my intruder's head and he offers a brief but surprisingly coherent summary of our exchange: "Oh feck—I'm in the wrong room." As quickly as he entered, he trips back out, scraping his nose on the doorframe on the way.

It's all I can do to resist calling my father in tears and telling him I want to come home. Instead, I give up on sleep altogether. At five A.M. I dress in the dark and head out to catch the earliest possible bus to Galway. At this point in my travels and in my life, I still regard changing course as a personal failing. I don't yet have the hindsight to realize that some places don't fit quite right, for whatever reason, so sometimes it's best to cash in your chips and give it a go somewhere new, even if a mere twenty-four hours before you didn't even know that place existed.

# [ 3 ]

*Our heroine undertakes a journey of insignificant length and*
*significant comfort to the west of Ireland. She relateth her*
*impressions of Galway, a very fine city, and explores the*
*traveler's constant companions—transience and loneliness.*
*She battles a mighty winged one and determines to find*
*gainful employment and permanent residence.*

I arrive at the station in time to catch the six-thirty A.M. bus to
Galway. The few times I took buses any distance back home, they
were filled with unkempt college students (myself included) and
what seemed like the entire population of smokers from any
given region. There was always one guy drinking in the back,
and far more than one on the Chinatown buses I rode to Manhattan to visit friends. Their don't-ask-questions seats smelled
like ash and sweaty bodies.

But the buses in Ireland are clean and new-looking. They're
painted with bright red stripes and sport a leaping red Irish
setter. The usual gaggle of twentysomethings is present, as disheveled and boisterous as their American counterparts, and
there is always a set of too-young Irish parents with their
mouthy kid, the mom telling a story about someone who is a

"gobshite" and the dad concurring this person is indeed a "fecking eejit." They wear matching tracksuits, as is the fashion here, though I never once glimpsed an Irish person out for a jog my entire time in Ireland. But there are also well-dressed elderly Irish on the bus, white-haired women perched demurely with handbags on their laps and becapped men making quiet conversation with the bus driver. Excited tourists ooh and ahh, and preteens in plaid school uniforms bounce on and off. Even the drunk guy seems slightly less smelly and offensive, like it's all a good laugh that he can't quite locate the equilibrium necessary to remain upright as he makes his way down the aisle. The whole experience is somehow neater and tidier, like Ireland itself, a journey after which you don't feel the need to peel off your outermost layer of skin in order to feel human again.

Everything here is smaller than in the U.S.—cars, houses, portions, people. Once we leave the bus station, it's a quick glide alongside Dublin's rangy River Liffey before we emerge out into the countryside. Small stone and stucco cottages set out on trim patches of grass line the roads. Moss has taken hold anywhere it can, growing like fur on the roofs. The more modern houses look ostentatious and out of place where they occasionally pop up, and the developments—where, as in U.S. suburbs, it's row upon row of the same—are positively embarrassing themselves among the quaint, aged homes. Stone fences in various degrees of disrepair partition the green pastures that stretch for miles in all directions, dotted with sheep and cows and the occasional trash-burning fire.

It takes only three and a half hours to traverse the width of Ireland's midsection, from the east to the west coast. We alight on Galway at the edge of Eyre Square, near John F. Kennedy Park, renamed after his 1963 visit, and it takes only a few minutes to cross it and find myself on the pedestrian-only cobblestone street that forms the center of this small city, whose population is about one fifth of Dublin's. Growing up, I'd always considered myself a city girl woefully trapped in a small suburb where the biggest attraction was the local swan pond. I vowed to slough off my geographical birthright as soon as humanly possible, which, when you're a good middle-class girl from upstate New York, means college. I have not been home for more than a few days at a time since my mom helped me tack my ratty Janis Joplin poster to the white wall of my freshman-year dorm room.

So I'm wary of the sense of relief sneaking over me as I drag my suitcase through Galway's compact city center. I pass between the unfamiliar shop signs that stand at attention on either side of the main thoroughfare: Vodafone, Cambridges, Boots, Eason's, Hynes, Flanagan's, Ladbrokes. It's ten A.M. on a Saturday, but, like me, the town is barely awake, bleary-eyed and uncoordinated. People in cafés halfheartedly suck cigarettes and stare blankly through one another. The street is currently cluttered with delivery trucks allowed to descend briefly to unload, their boxes disappearing into various back doors. The stench of stale beer lingers faintly in the air, whipped around by the heavy winds washing the city clean. From somewhere close by, the aroma of fried fish spills out onto the streets like a thick haze.

My new hostel is at the end of the main street. Outside the front door, a violinist tunes her instrument, case open and ready for donations. If my dad were here, he'd toss a dollar in. "So it won't be you one day," he'd say, half joking.

I started begging my parents to buy a piano when I was five, after my father played a recording of a haunting Chopin nocturne at dinner one night. My great-grandfather was a pianist who accompanied silent movies, so maybe my musical inclinations were genetic. Or it could have all started with my mother. When she was pregnant with me, she read the emerging literature on the connections between music and intelligence and often placed a pair of large headphones around her expanding belly. I can see her rocking back and forth in our favorite chair, eyes closed and head back, an old quilt across her lap, absorbing

Beethoven into our bloodstreams. She adores "Ode to Joy." Pure and direct communication, accessible without being ordinary, that's how Leonard Bernstein described it, though I've never asked my mother why it spoke to her.

My parents decided it was safer for me to try out the guitar first: smaller, less risky an investment in case the music thing turned out to be a whim. Also, my father had a guitar. We could play together, they reasoned, my dad conveniently forgetting that his instrument was more of a shrine to his sixties youth than anything currently getting much use. His father-daughter folk-duet dream died hard. Classical guitar, where you use your fingers instead of a pick to delicately coax the sound from the strings, and not rainy-day Bob Dylan songs, is where my heart was from the very beginning.

I was eight when I first laid hands on a viola, practically ancient in the world of string beginners. When I first dropped my long, thin bow down onto the strings, coaxing out deep, rumbling sounds from the belly of my instrument, the notes were wobbly, lilting at the edges of the pitch as opposed to cutting right through the center of it like they're supposed to—but I didn't care. In the beginning, all noises were equally beautiful and fascinating because I was making them. I'd press my nose against my horsehair bow and inhale the rosin slathered on. When I practiced for long stretches, the tips of my left fingers became stained charcoal black where the strings of my viola dug tiny canals into the soft flesh. Only my thumb remained pink, arched against the wooden neck that extended out from my viola's curved body, which protruded from my own jaw. In this space, squeezed between my left shoulder and chin, we fit together like puzzle pieces. For a long time, I remained convinced that it was us—us bendable humans—who were made for violas and not the other way around.

Once in a while my parents came upstairs after I finished practicing. My father would take out his neglected guitar, scratched and dull, and strum it while we sang Eagles and Peter, Paul and Mary songs. "Leaving on a Jet Plane" was by far my favorite, even though my mother sounded so sad when she sang it. She has a beautiful voice—soft but operatic. I searched their faces. They smiled at each other and at me, and I thought it must be the music making them feel that way, because outside that room, they frowned a lot.

Mostly, though, they stayed downstairs while I practiced, my mother making dinner and my father grading papers. When I practiced, I willed the music to reach them. I imagined the melodies drifting down the stairs and casting a happy spell over them like a net. Some days I didn't feel like practicing or didn't want to practice as long as I knew I must. But still I stayed up in that room for the requisite hours, whiling away the time with a book or journal. I didn't want to disappoint them. I wanted to be good. At the same time I knew that, although they loved music, classical viola was a foreign thing to them, to a large degree out of their grasp. And a secret part of me thrilled that it was all mine.

Like Galway itself, the hostel where I'm staying is smaller and less intimidating than the one in Dublin. The entrance archway is painted pale pink, and flower boxes sprout on the windowsills above it. Unlike in Dublin, my reservation not only exists but is extremely specific. I'm staying in room 114 in Bed 1. I insert my key into the door with a RESIDENTS ONLY sign and thankfully navigate only one flight of stairs to reach my room. Still I struggle to manage Big Red, hastily repacked this morning before my quick departure from Dublin.

My new hostel room is packed with four bunk beds. I booked an eight-bed dorm room this time instead of a four-bed one in the hopes of increasing my chances of girl roommates. Right now the room is blissfully empty, but I can tell from various items—

hairbrushes, a pink T-shirt, wedge-heeled sandals—that there are girls staying here. Again I wonder about the mysteriously small backpacks parked all over. Where are these travelers headed and for how long? I don't think of myself as one of them, just a girl in Ireland with a ridiculously oversize suitcase.

·I immediately feel more at home in Galway than I did in Dublin. No, not at home, exactly, but somewhere simultaneously foreign and intrinsically comfortable. There's no pleasant Canadian to keep me company, but I realize I actually want to go out and explore the cobblestone streets, pop into one of the unfamiliar bookstores, grab a floury pastry at the bakery I passed on the walk here. Plus, I need to start looking for a job and an apartment. This hostel is a little less expensive than the one in Dublin, but not much. If I budget twenty euros a day for food and twelve for my lower bunk bed, I have about two weeks before I go broke.

Galway's nickname is City of the Tribes, after the fourteen merchant families who bandied it about during the Norman era. It became the foremost Irish port for trade with France and Spain during the Middle Ages and the place where, many years later, George Moore traveled to meet up with William Butler Yeats to collaborate on a play. (I know this last random fact because I once randomly came across a diary entry of Moore's during this trip in which he called Yeats's laugh "one of the most melancholy things in the world," a spectacularly depressing description that has stuck with me.) Only a few feet from my hostel, the fast-flowing River Corrib gushes by, and if you turn left, you'll hit the Spanish Arch, an extension of the imposing, protective city walls that were constructed in the 1500s. If you look across the water from this point, you can see what's left of the Claddagh, an old fishing village that used to be all thatched cottages and Gaelic speakers and is these days know for its signature rings.

Perhaps I'm distractedly mulling over Galway's history, or ex-

amining the quaint shops and already filling pubs, or pondering
how Ireland has enough old castles that it can convert the extras
into banks, but one minute I am confidently wandering my new
streets and the next a pigeon flies straight into my forehead and
knocks me to the ground. I'm sitting dazed on the cobblestones
when a few kindly old Irish gentlemen, marveling at the impressive statistical improbability of such a thing happening, help me
to my feet.

"You all right, love?" one asks.

"Did that seriously just happen?" I say.

"He got you bang on!" which in Ireland means right square in
the bull's-eye that apparently is my face.

It's a startling beginning to an otherwise drowsy day. I walk. I
window-shop. I stop by that bakery for a piece of brick-dense
Irish soda bread. And I shyly enter a few bars and restaurants to
ask if they're hiring and hand over my carefully printed résumés,
which are regarded with the same level of scrutiny one might a
coaster.

"Come back in three weeks," they say, or "Try next door."

The sun emerges only in weak spurts, but it stops drizzling by
late afternoon. Turns out it doesn't rain all day long in Ireland, as
I had imagined initially, but it does rain for a portion great or
small of each day, leaving one to conclude that being a weather-
man in Ireland is about the biggest scam going. It's chilly, more
like early spring back home than summer, and I wrap myself in
my heaviest wool sweater. When my stomach begins growling,
I follow the delicious fish smell near my hostel to its source,
McDonaghs, and order fish and chips to go. I douse my meal in
vinegar, which, unlike the miniature packets of ketchup and tar-
tar sauce, is plentiful and free. I've never had to calculate my portions so precisely, have never had to worry about how spending
a measly euro on condiments will strain my meager budget.

Tucked away once again in my still thankfully empty room, I
drag a chair up to the small square window. I unwrap my dinner

and balance the contents on my lap. Already grease is starting to seep through the newspaper wrapping. Inside a deep, rich batter hides a piece of light, flaky cod. Thick potato wedges are getting deliciously soggy in the vinegar. The meal sinks like a stone in my stomach, just the thing after a long day wandering around a damp city. It's the end of my first whole day truly alone in Ireland, and even though I can tell already that I fit better in Galway than in Dublin, I'm lonely. Again I consider what exactly I'm doing here.

Over the next week, I meet other travelers staying in the hostel, and some of my loneliness dissipates. First there's Jeff. When I open my eyes the next morning, he is on his stomach reading in the bunk bed across from me, apparently having just exited an Abercrombie & Fitch billboard—chiseled arms, thick hair, freckles on his tanned neck.

We run into each other in the common room later in the day. I've been watching TV for an hour with two girls I don't know. They didn't say anything more than "hey" when I entered the room, but they didn't tell me to leave, either. I had this idea in my head that some guests in the hostel "owned" certain rooms, like the really popular girls in middle school owned certain lunch tables, but it's not true. Anyone can sit on the beat-up couch and watch TV. Nobody stays in hostels long enough to lay claim to anything, nor is it something anyone is interested in. There are hostels I'll encounter later on in my travels where people hole up for weeks and months at a time, but this one, like most of them, is simply a brief stop on the way to somewhere else.

"You're in my room, right?" Jeff asks.

I nod.

"If you're not doing anything, I'm going out for drinks with my friends. Do you want to come?"

I don't know how long you have to be celibate before people

assume you're doing it on purpose, but whatever the threshold is, I have surely passed it. I haven't so much as kissed anyone in over a year, since I shouted "Good riddance!" as my ex-boyfriend stomped away from our fifth tequila-fueled breakup. All of that changes my first night out in Galway. Jeff and I make out enthusiastically in the hostel's hallway, in that pawing, slurred way that seems so sexy when you're hammered, until we get caught by security cameras. A cryptic Big Brother voice rasps through an intercom: "Guys, we can see you down here."

In the morning Abercrombie & Fitch, like Matt the Canadian before him, is gone before I can say goodbye. This is fine by me, because I'm pitifully hungover. And embarrassed. I wait until all of my roommates leave before sheepishly sneaking out of the room.

The days begin to drift by. Late mornings I traipse around Galway, unsuccessfully applying for jobs. Every afternoon I wind up at a little café near St. Augustine Church, a few blocks from the busy main street. Here I always order the same sandwich— avocado and sun-dried tomato—and a cup of coffee, wolfing it down after subsisting until then on the hostel's free breakfast. Sometimes I leave after an hour or so, but often I stay two, three, or even four hours, eventually purchasing a scone to quell my guilt for taking up a table so long. I read or write or daydream or just people-watch, imagining the lives of passersby.

If ever there was a time before now when I woke up thinking, Now, is it Wednesday or Thursday?, I don't remember it. Since I was little, my schedule has been as regimented as soldiers marching down the lane, but not in Galway. New roommates chug like a locomotive through the hostel. Each day is a series of maneuvers around strange bodies to get in and out. At night I latch on to whatever new group has arrived and go out drinking with them. There's Paula and Marcel, beautiful traveling cousins from Puerto Rico; Michael, an American who has returned to Galway to pursue an Irish ex-girlfriend (I met her, and boy, is she out of his league, I'm sorry to say); three Brits here for a quick weekend holiday; and many, many more who are traveling for weeks, months, or years at a time. We usually end up in a dim multilevel pub called the Quays (which I idiotically pronounce "kways" instead of "keys" for five days until someone finally corrects me). The interior was imported from a French medieval church, complete with stained-glass windows and rickety pews. It's a place with different moods. You can stand in the middle of a churning bar crowd or tuck yourself away at one of the tables in the corner. It stays open far later than most bars, which in Ireland close by midnight so you can get tipsy and still fit in a full eight hours of sleep before work the next morning. Often I find myself stumbling home at two or three or four in the morning—no school or job to stop me. But the best thing about the pub is the music. Almost every pub we patronize has live music multiple nights a week, and the Quays is no exception.

Music is predictable. It is exact. No matter your interpretation—the tempo or volume or speed of your vibrato—a B flat is a B flat is a B flat. This was infinitely appealing for an anxious, watchful, perfectionist little girl who desperately needed the world to make sense, for things to be orderly. Girls like me choose horses, or eating disorders, or literature—we choose any number of worlds within which to disappear, but that dangerous energy has to go somewhere. For me it was music.

The passion that inhabited me while playing—the way that bodies sway in time, eyes close, chests rise and fall—came naturally. And the physical act of learning to play the viola itself was a methodical process. It was a formula. Practice and you get better. Practice longer and you get better faster. As with school, I knew the rules. My relationship with music was straightforward. I wanted to play the viola, and it seemed to want me to play it. We were in harmony.

Until my freshman year of music school. In college I practiced and practiced and practiced, emerging from my cavelike studio in the basement of the music building at the oddest hours. I was working harder than ever, but I realized in music school, surrounded by all these other amazing musicians, that I was no longer the best. Not now. Probably not ever. This hard truth took my breath away.

Music school was a seismic event that cracked my tough exterior, and apparently, my core was pure liquid terror. A few weeks into the semester, I started blacking out. I don't mean that I fainted during an actual performance, just that afterward I couldn't remember anything about it. When I played well, I was unable to explain it, as I was equally unable to explain my increasing failures. My body hurt all the time, and I no longer held my viola with the effortless adoration I used to. All my preparation was having the confusing, unpleasant effect of slowly but steadily draining my desire; the pleasure dripped out of my body like a leaky faucet I couldn't fix. Since I practiced so much—four, five, six hours a day—the skin under the left side of my chin was rubbed raw. It was red and unpleasantly thin to the touch, like an old woman's arm. After a few hours of playing, my shoulder would start to creep up, compensating for my weak chin. My back was sore and slightly hunched, and my neck protested my insistence on turning my eyes to face my fingers. I knew that I shouldn't need to watch them race along the strings. They're meant to find the notes feelingly, like a blind person, but I no longer trusted myself.

In Galway, at night, in the fiddle-soaked pubs, I can forget all this for a while. When I happen past a violinist in the street during the sober day, I feel a sharp pinch of sadness. I am full of regrets about giving up music. If I stand there listening for too long, I actually begin to feel a bit nauseated—as if the street is spinning. But there is something different about the nighttime bar music filled with exuberant fiddling and sweet guitars. The alcohol miraculously strips away the harshest feelings I harbor against myself, and I can sink down bodily into the melodies again without all the mental angst. I haven't been able to do that in the longest time. So I drink to be social. I drink to bandage my bruised ego after another day of fruitless job applications. But most of all, I drink to feel music again—to drown in it.

I'm living a life in Galway that's entirely unfamiliar from the one I left back home. Surrounded by strangers in a foreign land, where no one knows or cares why I'm here or where I'm headed next, it occurs to me that I can completely reinvent myself. And Ireland me would like another Guinness, please.

# [ 4 ]

*Our heroine takes up residence with three strangers of various and unaccountable natures, one of whom is an entirely different kind of girl species indeed.*

I have not contacted my parents since shooting off a brief email my first day in Galway, nearly a week ago. My father has written me numerous times since then. In each subsequent message, the all caps and exclamation points have multiplied.

> Subject: Hello!
> Subject: HELLO?!!
> Subject: Worried!!
> Subject: SERIOUSLY! CALL ME!!
> At the height of his frenzy, he refers to himself in third person.
> Subject: PLEASE CONTACT YOUR FATHER WHO DOES NOT KNOW WHERE YOU ARE AND IS EXTREMELY DISTRAUGHT!!!

Whoops. I'm not sure why it's taken me so long to get back to the Internet café. My father and I have a minutiae-sharing relationship, always have. We're two peas in a book-loving, film-going, pun-making pod. So my initial instinct is to spill my guts to him.

> *I'm lonely. I don't have any friends. The ones I make at the hostel keep leaving. I can't find a job or an apartment. I'm running out of money. This trip was a mistake. I have no idea what I'm doing here or why I came. I want to come home.*

I stare at that last line, stewing in the sorry reality my words have created. And then something very weird happens. As if I'm engaged in an eerie session with a Ouija board, my index finger slides toward the delete key, seemingly of its own accord. It pauses for a second and then presses down, erasing my email letter by letter, until "I" is all that's left standing. From there, I begin again.

> *I'm alive! No need to file a missing persons report, Dad, I'm still in Galway—safe and sound. I've been hunting for jobs, meeting lots of interesting people, and seeing what there is to see in this small town. Yesterday I went to the bookstore and bought William Trevor's* The Hill Bachelors. *Have you read him? He's wonderful, understated, all restrained, bubbling emotions. I miss you and I'll write more soon!*
> *Love,*
> *Rachel*

I hit "send." I don't know how to reconcile my urge to relate in the melodramatic detail that is our shared currency that I'm lonely and full of doubts with this new part of me who has held this information back and instead written a falsely cheerful email. Although I didn't recognize it then, this simple act was the beginning of the necessary process of truly striking out on my own. This summer away was my idea, however ill-conceived, and

I knew if I even hinted that I wanted to come home, my father would happily scoop me up and save the day. I could picture us hunkered down at the kitchen table back in his new Chicago apartment, discussing my future, eyeing each other across the fake fruit. The clock is ticking, after all. Soon I will be out there in the real world. I don't have an exact image of this place, though I understand it involves having my student healthcare taken away, and I'm pretty sure I no longer get an allowance.

If I asked his opinion, even if I just hesitated long enough to give him an opening, he would gladly decide my future for me. Being a professor, like him, is an ideal, predictable existence. So why not apply for Ph.D. programs now? Junior year is the perfect time—no aimless lag between undergraduate and graduate degrees. Or maybe I could get a job as an editorial assistant at a publishing house in New York, another popular job choice for bright-eyed English majors. He knows a few people, could call in some favors. Although we might decide on any number of career objectives now that I am no longer planning to be a professional musician, it is highly unlikely—no, we most definitely would *not* decide—I should spend a purposeless summer in Ireland. Why do I want to do this? What, exactly, is the point?

While my father's incomprehension is based on practical concerns for my future, my mother's hinges on hurt feelings.

"Why don't you come home for the summer?" she asked before I left. She means move into a spare room in the robin's-egg-blue house she recently bought with her new husband. It's set back on sixty acres, a few miles farther into the upstate New York countryside than where I grew up, a large enough piece of land for a garden and for my stepfather to hunt without fear (mine, not his) of accidentally shooting someone. Alongside her question about my absence is the unspoken accompanying question I can never figure out how to answer: "What have I done to drive you away?"

I don't want to face any of my parents' questions, so I send my mother an email with the same forced bright tone and log off. Besides, choosing this rosier version of my present state makes me feel a little more optimistic. And things *are* actually looking up on the job front. Yesterday afternoon, dripping wet and defeated after three hours of pavement pounding, I wandered into in a dingy little pub off the main drag. The place was deserted save an old guy in a red Patriots hat chatting away with a nodding young bartender drying pint glasses. A few seats down, a middle-aged man with puffy red hair sat hunched over some documents. He turned out to be the manager, Brian. I must have applied to every bar in Galway, so when he, like so many before, informed me that they weren't hiring, I found myself embarrassingly on the verge of tears. My soggy clothes and matted hair, sneakers so soaked they squished, must have added to the picture of pathos urging him to reconsider.

"Please," I begged. "I'll do anything."

His eyes were friendly, but I didn't think I had a shot in hell.

"Where are you from?"

"New York." I sighed, unsure whether I was strengthening or dooming my case.

"New York!" Suddenly, he was animated. "Ahh, New York is brilliant. Right, I'll tell you what. I'll give you a trial shift—just because you're a New Yorker—and we'll see how it goes. Come back tomorrow night and we'll put you on glasses."

So now I've got a night's work at a dim, dreary bar called the Hole in the Wall—exactly the type of time-forgotten place I imagined as the setting for my gloomy days in Ireland. Of course, I have no idea what it means to be "on glasses" or what I'll get paid for this mysterious position or even how long I'll work, but I don't want to give Brian enough time to change his mind or realize I'm from the cows-and-pastures part of New York, not the bright-lights part it's clear he's conjuring.

"Thank you thank you thank you!" I shout, backing out the door. In my excitement, I salute him, though I have never saluted anyone in my life, no doubt leaving him with the impression that he has just made a very big mistake.

But more than this new bit of luck, going home, so appealing an option when I arrived in Dublin, now strikes me as a solution that might not solve anything, that might, in fact, be the opposite of what I want. The fact that I can't sift through my own emotions and desires to figure out what precisely I *do* want is so infuriating.

As I'm gathering up my things to leave the Internet cafe, I notice a torn piece of paper tacked onto the pushpin-battered wall.

> *Female needed for 2-bedroom apt., 255/month,*
> *Presentation Rd.*

A small fortune, considering my lack of income, but it's still cheaper than remaining in the hostel. Like the job hunt, the apartment search has proved difficult. Even after waiting in line for hours with all the other desperate would-be renters to grab the latest copy of *The Galway Advertiser,* then throwing elbows to secure the nearest pay phone in order to inquire about the few rooms I can afford, I find that most of them are already taken, snapped up before the classified ad's ink has dried. I've looked at only one place so far. The rent is 325 euros a month plus utilities—an even more impossible sum. Plus, although my potential male roommate seemed nice enough, the apartment reeked of dirty socks, and there were unidentifiable red hairs circling the drain when he showed me the shared bathroom. Like my prospective job at the Hole in the Wall, the apartment on Presentation Road feels like my last hope.

There's a number with a name next to it: Carly. I rip it off the wall before racing out to call her. Every woman for herself.

"Can I come see the place, like, now?" Desperation drips from my voice.

"No worries. Whenever."

"Great! I'll be right there! Just give me twenty minutes." I slam down the pay phone with such nervous enthusiasm that the elderly woman manning the hostel's front desk clucks reprovingly at me before returning to her dog-eared romance novel.

It's a rare afternoon of blue Irish skies, at least for now, so sunbathers are perched on the River Corrib's grassy shore at the edge of the city center. The girls stretch back on their elbows, T-shirts yanked above their translucent bellies. The boys tap soccer balls. I hurry across the stony bridge to the other side of town, a section of Galway that is more residential, less packed with pubs and shops, than where I've been staying.

Carly is smoking a cigarette on the stoop when I arrive. Fine blond hair hangs halfway down her back. She's wearing a snug faded blue sweatshirt and dark blue jeans, a little ripped in the knees. She eyes me with surprised detachment, as if she has forgotten our recently organized appointment, but it's cool, she wasn't doing anything at the moment anyway.

"Hey," she says. "Come on in."

She shows me the room we would share. A tan backpack is spread out across her bed, its front section unzipped and tossed back like a curled tongue. The small bedroom houses two slim beds and a compact closet. An ugly green checkered curtain hides a sliding glass door that leads out to a little patio, where you would have a lovely view of the canal if someone hadn't decided it would be a splendid idea to erect a wall instead. Two rusty folding chairs occupy the concrete box, along with one wilting plant, drowning in the daily rains instead of flourishing.

Carly, an Australian, is on a one-year trip around the world. "Mum did the same thing," she tells me. "My grandmother, too."

It seems she is descended from a long line of adventurous

women, whereas my own grandmother's biggest trip is her yearly winter pilgrimages to Florida.

"You're the first American backpacker I've met." Her tone is positive, as if she's given me a compliment, which I guess she has (though my secret will be out once she sees my oversize luggage). Already I've been informed of a few particular American traits by others in the hostel: we are loud; we travel in big, obnoxious groups; we complain, demand, and laugh too heartily without just cause. A favorite statistic I've been quoted ad nauseam while traveling abroad: only 5 percent of Americans have passports. (It ranges from 3 percent to 10 percent depending on the teller, though the actual number is closer to 30 percent.) In short, we are not travelers. We are tourists—the ultimate dirty word among backpackers. And then there's our most egregious misstep: President George W. Bush. Oh man, do people hate this guy. The reactions of non-Americans to the fact that I come from the place that "elected" this language-butchering cowboy range from sympathy to disgust to stammering confusion. Often I must delicately extract myself from my government with surgeonlike precision in order to move the conversation to a new topic. If I'm feeling particularly impatient, I just give 'em the old 1-2-3: "Yes, I'm American. No, I didn't vote for Bush. Who here needs another Guinness?" Then I flash my toothiest American grin; no one radiates good cheer as Care Bear–brightly as we Americans.

"Want a cigarette?" Carly asks.

I've been noncommittally trying to quit for good since high school, when smoking was a statement of coolness unconnected to slight inconveniences like lung cancer, but I am auditioning for the role of the perfect roommate.

"Definitely."

We head outside. Carly props one of the decrepit chairs against the wall, then hoists herself up on top. I follow her. It takes us several tries to light our cigarettes with a pack of gray-

ing matches. We puff into the dusk and watch a swan family paddle purposefully downstream.

"See that railing?" she asks. A short distance to our right, a
yellow guardrail lines the edge of the water. "Kayakers launch
themselves off it." She shakes her head. "It's bloody freezing in
this country. Fucking lunatics."

"Totally."

I will agree with whatever you say. Just let me move in.

After another cigarette, we climb down to tour the rest of the
apartment which is no more than a second bedroom that the two
absent male roommates share, a grungy bathroom, and a small
kitchen/living room. A washer is hooked up next to the sink.
Wet socks and jeans droop from a clothesline suspended across
the length of the apartment. In the damp Irish weather, it takes
two or three days for anything to dry.

Carly plops down on the thrift-store leatherette couch, one
corner covered in brown crumbs that bounce when she sits. I
take the blue corduroy armchair stained with who knows what.

"The two guys who live here are decent blokes," Carly says.
"Portu can be a little full on. Within five minutes, he'll be telling
you that Spanish men are the world's best lovers. But he's harm-
less. Patchi is from Basque Country. He's on holiday in Scotland
right now. He's on the dole, that one, but not because he needs to
be. It's just more than he would make doing anything else.
Enough to go on holiday, right. And he's lazy. Bugger it. If I could
get the dole, I'd take it, too. Bloody European Union."

She shakes her head. I shake mine, too, though I have no clue
what we're talking about.

A few hours later, I'm moving in with three strangers.

"Bloody hell," Carly exclaims when I wheel Big Red into our
bedroom. "That thing's massive."

* * *

A few days later, a second small miracle occurs. I get offered a few shifts a week at a nightclub where I deposited one of the hundred or so job applications I've littered throughout Galway.

"You know how to work a till, right?" the broad-shouldered manager inquired at my brief interview.

"Of course," I said, nodding with supreme confidence.

Like being "on glasses," I don't let on I have no idea what a till is, much less how it functions. Unlike the pub, which is a dive but turns out to be a lively, friendly student dive once the sun goes down, the club is downright seedy. At the Hole in the Wall, I show up in ratty jeans and any T-shirt I don't mind stinking of beer for the rest of its natural life, but my club uniform is circulation-impairing black pants and a club-issued doily of a top that barely reaches my belly button.

"I think it's too small," I tell the owner, one hand instinctively covering my stomach.

"No love, it's perfect." He winks and shoos me upstairs.

I bartend from ten P.M. to four A.M., mixing cocktails and fumbling with the till, which luckily turns out simply to be the cash register. The club is three stories with ugly black-and-white-striped walls and plush round red seats. Each floor is darker and louder than the last, until finally at the top, you can barely see your hands to pour the drinks. The more popular Galway clubs, like GPO and Central Park, are packed with sweaty, dancing bodies all night long. But the club where I work is not popular. It is some morally suspect millionaire's hobby, and the girls who haunt its corridors are younger and drunker than the girls at other places. They bounce in around one or two after not getting in anywhere else or getting kicked out of everywhere else. They stumble around and flirt shamelessly with Simon, the cute red-headed bartender. Occasionally, the owner turns up with his creepy, balding friends. They gulp down free drinks with double shots, drape themselves across the bar, and leer at my exposed midsection.

The owner insists we stay busy at all times, and he dissects our every move on the security cameras. If we're not serving a drink to the dozen or so people who have shown up that night, we should be cleaning, slicing limes, or organizing the money so all the bills face the same way. At the end of the night, the bartenders sit side by side with the cash registers, counting our earnings under the boss's watchful eye. I'm flustered by the rapid-fire calculations and exhausted because it's four A.M. and I hate, hate, *loathe* it here.

"I'm quitting!" I announce to Carly at least once a day.

But my funds are dwindling fast, and I have made a pact with myself that I will not call my parents to bail me out. During my painfully long nights at the club, I often find myself recalling an Outward Bound trip I took when I was fourteen. It was two weeks of intense hiking, canoeing, and portaging with a dozen other teenagers in Maine's North Woods. This little nature jaunt was not my idea. My parents were preparing to separate at the time, and they wanted to give me something else to "focus on," as they put it. Why this something else had to involve possible bear attacks, I'll never know, but many years later, my father revealed they also thought the trip was a good idea because I was developing a bit of an attitude problem—a spoiled teenager's sense of entitlement. "We wanted you to appreciate what you had," my dad explained, then paused ominously before adding: "By taking it all away."

The first night on our trip we had to canoe several miles to the campsite. This was after we had been forced to go through our backpacks and hand over the shampoo (one of Outward Bound's mottos is to not leave behind anything in the environment that wasn't already there) and electronic devices (apparently you couldn't commune with the trees with Sheryl Crow blasting through your Discman). We had hiked what felt like three dozen miles in boots I had neglected to break in before the trip because, really, I don't hike. And now we were barreling down the Allagash River in the midst of the century's worst rainstorm. We were out there for hours, soaked and shivering, the rain beating us back with every paddle thrust. My arms ached; my head throbbed. I started to cry, but no one could tell because it was dark and pouring. I cried all the way to shore. When one of the guides gave me his hand to help me out of my red canoe, I couldn't believe I had made it. I felt this huge surge of pride, the kind that comes with totally reimagining your limitations.

Even though the physical demands of the club are nothing like Outward Bound, I find myself hearkening back to that night on the river because it's taking that same level of mental fortitude to stick it out in this disgusting place. Like in Maine, determination takes over, determination I thought I lost after quitting music and was certainly not expecting to find within the uninspiring confines of this depressing Irish nightclub. Each time I cash my minuscule paycheck, I'm proud that I'm supporting myself financially for the first time, however shabbily.

Life in our apartment on the canal is filled with delicious foreign food and cheap wine. We organize international cooking nights where we each contribute a native dish. I'm on my way home from a leisurely day of underemployment on just such an occasion when the aromas coming from our place assault me a few steps away from the front door: onions, garlic, parsley, and tomato. Inside, Patchi hovers over the stove, gently ushering the fragrant steam rising from a massive steel pot out the small kitchen window.

Patchi's soup has been simmering all day. At dawn I was annoyed to be awakened by blaring Spanish heavy metal and plates crashing around. Annoyance gave way to surprise when I found Patchi fully conscious in the kitchen at that hour, chopping carrots. Normally, he sleeps until around noon, when he emerges from his room looking like he lost a fight with an electrical socket. He'll absentmindedly scratch at his ample chest hair for a few seconds, then light a cigarette and shuffle into the bathroom.

Patchi's early-morning soup preparations remind me of my mother, the only other person I've witnessed toiling over an evening meal before the rest of the house has risen. She's a phenomenal cook who routinely presents food that looks like it belongs on the cover of *Gourmet* magazine, while the most intricate meal I personally have mastered is boxed mac and cheese.

"Want to help me, Rachel?" my mother would ask when I was ten or eleven or twelve—probably she tried multiple times to teach me how to follow a recipe.

My father would be parked in his big leather chair, grading papers with a special red felt-tip pen that I deeply coveted. I'd be next to him on the rug, reading, my knees curled against my chest, my back against his legs.

"Thank goodness for your mom," he'd say, winking down at me. "I can barely crack an egg."

"No, thanks," I'd always tell my mom, first unconsciously but then knowingly making one of a series of choices between my parents.

My mother has boxes of recipes, entire shelves of cookbooks organized by cuisine, then cross-referenced by chef and publication date. Each ingredient is precisely measured. She is skeptical about substitutions, while adding something new makes her positively dizzy with apprehension. Once when I suggested throwing in an uncalled-for handful of walnuts, she looked like she might faint. She grasped the edge of the marble countertop to steady herself. "I don't think that's a good idea," she whispered in a tone that really meant "Hell no, you maniac—go spread your anarchy in some other kitchen where they don't laminate their index cards." For my mother, cooking is like classical music— beautifully predictable—while what Patchi is currently doing—

tossing in a wide variety of vegetables and spices with no written guide to tell him when or how much—has the improvisa-
tional quality of jazz.

Patchi himself looks as frenetic as his cooking. He is tall with
wild, shaggy brown curls and could pass equally well as an eccentric Russian scientist or a prep-school misfit. Like Portu,
Patchi is ostensibly in Galway to study English, but he has made
little progress. Nor does he seem all that interested. While Portu
constantly tries out new phrases and asks me to define certain
words, Patchi speaks English only when absolutely necessary,
using Portu as his translator whenever possible.

The nights I work at the club, I don't get home until four or
five in the morning, just the time of day someone without a job
strolls in, too. So Patchi and I spend a lot of time together in front
of the television in the early hours of the morning, mostly
watching Ireland's version of *Big Brother* on one of our three stat-
icky channels. Unlike the U.S.'s weekly edited hour of *Big Brother,*
Ireland keeps cameras on the housemates twenty-four hours a
day, seven days a week. It's boring but addictive. Usually, I fondle
an open jar of Nutella. Every few minutes I absentmindedly
spoon a fudgy glob directly into my mouth, forgoing a utensil for
my finger when the idea of opening and closing the silverware
drawer is simply too exhausting. One time around four-thirty
A.M. we were knocked out of our trance when one of the contes-
tants jumped into bed with his housemate for what he must have
imagined (though, really, how could he?) was a discreet encounter. But mostly we just watch them sleep, half asleep ourselves.

Portu works in construction and keeps a much more regular
schedule. He kissed me lightly on the cheek when we first met,
then, as Carly predicted, immediately informed me that Spanish
men are the world's best lovers. He thinks this is something I
should be aware of, since I'm about to move in with an eligible

Spanish bachelor. He is engaged in a constant conversation of seduction with our pretty Spanish neighbors, three luminescent women who spend hours with him and Patchi in the kitchen, cooking and yelling, although Portu would say they are simply talking. At all hours of the day and night, I walk into a boisterous kitchen, five chairs smashed around our scuffed table. Spanish flies in all directions like misfired arrows, making it impossible for me to understand who is talking to whom. The conversation grows in volume and enthusiasm until everyone is out of breath. Once I asked Portu how he understands what anyone is saying, but he just gave me a sympathetic look like I was, sadly, not very bright.

Since Portu's English is decent, Patchi's is virtually nonexistent, and my and Carly's Spanish is barely coherent, we spend a lot of our time together nodding and gesturing wildly while attempting to reconcile who owes how much money for what and who left his toenail clippings all over the couch again. By the end of each conversation, we always believe we've reached a consensus, only to relive our misunderstandings the following week when the electric bill has not been paid by the designated person or we discover Patchi sprawled languidly out on the couch, blissfully chopping away at his feet with rusty clippers.

Patchi and Portu are terrible slobs. Their room is an explosion of clothes, empty bottles, and cassette tapes (apparently 2002 in the U.S. is 1990 in Spain and Basque). Both of them smoke nonstop and insist on crushing their butts out on our dinner plates. Carly and I strategically scatter more and more ashtrays around the apartment, but we never break them of this off-putting habit. Soon all our meals taste vaguely of ash, but by then I'm smoking so much myself that I barely notice. Unusual habits aside, they are extremely entertaining, friendly guys. Portu especially, his initial suggestive remarks more bravado than anything else, quickly becomes protective and dependable, like an older brother.

"That man has nothing to offer you," he concludes at a bar one night, gingerly extracting me from the nameless Irish guy I am drunkenly barnacled to.

Even Spanish heavy metal, which Patchi blasts during the rare moments he takes time off from his busy dole-collecting schedule to help clean up the apartment, is growing on me.

Portu's addition to today's meal is a Spanish tortilla. It's like a quiche—yellow, thick, and eggy. I stick my nose a few inches from it and inhale deeply, wondering if this is what Spain smells like.

"It's finished soon—only three more months," Portu says in English. He is much more proficient than Patchi, and I do not laugh when I correct his mistake, since last week I believe I asked him, in unintelligible Spanish, to "throw away any small children he found around the house," and he showed grave patience while correcting me.

Carly is preparing dessert. Three plates are piled high with lamingtons, an Australian concoction composed of sponge cake smothered in chocolate and coconut and filled with cream. She is elbow-deep in the sugary ingredients. I reach down for a taste, but her sticky fingers swat me away.

My roommates' creations cover every inch of the minute kitchen table. We have to balance our plates on the edge and support them with one hand while we eat. As usual, with the exception of the one night I offered up burned bruschetta, I've contributed only the wine—but lots of it.

After our third bottle, we decide the best idea we've ever had is to play a round of Burro. In this game, you're dealt four cards and you pass around all the rest in hopes of ultimately getting four of the same number. When a person achieves this magnificent feat of intellect, he or she sticks out her tongue. The last idiot to realize she is sitting at a table with three other idiots with protruding tongues loses. The loser acquires the letter "b," then, "u," then "r," and so on to spell out the word "burro," "ass" in Spanish. Whoever acquires all the letters first, loses. When Patchi is defeated, his determined punishment is to run shirtless around the apartment complex (apparently, the wine has transformed us into eight-year olds). We lose sight of him when he ducks behind the building, and when he reappears, he is inexplicably wearing only his boxers. When we ask him where his pants are, he shrugs and shakes his curly head around like he doesn't even know where *he* is, much less his pants, of all crazy things. After this, we uncap the whiskey, and thus I remember very little about the rest of the night.

Each of us hails from a different country, we have different languages and different accents and different reasons for coming to Ireland, but we fit easily together, as if we've known one another for many years. Or maybe it's precisely because we have just met and are bonded primarily by being travelers in the same place at the same time in our lives that it's so simple to be here together, for the four of us to form a ragtag little family.

# [ 5 ]

*Our heroine considers some advice from her unnervingly wild
new friend. She finds steady employment and an even steadier
drinking habit, though it is not her intention to imply that the
fine country of Ireland is in any way responsible for such
youthful debauchery, other than to note that it does have a very
high number of excellent bars in conjunction with an
overabundance of rainy days. Our heroine might choose
church, another fine, dry place in which to ponder
life's questions, but alas, she is Jewish.*

Carly has already been in Galway for eight weeks when I arrive.
She endures the six A.M. breakfast shift, while I toil late nights, so
our schedules don't overlap much. She loathes her café job as
much as I do the club.

"I'm only working to make some euros to spend traveling
around. The Australian dollar is worthless over here," she tells
me. "But I'm so bloody sick of the routine. And my boss really
gives me the shits."

Only young, foreign female backpackers work at the café, a
population of Italians, Kiwis, and Australians whom her boss
controls monetarily by paying them under the table and emo-

tionally by insulting them so ferociously that someone is always in tears by the end of the shift, although Carly herself doesn't seem like the kind of girl who cries at work—or ever, really.

Australians often head off to England for their gap year—a period of travel typically taken after college. Aussies have a yearlong reciprocal work visa agreement with England (when you're taught about the American Revolution in grade school, no one ever lets on that dumping all that tea into Boston Harbor has, sadly, curtailed your Commonwealth visa options). Many of them fly over after graduating and spend the year working in London and traveling on the side.

For Carly, however, traveling is the main dish, and working constitutes the crusty bread rolls at the start of the meal. Always wanting to be different, she chooses Ireland instead of England and comes over to Galway to work for four months, then spends the rest of her time backpacking across the continent. Eager to be the first to go off and try something new, she hasn't waited until graduation to travel for an extended period of time. I'm amazed to learn she has taken a year off in the middle of her degree to travel.

"What about your parents?" I ask, ready for her sad tale of exile.

"What about them? Mum's the one who suggested the trip."

"Wait…what?" It's too much to absorb.

"Mate," she says, "lots of people our age do this. Plus, my parents don't expect me to finish college when my mind is on travel. I won't get anything out of it anyway. University will be there when I get back."

Carly attended school full-time her first year but hated it. She wound up there by default, not wanting to go but not having any other ideas of what to do after high school and no financial means to travel. Her second year, she took only a class or two and spent the majority of her time at three different part-time jobs, slowly but steadily adding to her travel funds. The pièce de résistance was selling her horse, Ken, a formerly unruly colt she had diligently trained. After that, she was off.

"But *why* are you traveling?" I want to pinpoint her goal, to figure out how she is justifying this diversion from her studies.

"Why? To travel. To see the world. What do you mean, why? Because I want to."

I'm desperate to know exactly what her wants have to do with anything, but her definitive tone is intimidating. Carly has fearlessly forsaken the typical rhythms of adulthood that I feel pulling at me like quicksand, and struck out on her own. She blows along like the wind, a backpacker weighed down only by what she can carry. There is no plan, no predetermined outcome. She is confident and nonchalant in equal proportion to my paralyzing self-consciousness. I want to figure out how she has managed this.

I also want some of her boldness to rub off on me. For instance, Carly didn't find the apartment we're living in through an ad but rather when Patchi and Portu approached her in line at *The Galway Advertiser* and asked if she needed a room. She followed them back to the apartment right then and there.

"I mean, they could have been lying, I guess." She considers this briefly, then banishes the unpleasant thought, confident in her ability to handle whatever comes her way. "But whatever. It worked out."

I ask her how many people rang in response to the ads she put up, ready to bask in my victory against all the other potential roommates, knowing I'm the girl who was meant to live here all along.

"Mate, I put up one piece of paper in the Internet café. And you're the only one who responded."

I was constantly looking for signs about my life and thought that piece of paper was one of them. But Carly saw the note for what it was: a physical object expressing one person's need to be fulfilled by another person's inverse need, simple as that. It's clear from the start that Carly's world is black and white, whereas mine is ever-shifting shades of gray.

Our first few weeks in the house, Carly is aloof. Back home, I've always made friends fast and furiously. If we get along with someone, we American girls will throw our arms over each other's shoulders and declare our undying devotion after the first twenty-four hours together. This innate enthusiasm is something my as yet unmade Irish friends will rib me about constantly.

"Are you excited?" I'll ask about anything from a date with a cute guy to seeing a new movie.

"We don't talk about being excited, chicken," my friend Eileen will instruct, smiling. "In fact, I'm not sure we even get as excited as you Yanks in the first place."

By then I'll be immersed enough in Irish culture to be entertained by our cultural and personal differences, but Carly's indifference strikes when I am loneliest and could really use a companion. She already has her own cozy little social group, and in the beginning she doesn't make any effort to include me in it. Because she seems so carefree and confident, I assume she must simply dislike me, and it's only many years later, when we discuss these first encounters, that Carly explains that her initial detachment was, surprisingly, shyness, a trait that doesn't seem to mesh at all with her projected confidence.

When she's not waitressing, she's out with her Italian friend Gina or off to some new city on a day trip with Joanna—until she has an accident at work a few weeks into the summer. A fellow waitress tosses her a trash bag with protruding shards of glass that slice through her palm. Her hand is wrapped in heavy gauze when she unexpectedly returns home early one afternoon.

"Can't waitress with a dodgy hand," she announces, but she's grinning. Disability is awarding her a tidy sum, and she doesn't have to go back to the café for several weeks.

After that we're both around during the day, and she finally warms up to me. In the mornings, we settle in at a local café where I learn Carly, too, is adept at the art of stretching a snack for several hours. We vent about Portu and Patchi constantly leaving the front door open when they go out—not just unlocked but actually wide open. We have learned the Spanish phrase *cerrar la puerta* solely to admonish them, but it has no effect. While Carly and I agree this is reckless behavior that invites burglars and other miscreants—plus, Carly is sure that's how Patchi's sad little marijuana plant got stolen—for Portu and Patchi, it's simply a friendly invitation to anyone who might drop by, whether or not one of us happens to be home at the time. Carly and I also bond over the arrival of Scraps, the name we bestow on a stray dog who appears on our doorstep one day, alarmingly thin with tangled, greasy black and tan fur. We save the leftovers from our meals (hence his name) and leave him a little compost heap outside. At first he is standoffish—he'll take the food but won't let us pat him—but within a week he's tolerating our embraces of his dreadlocked mane.

Carly insists I try Vegemite, a disgusting yeast spread Australians are reared on and feel disconcertingly nationalistic about. It makes me gag, but she's convinced it will grow on me. She also introduces me to *Home and Away,* a dreamy Australian soap opera in which the characters discuss serious issues like teen pregnancy against an authentic beach backdrop with sand that glistens like diamonds and cushiony blue waves that definitely do not scream "abstinence." And she answers my eight hundred questions about her life, which seems so different from my own. In particular, I'm intrigued by this backpacking thing. I want to know exactly how it works.

"Buy a pack. Buy a plane ticket. And then just go. It's simple."

"For how long?"

"As long as you want."

"How did you decide where to go?"

"I thought of all the countries I wanted to visit and then picked some."

"Is it scary traveling on your own?"

"Scary how?"

"Like, what if you get lost?" This is a question my mother asked before I left, and it rather unhinged me because I have little faith in my ability to get unlost.

"You can't get lost when you have nowhere to be," she says cryptically.

One night we're in the kitchen polishing off our second bottle of bargain-basement cabernet when she asks why I've come to Ireland.

"I don't know," I say honestly.

"You don't know? You traveled to a foreign country alone for four months, and you have no idea why?"

"I just needed to get away." This sounds about right. I haven't told anyone about the various internal and external pressures awaiting me back home. In Galway, I've pushed aside those thoughts in hopes that they will magically disappear.

"Something more than getting away made you come to Ireland, I bet."

"Like what?" I ask, a little annoyed at being analyzed.

"Like…adventure," she announces triumphantly.

I emit a surprised snort. I search the room exaggeratedly, pretending to try and figure out if there is someone behind me or if she really is talking to me. "You are so totally and completely wrong," I tell her. "I look for lots of things, but adventure is not one of them." I've read the Greek epics. I've armchair-traveled with Jack Kerouac and Bill Bryson and Che Guevara, so I know how to categorize the idea of travel/adventure, but it does not coexist with how I picture myself—a sheltered, scared, predictable kind of girl, definitely not a girl who has adventures. I come from rooted people, people who prefer chlorinated bodies of water and career paths.

"Well, it could be. You should travel. Have you even left Galway since you got here?"

"I went to Limerick that one day..." I say. It's true I've been more living in Ireland than traveling here.

"Go see something! And you don't have to go home, you know." She's on a roll now. "School, your friends, your parents, whatever it is you've left behind is all going to be there when you get back. But I would be one hundred percent positive you really want to go back, because once you do, it's a lot harder to leave again." I can tell Carly revels in being the wise life guide. When the student is ready, the crazy Australian chick will appear, or however the expression goes.

I had never considered not going home. Like dyeing my hair fire-engine red or getting a belly ring, this summer in Ireland was surely a small, contained act of rebellion, a momentary hiatus from what was expected of me. In musical terms, we might call these moments embellishments or ornamentations of the overall coherent, predictable melodic line that was my life before things began unraveling freshman year in music school. Could I really stay away? Even asking myself the question feels monumental.

"I don't have any money," I tell her.

She scoffs as if I have raised a concern totally unrelated to what she's said, like lacking sunscreen in Seattle. "Get another student work visa. Where else can you go?"

I think back to the informational pamphlet I received with my four-month visa. "Well, I can work in New Zealand for a year or Ireland, England, and Australia for four months—"

"Come to Australia." It's a statement, not a question, as nonchalant a decision for her as deciding whether to wear her hair up or down that day. "It's awesome. You can stay with me. Mum and Dad love visitors."

Australia. I roll the word around in my head, trying to conjure up an image of myself there.

*   *   *

Less than halfway through the summer, Carly takes off to explore the rest of Europe and Asia, and I finally start getting enough shifts at the Hole in the Wall to quit degrading myself at the nightclub. Maybe it's because I am the kind of person who is perpetually trapped inside the recesses of her own mind—always thinking too much—that I've always been drawn to working in restaurants and bars, where the tasks are routine and blissfully physical. Waiting tables has a clear beginning, middle, and end. Take the drink order, bring the drinks, take the meal order, bring the food, check in, get the extra pickles, another round of beers, dessert, then drop off the bill with a heartfelt thanks. Those customers depart and new ones shuffle in and you have to figure out how best to serve them. Do they want a funny waitress or one who is serious and knowledgeable or one who leaves them the hell alone? Most just want an unobtrusive, smiling one. I can smile or not. Knowing who they want you to be is straightforward. You just have to be observant.

I'm more graceful as a waitress than I am in real life, deftly carrying three pitchers in one hand and two plates in the other or expertly twirling around a co-worker at just the right moment to avoid a collision. And I love the transient atmosphere, packed with creative types, everyone believing they are there temporarily, a fleeting stop on their way to something better. We banded together to weather unpredictable tipping, long hours, and customers who often treated us like complete morons, especially at the Harvard Square brewery, where I waited tables one summer. It's a skill I feel guilty about because it is blue-collar, nonintellectual work. My grandfather did not flee the Nazis so that I could serve food. My mother didn't climb out of poverty so that I could revel in my abilities to concoct the perfect apple martini.

So although I know my parents wish I was doing something more productive with my Irish summer, I long to lose myself in the restaurant/bar world again. And the dimly lit Hole in the Wall seems like the perfect place to do it. The bar is directly in front of you when you walk in. Four or five stools, wood with worn fabric, are where the regulars park themselves. The old guy I saw when I applied for the job is a fixture. He comes in early and often stays until closing, growing more and more incoherent as the night wears on. He cackles, "I get up with the birds and I go home with the birds!" and workshops the same three stories on repeat, as if those three moments constitute his entire life. When he's caught a cold, he exchanges his two-euro beer for hot toddies. Since he never swaps out the glass, you can tell how many he's had by the number of lemons piling up.

The Hole in the Wall's original rock walls have been plastered over, and now they resemble clotted cream. There is dark paneling everywhere, chipped wooden tables, and tiny windows with crisscross frames set deep into the walls like those of a fairy-tale cottage, perfect for when we pull the shades for a lockdown, where we hunker inside and drink until sunrise. The entire place has a fantastic slope. Walking into the back room is like an expedition aided by the dim lights of the old-fashioned gas lamps. The owner has hung pictures of himself with a multitude of winning horses taken during the yearly Galway Races, when the pub practically implodes with thirsty bodies. There's Guinness paraphernalia everywhere: GUINNESS FOR STRENGTH and GUINNESS EXTRA STOUT. As at the Quays, the benches that line the walls resemble pews, though the upholstery is worn from an altogether different type of devotion. There is a rumor—told with varying degrees of supporting detail, depending on the teller—that many years ago a nun hanged herself in the attic.

"On glasses" turns out to be collecting the dirty glasses from around the pub and returning them to the bartenders to load in the tiny dishwasher. One night a bartender makes the mistake of unloading a still-steaming pint glass with cold hands, and it explodes inside his fingers, rendering them as useless as Carly's for a few weeks. Unlike the club, the Hole in the Wall is packed almost every night. I push through overheated bodies to get at the stacked glasses that line every available shelf and threaten to topple off the rickety tables in the front room, where a few lucky groups have managed to score seats. I work for four or five hours at a stretch, sweaty and claustrophobic but elated to be employed.

After four trial shifts as a "glassie," I convince Brian to let me train on bar. Ever the dutiful student, I scrawl the following notes in my journal after my first lesson: Bud, Hein, Carlsberg = lagers = fizzy, let tap run for one second then tilt glass under, also Tennent's. Bloomers/cider—hold glass straight under tap. Guinness—tilt all the way for ¾ cup, let settle, then glass straight under and push handle back = perfect top-off.

Even with my shifts at the pub, I'm forever short of cash, and Portu is constantly lending me rent money. When Carly leaves, Portu and Patchi replace her with a girl who is the cousin of a cousin of someone Portu knows back in Spain, leaving me the only native English speaker in the house. I start hanging out more with my new bartender girlfriends. Instead of my previous sober afternoons, my days are now one long stint at the Hole in the Wall. I bartend three or four or, if I'm lucky, five nights a week, then end up drinking there or at another bar for the rest of the evening. After midnight, we spill into the clubs, dancing more than I have before or since, buzzing from vodka and Red Bull. I sleep until noon, then meet the girls for "the cure"—the Irish logic of banishing your hangover with more drinking.

My friend Dee is a skinny thing with a small smile, lovely dark hair, and pale Irish skin. Her father was a bus driver for many years, the route from County Clare to Dublin and back, and she tells me how she and her younger sister learned to roller-skate in the aisles. Una doesn't work at the Hole in the Wall with us but in the boots department at Top Shop. She's blond and bouncy and enviably fake-tanned. When she's drunk, she tells strangers she's related to Kylie Minogue, since they share the same last name. Siobhan is studying to be a nurse, a pursuit that unfortunately involves many early-morning exams. Eileen is the wild one who rides a blow-up green dinosaur around the pub when she's had too much to drink. (And we've always had too much to drink. Irish me turns out to be one hell of a drinker.) All the girls are funny and quick-witted, so much that I'm beginning to think of it as an Irish trait.

Halfway through the summer, I'm still broke, so I take our friend Gerry up on his offer to hire me as a flyer girl. This involves precariously tottering around the cobblestone main street in three-inch heels doling out two-for-one drink-special flyers to groups passing by. I decide this will translate on my résumé to "promotions assistant."

Everyone around me is in their early twenties. No one has anywhere to be, so we stay at the bar, drink cheap beer, and play old Irish love songs on the jukebox. There seems to be no limit to our days together. I've never had so many friends at once, whom I've liked so well, as I did in Galway, where I once felt so lonely and knew no one at all.

"Time to get off the Guinness," my boss, Brian, urges me discreetly one night, taking a gentle glance at my stomach. I look down, where my belly is indeed protruding more than when I arrived in Ireland three months ago. Back home, this kind of comment would have sent me spiraling into despair. Since middle school, I've struggled with body-image issues, like a lot of girls do, denying myself this or that and spending too much time pinching flesh in front of the mirror. So I'm shocked at this moment to realize that I haven't thought about my body in any self-punishing way in weeks, though by most standards I am woefully abusing it with cigarettes and alcohol. But my mind has twisted in a new direction this summer, and I've found it freeing these last few months to let go of some insecurities, large and small, or at least to put them on hold.

One night in early August, Eileen announces, "It's official, chicken. You're Irish." I surge with pride, as if I have passed a particularly difficult exam. It's exciting to fit somewhere when I have felt out of place everywhere for so long. It doesn't yet occur to me that this is simply my friend's way of expressing affection; she doesn't wish me to be anyone but myself, that, ultimately, I can't be. In Ireland, I become someone entirely different—a wild girl who stays out late, guzzles Guinness, tells coarse jokes, and says yes to every invitation. I let myself loose, a word that before never would have attached itself to me. That summer, maybe for the first time in my life, I existed wholly in the present moment, which is one of the liberating things about traveling to a place where no one knows you. I had no past or future, which suited me perfectly, since I did not wish to reckon with either.

# [ 6 ]

*Our heroine returns to her former life as a student, where she normally would be comforted by books and the lofty ideas contained therein, but finds herself unable to muster the necessary enthusiasm for anything but list-making and bellyaching. Somehow she finds the will to both graduate and entertain her relatives. An unexpected call answered.*

A week before the end of my endless Irish days, I call my father to test out the idea of staying. His silence blasts across the Atlantic.

"I don't understand," he finally says. "You want to graduate a year late?"

"Yeah, it's just a year. Plus, I can get lots of great student deals if I'm still enrolled in college." I'm repeating Carly's words, hoping I've imbued them with some of her unflagging confidence. Her mantra buzzes in my brain: What's the rush?

"Kiddo, I think you should come home, get your degree, and then examine your options."

"I just don't know what I'm doing with my life, Dad."

"Who does? I'll see you at the airport, okay?"

I'm not ready to go home, but I cannot locate the will necessary to defy him. I sigh heavily into the receiver. "Okay."

When I arrive on U.S. soil, my body recoils like a vampire's against the American summer sun. I'm even more ghostly pale than usual from cloudy Irish weather and drawn-out days in Irish pubs. My physique—though it was never profoundly muscular even in my wildest gym days—has softened like an overripe banana after four months of physical exertion limited to lifting pint glasses. I pepper my conversations with expressions like "shite" and "fair play to ye." It is my fervent belief that I have cultivated an Oscar-worthy Irish accent, though in reality I sound like the love child of the Lucky Charms leprechaun and Eliza Doolittle.

These summer souvenirs disappear a few weeks into my senior year of college, along with the rare moments of clarity collected in Ireland when I felt the freedom of a whole wide world opening up to me. The hours felt so expansive in Galway, like I was in an alternate dimension. Back home, time speeds up, and the unsettling feeling that it is running out attaches itself to me again, coupled with the paranoia that giving up music means relinquishing my one chance to be truly great at something, and now I will spend the rest of my life probably being—gasp!—ordinary.

Every morning I wake up in my dorm room thinking, Today is the day I will have a revelation about my life; today I will figure out what I am meant to be in the world. When nothing happens, I start making endless lists of possible careers, trying to take charge of my own destiny. I had a singular image in my mind for so long, could envision myself walking to orchestra rehearsals and teaching private lessons, but that picture is defunct now. Try as I might, I cannot see myself in my new future. Notebook pages with incoherent scrawling litter my bedroom floor like lily pads.

"Oooookaaaay, then," Erica concludes, popping her head in after class one night. "Time to quit popping the crazy pills and come out for drinks."

While I was disappearing into a faux-Irish life, Erica had experienced an altogether different kind of unexpected summer. Her art gallery internship turned out to be one long stretch inputting old show catalogs into an antiquated computer program. She didn't get to handle any art or even watch other people handling it. This semester she signed up for business classes, the beginning of her calculated transformation into a finance analyst; art has officially been relegated to a hobby.

It's a practical decision, the kind many of my friends were starting to make regarding their futures, but it depressed me nonetheless. I struggled with a romantic notion I had secretly nourished since I started playing music—that to be happy, we must make a career out of what we love most. I imagined us all as musicians and artists and philosophers. The idea of taking a job simply for the money was startling to me, and I was naïve enough then to judge others for it, even as I was in the midst of my own existential crisis. At least they were taking action. I was totally paralyzed with indecision. I had surprised myself by boarding that plane to Ireland, then sticking it out there and enjoying myself. After returning to college, I had a vague notion that I could do more unexpected, world-expanding things (maybe without so much Guinness). Travel guides had begun to crop up like weeds amid my textbooks. Every few days, I bid impossibly low on Priceline for cheap international flights, disappointed every time my fifty-dollar round-trip offer to Paris was rejected. But this new desire was all jumbled up with the various "shoulds" awaiting me in the U.S.—voices from others and from my own confused brain telling me what to do out there in the real world. There were so many voices swirling around in my head that I couldn't figure out how to strip them away and listen to the quiet yet insistent one humming softly in my subconscious, patiently waiting for an audience. It was that voice, I'm pretty sure, that led me to Ireland in the first place.

When I wasn't fretting over my life, I was studying. Ever since quitting music school in Boston, I had thrown myself into academics, the other area where I had always excelled, and was accepted as a transfer student at the University of Pennsylvania the spring of my sophomore year. I packed up my belongings and said goodbye to Copley Square and the Charles and hello to Ben Franklin and the Ivy League.

My first two friends at Penn were also transfer students. Jen, a five-foot rosy-cheeked spitfire, had upgraded from NYU but already knew scores of people at our new university. Some of her high school best friends are here, while the rest are sprinkled throughout New Haven, Providence, Boston, and New York City, which I do not realize until many months later are code for Yale, Brown, Harvard, and Columbia.

Tara, sick of the South, is a transfer from the University of Georgia. She is the first girl I've ever met who competed in honest-to-goodness beauty pageants, and she's the prettiest girl I have ever seen who isn't airbrushed. She has thick, curly black hair and foamy-green eyes. Her olive skin darkens exotically even on cloudy days, and her boobs look good in every top. Tara's only mortal quality is that she gains weight easily. To combat this, she survives on Clif bars and cafeteria salads and works out twice a day, although I find it hard to believe that an extra ten pounds would prevent men from running into solid objects when they pass by her any less than they do now. Tara doesn't have old friends here like Jen does, but she was in a sorority in Georgia, so she is an automatic member of the same chapter here. This provides her with a spontaneous social life. Even her good looks (an asset trumped only by family name) were not enough to overcome the religious barriers at her old school, where she was invited to join only the one Jewish sorority, but at Penn, Jewish students are a dominant force on campus. Many of the elite sororities are self-segregated Gucci-clad Jewish girls.

Life is flexible and beautiful to Tara, while Jen sees the world through slightly depressed glasses. I yin and yang between them, my energies shifting like a mood ring depending on who I'm with. And then junior year I meet Erica, who fits me just right. She's a transfer student, too, though a year behind me. We bond immediately over our shared confusion regarding the Italian language.

"What did she just say?" I whispered to her the first day of class.

"I have no idea. I'm just saying *sí* like everyone else."

"I think she's asking us about the weather."

"Then she should just look outside and stop torturing me."

I imagined life at an Ivy League university as one long stretch of parsing Hegel and pondering mind-expanding ontological questions, but instead I find myself in a land largely populated by rich sons and daughters more interested in designer handbags and fraternity parties than the brains they possess. Jen, Tara, and Erica aside, I can't find much to hold on to here; besides, I'm still reeling from leaving music school. My father the academic is thrilled that I've transferred to this elite institution, so I do not tell him one does not belong here simply because one attends. While any bright and diligent student can walk away with the degree, legitimate entry into this world depends on a specifically calibrated economic/social/regional pedigree, and the Friedmans from Syracuse, New York, simply have not inherited it.


At some point I am forced to ask myself, like all toiling away in the humanities, what I am going to do with my English degree. Yes, I have read far and wide. I can quote Marvel and Swift, Frost and Plath. I've been steeped in Austen, Dickens, and Dostoevsky.

I have committed certain pieces of wisdom to heart, most recently Oscar Wilde's "The aim of life is self-development. To realize one's nature perfectly—that is what each of us is here for." As my senior year draws to a close, I turn in my honors thesis: "Staging Silence: Reimagining the Women in Shakespeare's *Othello*." Yet precisely how a theoretical, experimental feminist rendering of a Renaissance play relates to my post-college plans remains unclear.

The English major "teaches you to think creatively and flexibly, to interpret, to analyze and communicate," my father tells me. However, it does not appear to come with a job title other than "poor shmuck who majored in English," and I'm pretty sure that's an unpaid internship. Maybe I should become an academic like my father. He gets to write books on pretty much whatever strikes his fancy, have summers off (not *off*, they all tell me, we're *working*), and spend a good portion of his time on a college campus in a kind of perpetual studenthood. But when I think about the years of my life involved in obtaining a Ph.D.—though it is a pursuit with a clear and definitive goal, and that appeals to me— I can't get excited about it. For starters, reading is such a pure thing, such blissful enjoyment, that I don't know if I want to professionalize it and risk, as with music, losing it on some level.

I poll my other English-major friends for ideas. Michelle is finishing up at Vassar. She considered going into publishing, but a recent depressing internship—the literary equivalent of Erica's archiving monotony—has convinced her otherwise. She, too, is contemplating her next move and, in the meantime, has accepted a nine-to-five job at an accounting firm in her hometown. When she graduates, she's moving back in with her parents in New Jersey. My friend Adam, who took to donning a red smoking jacket for inspiration while we were penning our theses (his on Poe), is off to Los Angeles to start his Ph.D. in American literature. He shrugs. "I have to do something."

We all do. It's what is expected. Besides, we have healthcare to worry about. And student debt. And making a contribution to society, making our parents proud, making something of ourselves that we can hopefully believe in.

Graduation day arrives like an unwanted houseguest. Inside the football stadium, parents crouch on hard white bleachers, hoping their camera lenses will zoom in fast enough to capture our speck-sized faces whizzing across the platform. It's nearly impossible to tell us apart in our cream gowns, so they flash our names on a large screen above the stage while a man adept at successfully pronouncing polysyllabic names under pressure introduces us. Our smiling professors sit in neat rows at the back of the stage. Their set faces remind me of those Semisonic lyrics—"You don't have to go home, but you can't stay here."

Two nights ago Jen, Tara, Erica, and I met one last time at our favorite local bar. We drank gigantic glasses of red wine and mulled over our post-college lives. Like hordes of other Penn grads, Tara and Jen are moving to Manhattan. Jen has been hired by Bank of Scotland and is anxious. "I start in three weeks. Can you believe it? Goodbye, summer vacations. Do you think I should go on Jdate now? I have a friend of a friend who's getting married to a guy she met on there. I don't think online dating services are pathetic anymore, do you? How else am I supposed to meet someone after college?"

Tara is spending the summer in Denver with her family before starting her job as a kindergarten teacher's assistant at the 92nd Street Y. "Woody Allen's kid is starting in the fall," she tells us in a hushed voice.

While Jen will make enough money to dull the pain of twelve-hour workdays, Tara's teaching gig pays too little to cover her expenses, so her parents have agreed to subsidize her rent. Tara is the least spoiled rich kid I know (she even has a personal philosophy against expensive underwear and T-shirts), but even she isn't willing to give up her city dreams over a little glitch like cash. Bohemia may not be dead, but no one I know from college has any interest in roughing it. Erica is working for a family friend who owns a real estate company. She still has a year of college left, and I deeply envy her this extra time to figure things out.

What are my plans for the summer? I'm staying right here in Philadelphia. My friend Bindi is heading to Washington, D.C., for an internship, and I'm subletting her minuscule studio apartment. I've gotten a job as a bartender in an Irish pub not far from campus, a sad attempt to re-create my lost Galway summer.

After the graduation ceremony, my family heads to Old City for dinner. I bring Erica to help me keep an eye on everyone. My parents have been divorced for six years, and each believes he/she has sacrificed the most personal comfort in order to have one joint meal. It is no exaggeration to relate that I have been dreading this dinner since my first day of college.

Up until this point, I have been distributing my time equally between my relatives: Independence Hall with Mom's side, Rittenhouse Square with Dad's, breakfast with one group, lunch with another—all punctuated by blissfully quiet taxi rides that I never want to end. "No rush," I want to tell the driver. "In fact, why don't you move into the bus lane, and we'll really take our time." I rest my head against the dirty leather and pray for red lights.

My parents, in true competitive form, have brought an equal number of allies, seven relatives each. Erica and I occupy the middle chairs across from each other, cutting the two sides neatly in half. We are Switzerland. Every time someone rises to walk to the other side of the table to chat amiably with someone from the past, I stare at Erica with alarm, and she mouths "It's okay" across the table.

When we sneak away to the bathroom, I announce that I'm eloping.

"With who?" she wants to know.

"Not now. I just mean when the time comes. This way we won't all have to be in the same room together ever again."

"It's really not that bad," she says, bending toward the mirror to apply more mascara. "Everyone is getting along great."

She is right, actually, but I am less prepared for things to go well than badly.

Back at the table, everyone has a glass of bubbling champagne.

"Welcome to the real world," my sister toasts, and everyone laughs but me.

If at this point I revealed that I never saw Carly again, it would not surprise anyone who has traveled. Our time in Galway was brief, a matter of weeks, and our friendship incited by proximity and personality. But it turns out our two lives were not nearly finished running parallel. While I returned to college, Carly continued traipsing through Europe, Morocco, and Asia for the next few months. She sent emails from Paris and Amsterdam, Hong Kong and Laos. Eventually, though, her funds ran out, and she went home, too.

We've been out of touch for several months when my cell phone rings a few weeks after graduation. "So. You've finished uni. Good on ya. Now—when are you coming to OZ?"

"Carly!"

"Owzitgoin?"

"Pretty good, I guess. Well, shitty, actually. I'm stuck in Philadelphia, waitressing, no clue what to do with myself."

"You're not stuck anywhere," Carly declares. "C'mon. Stop whinging. Listen, work for a few months. Save up and book your ticket to Australia. Mike's gone O.S. until December, so we've got a spare room. You can stay with my family and travel all over Australia."

Mike is Carly's twin brother and "O.S." stands for "overseas," where he has recently ventured for his own version of Carly's gap year. Everything this past year had been so blurry that the sheer force of the statement that hurtles through my brain next hits me like a wayward pigeon: I want to go to Australia. The clarity of it, after so much indecision, is dizzying. I had gone to Ireland on a whim to try to escape my life, but some hidden piece of myself was uncovered there. Being a stranger was invigorating. Maybe I am a traveler. There's only one way to find out. There are, of course, some practical issues to address.

"Will you take me to the set of *Home and Away*?"

She laughs. "Just book the ticket, mate."

# Part Two

# Australia

# [7]

*Our heroine alights on Australia, a faraway land she has only read about, and not much at that, and is ferried to the exotic suburbs of Sydney by her native friend and guide. Though she is much jet-lagged and rather perplexed by her host's progenitor— a skilled caller of birds—she nevertheless finds herself quickly and comfortably ensconced in her welcoming new abode.*

The Sydney airport is all wrong. In Dublin and New York, the security agents are pale and lifeless. They begrudgingly scan suspicious bodies with beeping wands or eye you accusingly after discovering the pair of tiny cuticle scissors you've unintentionally smuggled in your carry-on luggage. "What's this?" they ask, as if they don't already know, then drop it with a ping into the metal trash can. You expect to be treated like a piece of gum on the bottom of someone's shoe at the airport. After all, it's a serious place where very serious business is happening. You strip down to a single layer of clothing, remove your shoes, pack your toiletries in minute see-through bottles, extract your laptop from its carrying case, look as serious and nonthreatening as possible, and hope you make it from point A to point B without incident. Post-9/11, that's all we ask.

But in Sydney, it's different. All of the very serious business is happening here, too, but people are tan. They're helpful. They're *smiling*. Even the beagles sniffing your bags for drugs seem to be grinning pleasantly. The one exception is a morose X-ray technician who scolds me for not declaring my vitamins as "organic medicine," but she's unconvincing, like an actor playing a character whose motivation is unclear.

The passport control agent is a painfully good-looking Brad Pitt type with lean, muscular arms. His bronze skin glows like he was at the beach mere moments ago, and if he shook his thick blond curls, flecks of sand would fly out. I am adrift in those curls, blissfully unaware that my tangled dark hair is unattractively matted on the left side of my face, on which I've been dozing for the past twelve hours.

"Where are you staying?" he asks.

"In Sydney." I bat my sleep-crusted eyes at him. Surely his next question will be "What time should I pick you up?"

"Where in Sydney?"

"Ummm...near the beach?" Carly's address is scrawled on a piece of paper somewhere in my bag, but my synapses are all jet-lagged.

"Okay," he says patiently. "Bondi Beach?" He's willing to keep this up, but it's clear our date is off.

"Yes, that's the one!" (Carly lives in the complete opposite direction of Bondi Beach, actually.)

"Is a mate picking you up?"

When I say yes again, he seems satisfied. At least a geographically challenged American won't be wandering around his country unattended.

Here is what you should know about Australia. It's rotten with kangaroos. In Sydney, the government employs a handful of roo-shooers whose sole responsibility is to shoo them off the Harbour Bridge around five A.M., before the daily commute begins. It's a dangerous, delicate job, because if you cross a kangaroo, your reward is a swift kick in the gut. Australia is also home to the infamous drop bear. Delicately perched in any number of native trees, these creatures (which resemble koalas) have been known to descend onto the shoulders of many an unsuspecting tourist. You'll notice the locals give the trees a wide berth, and you should, too. They'll claw your eyes out, given half a chance. Hoop snakes are perhaps the most terrifying of all. This creature grasps its tail in its mouth to roll after its prey. Contorted like this, it's terrifyingly fast. One was once clocked at over sixty miles an hour. The hoop snake has a stinger on the tip of its tail, so highly venomous that any unfortunate tree it brushes past instantly withers, turns black, and dies. If you encounter a hoop snake in the wild, run uphill. That's the only way to escape.

All lies! Every word. (Except the part about kangaroos kicking you in the gut—that happens.) All this misinformation about Australia is compliments of Carly, who randomly dropped these faux facts in Galway, apparently for her own amusement. Now, four and a half months was long enough to discover the Irish's impressive gift of spouting complete bullshit with a perfect poker face. (Eileen once told a group of wide-eyed American college students that she had been to America only once, since it was such a long swim.) But Carly is the only Australian I know, and I consider us friends, which in America means she should have dissolved into sheepish giggles at some point. But she didn't. Thus, her tales have morphed into myth since we first met. So when I call her a few weeks before my October departure date, asking to be reminded again what to do in the event of a hoop-snake confrontation, she laughs so hard she starts to choke. "Mate! You don't still believe that, do you?"

However, just because these particular gems are untrue doesn't mean Australia is anything like Ireland, a country with no snakes (apparently, Saint Patrick drove them all away) or major variations in the temperature (the only way to tell the difference between summer and winter is to measure the temperature of the rains, so the saying goes), whose tidy green belly can be traversed over the course of a leisurely afternoon. Although opinions vary some, it is generally agreed that Australia is home to at least six of the world's ten deadliest snakes. There are also the saltwater and freshwater crocodiles ("freshies" are less dangerous than "salties"—which aren't considered man-eaters but will happily take a nip/tuck here or there if bothered; so go the distinctions one must comfort herself with in Australia). As part of their standard coursework, school-age Australians learn not only how to navigate colossal, pounding ocean waves but also strategies for surviving a shark attack. Amazingly, a little unassuming guy, the box jellyfish, is quietly responsible for more deaths in Australia than snakes, sharks, and saltwater crocodiles combined. Perhaps most remarkable, the deadliest creature of all in Australia is—wait for it—the gum tree. That's right, a *tree.* Gum trees practice a form of triage where they cut off the water supply to one of their limbs if there is a drought, and there is always a drought in Australia. Eventually, the spurned branch dies and, with alarming frequency, breaks off and whooshes down onto an unsuspecting camper fast asleep in her tent, or crashes through the roof of a pensioner who has just settled in for a relaxing cup of tea.

But I don't know any of this yet. The only thing I really know about Australia once Carly has dispelled her tall tales is that it is a great open expanse of land, as big as the United States with one eighteenth the population. Ireland was a tiny island a mere jaunt across the pond, but it will take almost twenty-four hours to reach Australia. Somewhere over the Pacific, I'll lose an entire day and, an ever trippier feat, on the way back arrive earlier than I left. In Ireland, I was able to escape for a while, but in a place like Australia, I might truly be able to disappear.

\* \* \*

A few weeks before my twenty-second birthday, I break the news to my parents that I'm leaving again.

"And then what?" my father asks.

I answer his question with one of my own. "Who knows?" I shrug and look up at the ceiling, as in "only the universe holds those heavy secrets, man." I say, "I'm only twenty-one years old."

These are Carly's words tumbling out, but treating my father like an oppressive regime attempting to get me to fall in line is easier than saying "I don't know." All I know is that I want to leave again, though this time it feels distinctly more like running toward something than running away.

My parents are understandably confused, as anyone would be when caught in the whirlwind of another human being's one-eighty. Who can blame them? Australia constitutes an even bigger rebellion than Ireland for me because I have my degree now, though I have no idea what to do with it other than let my mother frame it, then allocate it to one of the cardboard boxes in her basement, storing sections of my life. Still, I'm a bona fide college graduate and can officially start my real life, whatever that means. And real life does not appear to be four months in Australia. Plus, contrary to my general conversion to Carly's mantra, "What's the rush?," a part of me does worry about falling behind my peers, about further divesting myself of material goods through travel at the same moment when they are beginning to accumulate apartments and careers and relationships. I have no boyfriend. No childhood home to return to. No grown-up job offers (no doubt because I haven't applied for any). And now no degree to finish. I'm completely untethered. There is the smallest possibility that when I go to Australia, I might float away forever.

Despite their concerns, both of my parents, as always, find ways to support me. My mother donates frequent-flier miles. She cuts up thousands of tiny squares of paper—one for each mile—

and puts them all in a little plastic bubble container like the ones they hand out at weddings. When I open it, white confetti spills like snow into my lap. My father's graduation gift is five hundred dollars, and I have fifteen hundred saved in tips, enough to get me through my first month if the Sydney job market proves as difficult as the Galway one.

In certain ways, leaving is easier this time. I've proved that I can navigate new cities, cobble together a living, and convince a foreign bank to give me an account. (In Ireland this endless process involved stacks of documents from my landlord and employer, plus testimony from everyone I knew that I did, in fact, exist.) After Carly picks me up from the airport, I'll stay with her family for a few days while I get my bearings and find a cheap apartment. No deranged Irishman will stumble through my bedroom door at four A.M. My load is physically lighter, too. I exchanged Big Red for more practical luggage: one carry-on black suitcase and a real backpacker's backpack, shiny silver and black. It represents a change in the way I move in the world—a new mobility.

Carly is waiting for me after I make it through customs. She emerges from between two tall men in suits, remarkably transformed since we said goodbye in Galway a year ago. Gone is her uniform of holey khakis, drab wool sweaters and muddy sneakers. Now she's clad in neon-green shorts and a thin cotton tank top with VOLCOM splashed across her chest in big blue letters. Her formerly long, limp hair has been cut short; stylish layers frame her heart-shaped face. But it's not her haircut and outfit that make her unrecognizable for a few disorienting seconds. She has lost weight, a good fifteen pounds. She hugs me with tan, sculpted arms. I've missed this girl.

"Welcome to Australia!" she says. "Let's get out of this bloody airport."

By the time we reach her car, I'm sweating. I flip my shoulder-length hair up into a bun, roll up my jeans. We throw my bags into the trunk (the "boot" here), then Carly yanks off her flip-flops and tosses them through an open window into the backseat of her little red Barina.

"Much better," she sighs, as if the flimsy half inch of rubber between her and the ground were as constricting as Chinese foot-binding. She pushes in the clutch and brake with bare feet, throws the car in reverse. I've never seen anyone drive without shoes. I want to point this out, but I know I'll come across as prim and worried, so instead I say, "I can't drive a stick shift."

"It's called a manual, mate. 'Stick shift' is a bit rude."

In Ireland I learned that "rude" can mean vulgar. After my first shift at the Hole in the Wall, I made the mistake of asking if anyone could give me a ride home instead of a lift home, essentially propositioning the entire male staff. It had taken a few confusing moments and a sympathetic girl bartender for me to realize my mistake. Now it takes me only a second to realize I've used a euphemism for male genitalia.

The Sydney sun is relentless. Growing up in upstate New York, one of the grayest parts of the U.S., meant whole weeks might pass with no more than a fleeting ray of light, a momentary sun escape before it was swallowed up again by dense, omnipresent clouds. In middle school, my friends and I heard a rumor that people who overdid the sunbathing in places like California and Florida were often instructed by their doctors to move to either Seattle or Syracuse, the same way Victorian patients were once encouraged to depart for the country to cure their urban ailments. We never verified these details. We didn't need to. Every day we saw the effects of a sunless city on people's dispositions. When you're little, you adapt pretty easily to your environment (especially when you have no point of comparison), but some of the adults we knew struggled mightily. Tanning was an incredibly popular antidote, and a few of my friends' parents forever looked like they had just returned from the Caribbean, their brown faces oddly out of place shoveling a foot of snow from their driveway or bundled inside a heavy fleece jacket at the supermarket.

"Check it out." Carly sticks her right arm out the open window to point. She smiles broadly, waiting for my reaction. Light ricochets off the Opera House's enormous sail-like appendages, which yawn and stretch toward the sky. The striking centerpiece of the city is set out on its own little tip of the harbor, and boats race past, leaving frothy white streaks. The color of the ocean is what could only be called Sydney blue, a soft, shimmering, incandescent shade that is so inviting, the bodily urge to dive in is overwhelming. It hits me that Carly's drastic physical change mirrors her environmental one. After spending your entire life in a place that virtually bathes you in beauty and light, how could she fail to be depressed in lively but granite-sky Galway? Being a die-hard bookworm, and later bar worm, I was at home in a place where the rain gives you an almost daily excuse to avoid any outdoor excursions, not to mention the fact that the most glamorous body of water in my childhood was the Erie Canal. But Carly dreaded those long, chilly days cooped up on an island where even the ocean held no appeal.

Now we are up and over the Harbour Bridge, where Carly teases me about the roo-shooers again, Sydney receding in the distance. Carly's family lives twenty minutes north in a suburb called Forestville. The landscape is greener than I expected. Ridiculously, I had imagined the whole country as one great desert, Australians camped out like Bedouins along the way. On the side of the road, a sign announces that the fire danger today is high, greater than low or moderate but not as treacherous as very high or extreme. The decades-long drought has intensified over the past four weeks. You have to wash your car on the grass to conserve water.

Carly's family lives in a typical suburban house. It's two stories, cream with a green roof. But the backyard proves this is where the points of reference to the Northeast neighborhoods of my childhood end. There are three robust palm trees Carly's parents planted when they moved in over twenty years ago. A hammock droops leisurely between them. All sorts of exotic flowers are in bloom: hibiscus, hydrangea, bougainvillea, bird-of-paradise, daises, may. Ripening fruit dots the mandarin, lemon, and orange trees. A blue-tongued lizard who lives under the rectangular pool is currently sunning herself on a section of concrete. A faint buzzing sound, crickets and other creatures I cannot yet identify, hums through the air, giving me the sense that the whole place is vibrating, teeming.

Sebastian, the family Maltese, greets us at the door. He licks my ankle once, then sprints away.

"Poor Sebby. He misses Mike," Carly says.

We walk through the carpeted hallway, past her younger brother Steve's room, an explosion of T-shirts and smells not entirely unlike Patchi and Portu's man-cave back in Ireland. In the kitchen, I freeze. Carly's mom is naked.

Carly chuckles. "Mum and her friends made that calendar to raise money for a charity."

"No *way*," I whisper in awe.

My own mother won't even wear a swimsuit without one of those little matching skirts, much less go the Full Monty for strangers. Even though it is the beginning of October, Muriel is still on display in all her September glory, looking wistfully over her bent knee against an ocean backdrop.

"Dad won't change the month," Carly explains before I have a chance to ask.

She leads the way to Mike's currently unoccupied bedroom. It's next to Carly's, with a wardrobe that abuts hers. It smells like fresh linens. All I see is the bed. I zoom in on the pillows, soft and plump. "Thanks, Carlz," I slur, dropping my backpack.

Sebby plants himself in the doorway. He cocks his head to one side, a look that says "And now you're sleeping in his room?" before promptly dismissing himself again.

"Are you tired, mate?" Carly asks me. "Why don't you have a little lie-down? I'll give you the grand tour when you wake up."

I drop heavily onto the edge of the bed. "I'll just rest my eyes for a few minutes."

"No worries. Sleep as long as you like."

These are the last words I hear before collapsing coma-like for the next twelve hours.

"Oi! Carly! Get your mate up. There's a kookaburra!" An excited, disembodied voice floats into my room.

"Dad, let her sleep. She's jet-lagged."

A soft knock.

"Hello?" I say.

For a second I think I am back in my dorm room, annoyed that Erica is making so much noise this early in the morning. And then I remember. Sydney. Carly. Houseful of people who I thanked for their hospitality by falling asleep before meeting them. I sit up with an embarrassed gasp, but the grinning man peeking into my room is unconcerned with formalities.

"Good on ya, Rach. You're awake," he says, as though I've accomplished a magnificent feat before even getting out of bed. He beams at me.

"Hi." I'm not sure what to do next.

"Dad!" Carly bursts in. "Leave her alone."

"No, it's okay," I say. "I was just getting up." It's sinking in: I'm in Sydney. I'm in Sydney. I'm in Sydney!

"Listen, Rach," Pete rushes on, ignoring us. "There was a kookaburra outside. If you hurry, I might be able to get him back."

"Oh, wow, a kookaburra!" I exclaim as he rushes back down the hall.

The fact that I have absolutely no idea what he is talking about must be obvious to Carly, who clarifies: "It's a bird."

Before I can ask how exactly her father plans to get this mysterious bird back, I hear my answer. "Koo-koo-koo-koo-koo-koo-kaa-kaa-kaa!" reverberates throughout the first floor of the house. Instinctively, I cover my head in alarm. But the sound is coming from outside, where we soon discover Pete balanced on a lawn chair on the back porch, yodeling through cupped hands into the trees. "Koo-koo-koo-koo-koo-kaa-kaa-ka!" fills the air like maniacal laughter.

"Is he okay?" I turn around to ask Carly but instead come face-to-face with her fully clothed mother, Muriel. Carly is behind her, doubled over laughing.

"Oh, Pete," Muriel says with a sigh, but she's smiling, too. "Stop shouting into the bush." She turns to me. "G'day, Rach! Don't mind Carly's dad. He's just dying to show you the local wildlife. Come inside and have some brekkie."

Previously only close family and friends called me Rach, and only when I was very young. In the way that Debbie Gibson became Deborah when her illustrious teen-idol career ended, I killed this truncated version of my name pretty much as soon as I was old enough to speak, along with my dad's embarrassing pet name, Rachie Bachie. But here it's immediately apparent that Rach is the unabashed property of an informal population who shorten anything and everything without ceremony or permission: afternoon is arvo, sunglasses are sunnies, chocolates are chocys. I could rail against it, but what's the point? When twenty million people decide you're Rach, you're Rach. Besides, there is something about the Australian wink, nudge, and shrug of an accent—and the Dawsons themselves—that makes this immediate intimacy feel natural, comforting.

Muriel looks a little like my mother. They have the same chestnut-colored hair, my mother's light or dark depending on the season. Neither wears much makeup, maybe a few strokes of blush or a little eyeliner, but nothing more. Each woman is slim and graceful, though Muriel's figure, like Carly's, is sturdy and athletic, whereas my mother and I have softer, more bookish physiques. It's strange how you can see your own future in your mother's body.

Carly has pulled herself together by this point. She follows us into the kitchen. Pete is close behind, making excuses for the kookaburra's poor showing. "Next time, Rach. Next time. Now, then. What's on the agenda for today, girls?"

"Come on, Pete. Let her have a chance to catch her breath," Muriel admonishes.

"We are so thrilled that you're here—just thrilled." He opens an enormous newspaper, *The Sydney Morning Herald.* "Here you go. That'll help you get acclimatized." Pete hands me the World section as if we've been sitting down to breakfast together for years, and in a just-entered-an-alternate-reality way, it kind of feels like we have.

# [ 8 ]

*Our heroine embarks on a brief journey to the Outback, wherein she meets a rock of indecent proportions and heat of insulting voracity. Locates gainful employment of coffee and curry, philosophizes and questions—questions and philosophizes.*

Amazingly, I get a job on my third day in Australia. I'm hired at a restaurant in Manly, an upscale beach town southeast of Forestville. The trip out there will take me at least an hour (and two buses) each way, but I accept the position on the spot, afraid to test my luck. That night at dinner, I deliver the good news.

"Thank you so much for having me," I say to Pete and Muriel for the fourteenth time. "Now that I have a job, I'll start apartment hunting. I don't want to inconvenience you for too long."

I wait for their inevitable praise. What a responsible houseguest I am, how impressive it is I've already found a job, how thoughtful already to be considering finding an apartment while still in the capricious throes of jet lag.

"Apartment?" Pete says.

On the heels of his question is Muriel's no-nonsense counsel: "Don't be daft! You're staying with us while you're here. We have to show you around."

"Well…" Surely they can't want a visitor for four whole months. I was brought up to believe that anything over a long weekend verges on impolite, even if your hosts are too gracious to say so.

"Now, hang on a mo', Rach." Muriel again. Her expression is serious. "You're only here for four months, and you have to travel the entire continent of Australia. You can't afford to pay rent and save any money to travel. Your parents sent you all this way, and we wouldn't dream of dropping you off in the middle of Sydney to fend for yourself."

Well, sure, I'd considered a few weekend trips here and there, but traverse the entire continent of Australia? Yet now that Muriel has taken rent out of the equation, the possibility of traveling—really *backpacking,* as Carly was doing when we met, but I have never experienced—presents itself in all its alluring, terrifying splendor.

Muriel isn't finished. "What's more," she says, "I think you should quit this job. How much are they paying you?"

"Nine dollars an hour."

"Outrageous!" she declares. "In downtown Sydney, you'll make double that. But that's not the issue. You definitely do not want to miss seeing the Aussie Outback. In a few months it will be full-blown high season, and the tickets are going to get more expensive. You should go now if you have any hope of finding a good fare."

"Plus, it's only going to get hotter. You should definitely quit, mate," Carly agrees.

The verb is a sore spot on my tongue. I've never quit a job. I've had jobs where the owners knew I was there only a certain time: the school year, the summer, a stint over winter break. But I've never left without warning, definitely never quit before I've even started. Plus, since leaving music school, I've developed a complex about being branded a quitter. I have incorrectly concluded that quitting is not a choice of one thing over the other but rather a comment on one's character, no matter how trivial the commitment or how great the opportunity on the other side of quitting is. I'm also a die-hard people pleaser, and the idea of disappointing a restaurant manager I've spent a grand total of five minutes with sends shivers through me. Not to mention that it's one thing for Carly to tell me to give up my job, but her *parents* want me to quit? Two adults are choosing travel over employment. Can they be serious?

"Quit?" I say.

All three of them nod emphatically.

"And go to the Outback...now?"

"I'd leave in the next few days, if possible," Muriel says. "The sooner the better."

"Now Carly, what are you going to show Rach while she's here?" Pete asks, the previous topic nonchalantly discarded now that the Dawsons have stated their positions. "There's the Opera House, Botanical Gardens, Powerhouse Museum, Hyde Park Barracks—"

"All right, Dad." Carly rolls her eyes. "I've lived here for almost twenty-two years, so I'm pretty sure I know where to take her."

"Now, darling, come on. I'm just trying to help. What's the plan?"

Aha! He wants us to have a plan. This is more like it. More parental.

"Tonight I'm taking her out for drinks to celebrate her liberation from the drudgery of employment."

"Excellent!" Pete says, clinking my wineglass. "That's the stuff." And once again I lose my bearings in this strange new universe where none of the rules of my old life seem to apply.

My hands are shaking when I call the restaurant to tell them that I won't be in tomorrow for my first shift. I expect no less than the earth to crack open and swallow me, such is the extent to which I'm defying my own natural laws. But of course no such thing happens. The manager sighs "All right, then," and hangs up. As on that first day in Galway drinking Guinness with a stranger, I feel a twinge of excitment, like maybe I do have a say in my life after all.

"What should I have?" I ask Carly when we're waiting in line at the bar.

"Do not get Foster's. Everyone thinks that's what Australians drink, but we don't. It's absolute shit. Victoria Bitter is the cheapest, but it tastes like cat piss. There's Tooheys New or Carlton Cold, but I'm having a Malibu and pineapple. Why don't you give that a go?"

Carly's two closest friends, Jessica and Natarsha (Jess and Tarsh) meet up with us a few minutes later. They're a year younger, in their last year of university, and both planning postgraduation trips abroad. Jess is headed to England. Tarsh is saving up for Nepal.

"So…how long are you going to travel?" I ask.

"A year or two," Jess says.

"Not sure," Tarsh says.

"Your parents are okay with this?"

"Okay with what?"

"Traveling indefinitely."

"Sure. Everyone does it."

"My parents did a gap year when they were my age." This from Tarsh.

Though the gap year hasn't caught on in the U.S., it's typical in Australia and other countries. However, it's one thing to digest an entire country of young people wandering the globe and altogether something else to picture my parents hoisting up backpacks, heading off toward unplanned adventure—toward anything unplanned.

"So you're saving up right now to go traveling?" I ask.

"What else would we be saving for?"

"What about student loans? Won't any of you have any student-loan payments?"

"Student loans? No. We've got HECS."

HECS stands for Higher Education Contribution Scheme, which is a colorless appellation for a concept that totally blows my mind. Tarsh and Jess explain how the government fronts the bill for your education, which you then have the option of paying back through the tax system once your income reaches a certain level. The bill is taken right out of your paycheck a little at a time, week by week. University isn't free here, but it's light-years less expensive than many of our universities. And—get this—if you have to live away from home, the government gives you an allowance.

"The government *pays* you to go to university?" I marvel.

"Too right," Carly says.

My parents struggled to pay for my education once I abandoned music and the hefty college scholarship that accompanied it. They had been saving since I was born, but still it wasn't easy to shell out over thirty thousand dollars two years in a row. We were in that middle-income bracket—too well-off for financial aid but not wealthy enough to comfortably weather the ever bulging tuition. Still, they managed it. Not being saddled with student debt, the kind my mother was paying back for her late-in-life law degree, is a huge gift, one I do not fully appreciate at the time. After my loan-free bachelor's degree, I am understandably on my own financially.

"We're tapped out, kid," my father summarizes.

My mom says, "Just keep in mind when you're choosing a career—money doesn't solve everything, but it sure makes life easier."

I relay all this to the girls, concluding with "And if you don't have a good job, you can't get good healthcare." It's the Australians' turn to express shock.

"Healthcare, massive student debt," Carly muses. "No wonder Americans stress about starting careers right away. Bloody ridiculous."

"No wonder they barely travel," adds Jess.

I had never thought of it that way. During my summer in Ireland, I had encountered the widespread belief that most Americans don't travel because they are uninterested in "anything beyond their own backyard." It is often assumed that willful ignorance is our regional affliction, same as Parisians are rude and Germans scarily well organized, but in Australia I consider that maybe the whole U.S. system is somehow complicit in keeping us at home. In addition to the baggage of debt and healthcare, however, there does seem to be a nebulous cultural value American society is missing, though I don't believe it's lack of interest in the larger world. In Australia travel abroad is considered a key component of a well-rounded life, its own kind of necessary education, whereas I know many people back home feel my four months here are somehow shirking my responsibilities as an adult. These Aussie girls are free to set their own courses in the world, to meander and experiment. Their travels are not bumps along the road—they are life itself. See the world and then come home and decide who you want to be in it, not the other way around, as seems the general trajectory in the U.S.

I thought Carly might go with me to the Outback, she's been there twice before. Even after I find a good Internet fare, it's not a cheap jaunt, and she's working heaps to save up for travel in addition to taking university classes, so she stays behind while I heed Muriel's advice and fly out alone a week after arriving in Sydney. The night before my trip, Carly helps me pack. I pull my pristine backpack out of the closet, unzip it, and then proceed to stare intently at it, as if I'm attempting a Jedi mind trick.

"It's not going to pack itself, mate."

"I know. It's just so small." I put my hand inside and prod the fabric, gauging the empty space.

"She'll be right. What do you need other than a T-shirt, a pair of pants, and sunnies?"

"I don't know." Forget that Carly is perfectly content with just one of each of these items for five days (and that she has failed to mention underwear). I've never been to the Australian desert; the closest I've come is Outback Steakhouse. Surely it's a place that requires options. Leaving Big Red behind makes me feel like I've already whittled my worldly possessions down to the absolute necessities. Imagining going somewhere new with less seems impossible, even if it's under a week. If my future self had revealed to the present self that soon I would be the proud owner of only a handful of possessions, traveling with a small pack for several months somewhere I had not yet imagined, I would have laughed in my own face. Right now I'm finding it difficult to let Carly convince me that, no, I don't need to bring four novels on a five-day trip. I don't need to cart along my full-size bottles of shampoo and moisturizer.

In the end, she packs for me: two short-sleeved T-shirts, one gray tank top, one long-sleeved tee, my favorite purple sweatshirt for cold desert nights, blue capri sweatpants (oh, how I wish someone had told me how hideous these looked, even for the Outback), a pair of gray socks, sneakers, green Tevas, six pairs of underwear, 50 SPF sunscreen, a small bag of toiletries, my camera, my journal, and a copy of *Aman: The Story of a Somali Girl* that Muriel lent me a few days ago.

Carly helps me hoist the pack up onto my shoulders, then buckles me in: one thin strap across my chest and another around my waist to prop the pack firmly atop my hips.

"Look at you!" She preens like a proud parent sending her child off to the first day of school.

Carly's parents pop their heads into the room. "Look at you!" they exclaim.

"One sec, Rach." Pete sprints out of the room and returns a moment later with a floppy wide-brimmed blue hat. He drops it onto my head. "There you go, mate. That sun will give you a thrashing if you're not careful."


After three hours on a bumpy flight, I land in Alice Springs, or the Alice, as it's familiarly known. At the baggage carousel, a man whose leathery skin looks like he's spent the last ten years directly under the central Australian sun walks straight up to me and greets me using my full name. I let this psychic lead me out to the parking lot, where he thankfully does not abduct me but instead deposits me at my white tour van and promptly disappears like a mirage. Nine other travelers are already belted in, slouched and overheated with eyes closed while the air-conditioning does its feeble best to combat the ninety-five-degree heat. My fellow travelers include Stomatos, a good-natured but bossy Greek guy who offers his expert opinion on everything from how long dinner should take to prepare (versus how long it's actually taking) to which branches work best as firewood. Stomatos is traveling with Mauricio, a Mexican guy he met on the road, and with whom he's decided to return to Mexico in a few months. Also on board is Tobias, a German who teaches primary-school art and is planning to propose to his girlfriend of eight years when he returns home in two weeks. Quiet Tobias, soft-spoken and reserved, shocks us all the second night when he gets drunk and uses a nearby tree to execute a pole dance (he's surprisingly limber) to a Britney Spears song. There are three Irish girls—Sinead, Aiofe, and Eva—two on working holiday in Australia and the third visiting them. Sandy is an American girl on her way to teach English for a year in China. She is visiting her Australian friend Miranda, a lobbyist in Canberra. Finally, there's Orly, an Israeli woman who pines constantly for her lost

New Zealand boyfriend, with whom she has broken up because her trip is nearly over. In a week, she will be back home.

We exchange all the usual getting-to-know-you travel questions. Where are you from? How long are you in Australia? Where have you been so far? What do you do back home? When I tell people I'm from New York, I get the familiar reaction. First they praise Manhattan. They marvel at the skyscrapers, the Broadway lights, the celebrities. Many of the people I meet traveling have been there, and others want to visit. Since that rainy day when Brian mistook my identity at the Hole in the Wall, I've tried countless times to clarify that I'm from upstate New York, a good five hours from Times Square. When I explain that New York is a rather large state, not just a city, I'm appraised warily. Or greeted with pity, like, "Sweetheart, even if you're *not* from Manhattan, wouldn't we all be better off if you pretended you were? Isn't it without a doubt better than wherever you grew up?"

I'd be happy to go along with this, absolutely thrilled to misrepresent myself as a sophisticated city girl, if doing so didn't mean laying claim to a tragedy that doesn't belong to me in the same way it does to true Manhattanites. Still, some backpackers seem determined to intimately attach me to that terrible morning. What usually happens immediately after the New York cooing is the uncomfortable onslaught of 9/11 sympathy. In Ireland, it was pure, unchecked empathy offered up with a slow, sad shake of the head. That was in 2002. Now it's 2003, and Bush has declared war on Iraq. Sympathy is still expressed, but after it come all the questions, none of which I can answer. All I can do is speak for myself, express my own regret and confusion, and feel the growing discomfort of that no longer being enough.

We reach our campsite just before sunset. Dinner our first night is a massive pot of stew into which our guide, Leah, tosses a variety of vegetables and an unidentifiable meat she claims is chicken. For dessert, I teach the Irish girls how to make s'mores.

No graham crackers or marshmallows are on hand, so we put pieces of a Flake (an Australian brand of chocolate bar) between two mini-chocolate-chip cookies and roast them in a pan over the fire.

Around nine, when all the various fireside conversations have petered out, we unroll our sleeping bags (I surreptitiously but violently shake mine free of any lurking desert creatures). Leah hands out the swags (a waterproof shell made of canvas, similar to a tarp) that will serve as an outer layer to keep us warm. The temperature has dropped drastically since the sun set. I hop inside and zip myself up, then flip over onto my back. The sky is a planetarium of stars, completely unimpeded by clouds, trees, lights, or smog. It is the starriest sky I have ever seen. Soon the only sound is the others breathing, all of us cozy in our swags with full bellies, enveloped by the vast quiet. All along I've thought the best way to keep out all the voices in my head directing my life this way and that was to stay busy, to distract my brain from itself, but it's this profound silence that releases me from worry. Only a single strain of thought runs through my head like a simple melody: this is exactly where I want to be, out here in the world. At some point I fall asleep, but I have no sense of exactly when, because I see that starry sky all night long in my dreams.

Leah wakes us up at four A.M. with determined perkiness. We pull together tea and coffee and toast, then stumble off to the ramshackle restroom, a tin structure housing two mirrors, two sinks, and two outhouse-style bathrooms. I am the last girl to finish getting ready, and although I take barely ten minutes, the campsite is eerily deserted when I emerge. No van, no swag, no backpacks, not even my own. It's happened. I have been left in the middle of the Australian Outback. Now I'll be bitten by a venomous snake and die a slow, painful death. As I am somewhat gleefully considering how sorry Carly will be for sending me out here alone, the van, an apparition out of nowhere, barrels toward me. It slows down long enough for Tobias and Stomatos to yank me inside, like in those films when the hero sprints to catch a moving train, before we are off again, racing to beat the sunrise we want to witness from a lookout point half an hour away.

The next three days are an unconventional routine of hiking, driving, sunrises, and sunsets. Each morning Leah hurtles breakfast at us with the same willful cheeriness, then we race off somewhere to marvel at the various shades of lightening or darkening sky. Hands down the best sunrise/sunset presents itself at Ayers Rock, or Uluru, as native Australians call it, the monolithic sandstone rock that graces at least half of all Australian postcards. I take no fewer than thirty photos each of the sunrise and sunset at Uluru. The sky turns so many magnificent shades of red so swiftly that I'm never sure where the pinnacle of beauty is. So I snap away, we all do, witnessing nearly the entire event behind our lenses.

Uluru holds great spiritual significance for Aboriginals, and they don't want you climbing it. Our guide tells us this, as does everyone else who works at and around the rock. There are other reasons not to climb. It's steep, the sun is merciless, and more than thirty people have died so far attempting it, even though there is a clearly marked section with a rope to hold on the way up.

Despite these compelling reasons, people do climb. When we arrive, a steady stream of ants is marching single-file up the rock. Our group chooses instead to do a four-hour walk around the monolith's base, marveling again and again at its enormity and at such unforgiving heat when it's not even ten A.M. Not only are you discouraged from climbing Uluru, you are also reminded that it's not a souvenir. Yet people abscond with bits of red rock, stuffing them boldly in pockets and backpacks and returning home with them. Only something strange has been happening over the years. Tourists are returning the stolen sandstone in great numbers, posting pieces back, often at great expense, and begging the site's employees to return them to their place of origin. The notes give detailed directions about where this or that rock was abducted, followed by profuse, shamed apologies. Since picking the forbidden fruit, terrible things have happened. One woman's note describes a sudden illness, another a series of pets' deaths. Trauma after trauma is related, each person convinced that these troublesome events are tied to the contraband.

It's a satisfying form of justice. The rock is where it's meant to be, where it's fated to be. Its resolve to remain is like a force field—after all, it cannot speak for itself, and though the Aboriginals do their best to protect it, their warnings too often go unheeded. Or maybe the rock is more like a magnet calling itself home, bringing back the various bits of its lost body at whatever cost.


When I return from the Outback, I renew my job search. Luck strikes again days later, when I'm hired at a café to work the cash register and assist the barista during the busy morning shifts. The café is the bottom level of a massive office building in downtown Sydney, tucked down the street from the Parliament House, whose colonnaded verandah reminds me more of an old-time saloon than a government building, and a few blocks east of the Domain, the city's large open space that hosts dozens of amateur rugby and soccer leagues, outdoor concerts, soapbox orators, and general lazing about.

My shift starts at seven A.M., which means—and I can feel the exhaustion creeping over me even at the memory—I have to get up at five A.M. to shower and eat, then walk fifteen minutes to the bus stop at the end of the Dawsons' street to catch the six-twenty bus into the city. Getting up early for a spectacular sunrise is one thing, but this routine, well, it sucks. I must resemble a groggy noon-hour Patchi, but luckily, no one is awake to witness it—or have the unfortunate task of attempting conversation

with me. The bus drivers here wear white kneesocks. That surprising uniform choice is all I'm capable of comprehending at
six A.M. The first few mornings, the promise of the heart-stopping
Sydney Opera House, rising like a beacon to my left as we cross
the Harbour Bridge, is enough to keep me awake. But soon even
this becomes routine. I drift in and out of consciousness, willing
my body to wake me at the right stop. The upside is that I finish
work at one-thirty P.M., giving me the afternoons free, and the
pay is pretty good.

When I arrive at the café, I greet Joey, the barista, with a
sleepy nod. He slips me two shots of espresso, which I throw
back like tequila, visualizing the caffeine coursing through my
veins. Even with the coffee, I'm never fully awake, just jittery.
That doesn't help my performance, which is—and this is an
understatement—woeful. It is so woeful, in fact, that I wonder if
I have imagined being a good waitress up until now.

My current position is not technically waiting tables. There is
a restaurant section, hard white plastic tables with sleek, aerody-
namically curved wooden chairs, where businesspeople gather in
their summer suits for a quick lunch—a chicken sandwich with
basil mayo, say, or a light salad Niçoise. But I'm working the
breakfast shift, and the customers are in a rush to get upstairs to
their law or tech or architecture firm, where they might order
toast with Vegemite or muesli with yogurt, banana, and honey,
but where they always line up in front of our shiny rectangular
counter, with two hulking coffee machines at one end, and order
a coffee of some kind. Their choices: cappuccino, flat white, latte,
long black, double espresso, espresso, macchiato, piccolo, long
macchiato, or Vienna coffee. Simple enough, except that it's not,
for several reasons. The first is that Joey has been working at this
café for several years, and his brain is a hive of customer names
and orders. Like any self-respecting Aussie barista, he knows
them all, and he knows what they drink.

Joey moves with robotic precision, first running both hands

from his temples to the back of his skull, matting down his loose shoulder-length curls, a lion coiffing his mane. He smoothes his long white apron, then places his hands on his hips and stares meaningfully at the coffee machine for a few intimate moments, two athletes in a huddle. Finally, ready for battle, he begins to make coffee. One right after another, they fly from his graceful hands, hissing steamed milk punctuated by the blunt knock of coffee grounds being dumped into the garbage can after two perfect espresso shots have been drained from them. All the while he calls out his g'days to the customers, asking them if they want the usual, which they always do. The regulars expect to have their coffee prepared and waiting for them by the time they reach me at the cash register.

Everything happens at warp speed, hundreds of suits revolving like a dry cleaner through the café doors. My job is to cap the coffees, give them to their owners, and make change with their colorful Australian dollars. Unlike waiting tables, though, there is no time to develop a rapport. It is a factory line, and one screwup throws off the whole team, the team being me and Joey and the screwup being me. I, too, am expected to know these customers by name and coffee preference, but their friendly faces all blur together, and after a few days, I recall only the two customers who have hit on me and a man on crutches. What's worse is I can't understand people's accent, so I mistake "skim cap" for "skim flat" or "cap" for "mach," all the while cursing Australians' insistence on shortening words that are not overly long to begin with as Joey is cursing me for getting all the orders wrong and wasting more than I make all shift in mistakes. While Carly's family seems to understand me fine, here people have trouble with my accent, too, calling me Rita over and over. Not being understood and not understanding them is infantilizing, and it's even more disconcerting because we are supposedly speaking the same language.

It should be clear by now that Australians take their coffee *very* seriously. Starbucks went broke here, which pretty much says it all. So although they say "no worries" and smile politely at me when I butcher their order for the fifth time, Joey assures me that I have ruined their morning. One day it gets to be too much. I call out two cappuccinos instead of two skim cappuccinos, thereby causing Joey to nervously run his fingers through his hair, a precise coiffing, as I've described, meant to occur only *at the beginning* of the shift. This is not good. Next I hand two people the wrong trays, forcing Joey to make eight new drinks when they discover my mistake. He halts the line in order to scold me like a naughty puppy in front of everyone, and suddenly, I can't cope. I flee to the bathroom, locking myself behind the red stall door to release my embarrassed tears. The owner, a minute Italian woman with copper-pot-colored hair, knocks gently.

"Do not worry," she says. "When men get frustrated, they hit someone, and when women get frustrated, they cry." I crack open the door. "Pull yourself together." She places her child-size hands on my shoulders. "You really do make a lot of mistakes, no?" And I do, there's no way around it.

My second job (as in Ireland, I need two, but instead of barely working part-time, I manage to log almost forty hours a week in Australia) is at an Indian restaurant called Aki's, in Woolloomooloo Wharf on the eastern edge of Sydney. It's fine-dining Indian cuisine—four words people don't expect to hear strung together. The owner and head chef is a middle-aged Indian man who opened his first bustling restaurant in a Sydney suburb and has decided to stake his legacy in a strip of expensive eateries on the water. He hires me a week before the restaurant is set to open. When I arrive for my interview, plush maroon cushions are being fitted on long benches. An upstairs cocktail bar overlooks the larger dining area, where sleek black chairs surround white linen-clad tables. There is outdoor seating where you can watch the boats slide in and out of the harbor. I myself could never afford to eat here, but luckily we're often fed heaping portions of butter chicken, sweet mango chutney, and crispy pap-padums. Before each shift, the entire staff downs a shot of Sam-buca.

"See how we are now?" the owner will say, sweeping his ring-adorned hand around the room. "What we are doing now, I want us to be doing always. We are a family, we eat as a family, and we drink as a family."

At Aki's, I perfect the art of folding a tablecloth in both the French and Italian styles, a skill I'm still hoping to be called upon to use one of these days. I learn how to delicately unfold a ba-nana leaf in front of a guest, exposing the perfectly grilled piece of barramundi fish inside. And I wait on a number of famous Australians whom I have never heard of: John Laws (the Aus-tralian Rush Limbaugh), Andrew Johns (the best rugby player in the world, according to the Dawson men), and Neil Perry (popular TV chef). Most shifts I'm the cocktail waitress upstairs, where the rectangular tables are so low to the ground that I have to practically kneel in order to serve drinks, carefully lifting mar-tinis one by one off the black tray balanced on my left palm. We all wear crisp ankle-length black aprons and black tops. One of the gorgeous Indian waitresses gives me a sheet of sparkly stick-on bindis, and I carefully center one on my forehead before each shift. This is not a uniform requirement. I just love the way they shimmer in my peripheral vision, as if I'm emanating my own light.

Hands down, the best part of working at Aki's is its location. It's at one end of a long wharf; it's also opposite Russell Crowe's house, and though I am vigilant, I unfortunately never catch a glimpse of him. Every shift I ask to work outside, please, and my day is a constant series of attempts to prevent the tablecloths from blowing away. With few customers wanting to sit in the hot sun and eat curry (not what we serve, but it's what people *think* we serve, which makes for a pretty rough time unveiling an In-dian restaurant in the middle of a Sydney summer), I am free to lean against the hostess's podium and stare down into the ocean. It's as difficult to describe the sea as it is a piece of music. I want to use undulating rhythms, words like "lilt" and "eddy," but really what does that tell you about how I lost myself like Narcissus, somehow lost all sense of where I was or the time of day. I'd imagine pitching over the side, then shooting out like a spark under the water, past the wooden stakes of the wharf crawling with fish and seaweed, into the harbor, where the ferries circle, before finally making it out to the deep sea, where the color deepens from Sydney to Pacific blue and there is nothing but ocean for miles in all directions.

When I'm done with work, I sometimes saunter across the road to Harry's Café de Wheels to devour a steaming chicken pie on a bench overlooking the sea while the pigeons dive for scraps all around me. Like the coffee, an Australian pie is an art form. The meat or vegetable is enclosed in a pastry about the size of a man's palm, the bottom thick and doughy and the top greasy and flaky. The first bite is warm and buttery, the last a minor tragedy. My diet at this point consists mainly of the four major food groups: Indian food, chicken pies, Tim Tams (two layers of chocolate biscuits with chocolate cream filling in the middle, the whole sugary fiesta coated in more delicious chocolate), and mangoes, which I devour so voraciously that Muriel buys them by the box load. Is it any wonder I'm steadily gaining the fifteen pounds Carly has recently lost?

The restaurant is a better fit for me than the café, but I'm having a tough time focusing on the work. Maybe it's the ocean, or the newness of Sydney, or the fact that the service industry here is not based on tips. Carly says the system is better. Everyone gets a fair wage. But I argue that a performance/reward system makes people work harder, go that extra mile.

"Why do I need my waitress to go an extra mile?" she asks. "I just want to eat."

"Because it makes people feel good."

"Why do I need a waitress to make me feel good?"

"That's the agreement," I say. "You get to feel good—to feel like you're the only customer who matters in the whole world—and I get a tip."

"That's demeaning."

"For who?"

"For everyone involved."

"No, it's not. Plus, if you don't get a tip, how do you know if you're any good at your job?"

"I just do," Carly says, thereby efficiently summing up our different personalities.

Unlike the Hole in the Wall (or any other place where I've worked), I don't get into a restaurant rhythm in Sydney—going out with the other staff at night, waking up hungover, dragging myself to work, repeat. For one thing, the bus doesn't run regularly past ten P.M., and it's the only way to get home. When I take it at night, I have to creep back to the Dawsons' house in the dark, no streetlamps on the suburban road to illuminate my path. But more than that, I simply prefer hanging out with Carly or, when she's working, her parents. Sometimes I meet Pete at his office for lunch; he's an accountant. Other days Muriel takes me to the fish market in Glebe, where pelicans line up like schoolchildren at the end of the dock, or we'll go out for a leisurely coffee together. I find an easy place within their family. I fit.

Muriel and I exchange ideas—mine burgeoning and hers long-solidified—about healthcare, education, war, and travel, issues that, before now, I've barely considered. The world, of course, has changed dramatically since 9/11, and I'm of the right age and disposition to start giving this some thought, especially ensconced in a country with a perspective different from America's.

The current Howard government has sent Australian troops to support the war effort, a development increasingly unpopular with the people. While they are offering this assistance, Australians find themselves (like other nationalities) under increasing scrutiny when they enter the U.S., and this further irks the nation of avid travelers. Headlines abound: ATTENTION, PASSENGERS: QUEUING FOR THE LOO IS FORBIDDEN FOR 14 HOURS, describing the new prohibitions against congregating near the bathroom during the fourteen-hour flight from the United States to Australia, and SECURITY RANKING FOR ALL U.S. TRAVELERS, outlining how all travelers boarding at U.S. airports will be given a score and color that rank their perceived threat to the aircraft.

"One day we'll all be citizens of the world! No more passports. No more visas," Muriel declares one tipsy evening. We clink our wineglasses together, pleased to have solved many of the world's most pressing problems at the kitchen table.

Sometimes Carly meets me at Aki's after work. Damien, a skinny bartender, sneaks us the cheapest bottle of wine the restaurant sells, and we find some empty seats down at the edge of the wharf, past the slew of seafood restaurants offering high-priced oysters and king prawns.

Carly sighs. "I'm so sick of Sydney."

"Sick of Sydney?" It seems impossible. To me, Sydney is an Eden. The sun wraps you in its warmth like an old baby blanket. Sure, it's a baby blanket likely to give you skin cancer, but after twenty-one years on the overcast East Coast, I'm willing to take my chances. The ocean is such a glittering shade of blue that I can't bear the thought of the murky, freezing Atlantic back home. We're so close to a handful of beaches that we swim in the ocean almost daily, an insane luxury. The first few times I got pulled under by gargantuan frothy waves, but I've learned how to duck below the water when they crash overhead. I swim farther and farther out, where the water grows calmer.

Swimming lessons are compulsory for all schoolchildren here, and sometimes I catch a glimpse of enthusiastic kids in matching red swimsuits out for their ocean recess. Playing dodgeball in the dead grass or sliding down a greasy fireman's pole set up in the middle of an uninspired concrete playground, both activities I cherished in elementary school, seem a bit depressing when viewed through Australian sunnies. I'm settling in nicely to Sydney life. My normally pale white skin has reached back to what must be some long-lost Mediterranean roots and darkened admirably. My nose has broken out in freckles, something it hasn't done since the carefree summer vacations I spent at Club Med with my parents when I was a little kid. How could Carly possibly be sick of Sydney, a place I feel like staying forever.

"I need to go somewhere new," she says.

If my own restlessness is a dull itch I can't quite scratch, Carly's is a gaping, bloody wound that refuses to heal. No matter how she puts pressure on it, in Bangkok or Marrakech or Prague, within a few days of her return to Sydney, it breaks wide open, the monotony of her native land gushing forth.

Carly has been home for a few months when I turn up in Sydney. She hasn't saved up enough money for another trip, but she's aching to hit the road. In the meantime, her reentry into Australian life has been bumpy. She's addicted to the rush of being a foreigner: new cities, new people, new food, new languages. Australia marks a return to the predictable—and a place where she doesn't quite fit anymore.

Carly has known for a long time that Sydney is not her place in the world, just as I have always suspected Syracuse, New York, isn't mine. The geographies of our childhoods don't quite suit either of us, something we have in common. But she's more displaced than usual after her travels. Everything here is the same, or so it seems to her, while she is definitely different after her journey. Her friends can't relate to her experiences abroad because they haven't traveled yet, so she's greeted by sharp loneliness back in Sydney.

"You're kind of the only person who gets me," she says.

I am in that same place, where my ideas and experiences and desires are expanding. I'm in that traveler's space with her.

Carly longs to be back in the world of backpackers, bohemians whose values differ from those of the typical middle-class Northern Beaches Australian girl. She has never been compelled by the traditional trajectory of a short stint abroad, then back to Australia for the beach lifestyle: relaxed, comfortable, and predictable. She knows that her gap year was only the tip of the travel iceberg for her, and she's desperate for more adventure. Her mates are living a life of health, sun, and the day-to-day, which is all well and good, but Carly wants more of a challenge. Her friends are content in this environment, but she gained a more global perspective from meeting all sorts of travelers abroad. She misses talking world politics and philosophy. And she has become quite a minimalist, so it's hard to refocus on material desires. Although Carly would always have a shared history with them, she was out of sync with her childhood friends, and with Australia.

Other than traveling, Carly has no specific image of her future and is okay with that, whereas I'm still struggling.

"I don't want to be a waitress," I tell her as she pours me another glass of Shiraz.

"You're not a waitress. You're just waiting tables."

"Aren't they the same thing?"

"Definitely not. It's just an easy way to make some cash," Carly says. "It's a long road, mate."

A long road. What's the long road? Is it traveling around Sydney? Or is it returning home? Is the long road the rest of my life?

When I was in my early teens, my viola teacher, Ms. Sasson, had an older student, a doctor my parents' age. His lesson preceded mine, so when I arrived early, I made myself at home on the couch and listened in. Inside the closed doors, it sounded just like any other lesson, except that he called my teacher by her first name, something I would never dream of doing. But when he emerged in his plaid collared shirts, I was always a little sad to see him. He was a friendly, distinguished-looking man, but definitely old. Secretly, I thought taking lessons alongside all these young, ambitious kids was depressing. It was obviously far too late for him to have a music career, and it didn't ever occur to me that this wasn't his goal. Back then I was smug in the knowledge of my own true purpose. That saving lives might be his purpose—or worse, that one might have no purpose at all, that all we have is the present moment and what we make of it—was unimaginable.

And so you see our twin problems. I could not get a fix on any one thing because I was always stressing about what I was truly *meant* to do and be, especially after giving up music. Carly could not stay put because she was constantly chasing happiness, searching for it in every foreign nook and cranny. My purpose and her satisfaction were equally illusive things, both of us so desperately trying to figure out our places in the world. And we were both restless, no doubt wanderers at heart—travelers.

We're bouncy drunk when we leave the restaurant a few hours later. The sun is setting, and by the time we reach the Domain, it's nearly dark. Stumbling, singing old show tunes, we tramp through the green. I'm behind Carly, following her to the other side of the city to catch our bus. Something drops in the grass. I bend down and scoop up her scuffed leather wallet. One step later, I find her sunglasses. Her purse must have ripped open, because she is shedding belongings like bread crumbs: lip balm, hair tie, ticket stub, cell phone. When I finally catch up, my hands are full of her things.

"Huh!" she says, delighted. "Where did you find all that?"

We stuff all of it inside my bag, her broken purse, too, and keep on walking.

# [ 9 ]

*Our heroine learns much about the so-called Down Under and the people who reside therein. She considers the nature of families and homes, dingoes and the British. Resolves to avoid encounters with magpies at all costs.*

My arrival in Sydney provides the perfect excuse for Carly to perform a favorite role of hers—that of all-knowing guide. If she herself can't travel again quite yet, at least she can witness Sydney through the wide eyes of someone seeing it for the first time.

We hit all the typical tourist sites. There's the Aquarium, a low, sprawling structure at the edge of lively Darling Harbour. The Aquarium is currently capitalizing on the success of *Finding Nemo,* an animated film about a young clownfish's adventures away from home. A massive tank houses numerous orange-and-white-striped Nemos flapping in the dull water, while all around me little kids and their parents, each more original than the last, shout, "I found Nemo!" Okay, okay, I shout it, too. That movie really brings those darn fish to life, plus I totally *get* the storyline, you know? Carly rolls her eyes and tells me I'm blinding the fish with my flash. I snap shots of Nemos 1, 2, and 3 as they snake

along the edge of the tank, up to the very top and then, after realizing there is nowhere else to go, back along the sides.

We check out the Hyde Park Barracks Museum, up on Macquarie Street, named after Lachlan Macquarie, an early governor
of New South Wales. The museum has transformed itself several
times during its life. Some of the first convicts, mainly from Ireland, were housed here between 1819 and 1848. The men, transported far from home for both petty and significant crimes, faced
the involuntary task of fashioning the new city.

We visit the Opera House, which is most spectacular from a
good distance. Up close, you can discern each individual corru-
gated tile, and the overall effect is lost, whereas from farther
away, the layered roof shells undulate like waves. One day Carly's
friend Simon, a Qantas pilot, takes us for a flight over the harbor.
From that high up, the Opera House reposes like a queen amid
her sailboat subjects. We stare down at determined tourists inch-
ing up the sides of the Harbour Bridge.

One of the best spots in Sydney is the Royal Botanical Gardens, a large expanse of blossoming land abutting the Domain,
located between Macquarie Street and Woolloomooloo Wharf. It
brims with sublime flowers whose names I've all forgotten. It is
also home to a good number of sulfur-crested cockatoos, my absolute favorite Australian birds, even more than the kookaburra
with his psychotic laugh. The cockatoo is a type of parrot. It has
a white body, a black beak, and a canary-yellow cowlick that
fluffs out into a hell-raiser Mohawk when it's pissed off. It's an
awesome bird.

There are countless astonishing birds and animals in Australia, though many of them have off-puttingly sharp fangs and
talons. And that is why Carly takes me to the Featherdale Wildlife Park, a short drive from Sydney, to observe them up close. It's
a petting zoo for the deranged, harboring only a handful of native animals that are safe enough to come within kicking distance. You can hand-feed green pellets from an ice-cream cone to

a scruffy kangaroo or wallaby (similar to a kangaroo but smaller). You can cuddle up to a fuzzy koala as he lazes like a portly, drunk man on his gum tree. Nearby, the laughing kookaburras are perched like professors, and the Tasmanian devils (a carnivorous marsupial with rodentlike features) run in endless, loping circles. It's a parade of strange new creatures: wombats (marsupials again, with some rodentlike features, though furrier and less angry-looking than the Tasmanian devils), goannas (like lizards but uglier), lorikeets (rainbow-colored parrots), Cape Barren geese (known as pugnacious and intolerant of other birds), and the all-time winner for scary-as-shit birds, cassowaries, large, flightless, with a Cruella de Vil nail on the middle of three toes that can easily sever a limb or eviscerate an abdomen.

Museums, gardens, aquariums, and petting zoos might be considered my formal Australian education, secondary to the informal, far more colorful instruction Carly and her family and friends provide, what I'm absorbing by osmosis living here.

First, the 2003 Rugby World Cup, held in Sydney—where the Australians ultimately lose to the British in the finals—provides an opportunity to see the two countries' complex relationship. The sweeping generalization is this: the Australians firmly believe that the English are arrogant and aloof, while the English arrogantly and aloofly dismiss the Aussies as immature and uncouth. (This was concretely illustrated by an unfortunate British girl someone brought to the Dawson family Christmas, who was met with stony silence after her ill-timed joke: "What's the difference between Australia and yogurt? If you leave the yogurt out, after a while it will develop a culture.") England is the country Australians love to hate, and nowhere more than in sporting matches does this typically good-natured but competitive rivalry have as much room to express itself amid patriotic face painting and beer guzzling. Britons pour into the country to attend the match, bringing with them the rain that ends a six-week uptick in the drought, and inciting Carly's younger brother, Steve, to amble around the house despondently for several days muttering, "Bloody Poms." (This is an expression the Australians have twisted back on the British, the assumed originators, that supposedly stands for "prisoners of mother England.") Even after the match ends, the two proud nations can't let it go. Egging them on is the fact that the ball used by British star kicker Jonny Wilkinson to score in the ninety-ninth minute of the final disappeared into the Australian crowds afterward, and the British are demanding its return. An article in *The Sydney Morning Herald* entitled "Why the Poms Have No Balls" argues: "Since the British refuse to return the Parthenon sculptures, the Sphinx's nose, and various Aboriginal skeletons to their rightful owners, Spike [the writer] doesn't think they are on very high moral ground when it comes to some sweaty old piece of pigskin. We shall not succumb." Points of contention between the two countries are never wholly about the present moment but always threaten to hark back in time as far as necessary in order to prove who is right and who, in common parlance, is a complete wanker.

And if there is one thing Australians can't stand, it's a wanker. One day we attend a cricket match where an off-key chant I can't make out starts to ripple through the crowd an hour in. I lean over to solicit an explanation.

"They're saying the members are wankers," Carly informs me.

"Why?"

"Because the members are wankers."

"No, why are they wankers?"

"Well, look at them, all snobby in their box seats." She gestures disgustedly toward them. "Plus, didn't you see how they wouldn't do the Mexican wave a few minutes ago?" (Another random difference: many outside North America apparently call it "the Mexican wave" instead of plain old "the wave," since the first time any international viewers witnessed the phenomenon was on the televised 1986 World Cup in Mexico.)

These affronts, essentially one bunch of Australians acting "too good" for another group of their fellow Aussies, are unacceptable. It's an example of the Australian expression "tall-poppy syndrome." Carly puts it succinctly: "Poppies grow taller than the grass, so they get their heads cut off by the lawn mower." Others have attributed its etymology to the world wars, where ANZAC (Australian New Zealand Army Corporation) forces fought many deadly battles on poppy fields and where, if you stuck your head out of the trench, you were likely to get shot. Regardless of its origins, this phrase showcases a major cultural difference between the U.S. and Australia. Australia is a proudly egalitarian, community-based society where the group reigns supreme, whereas the U.S. is a staunch meritocracy with the individual as the prime unit. So while Americans love first to build up a homegrown hero only to take schadenfreude delight later on if he/she gets knocked down, Australians prefer to skip the building-up part and go straight for the knocking down. This way, no one gets to thinking he or she is better than the neighbors, when everyone should be equal.

I quickly discover Aussies have a strong sense of humor, the kind in which anyone or anything is fair game. The only exception seems to be their origins as a penal colony. Though Australians live in a developed, democratic, educated, and multicultural society, media representations of them often stereotype. Carly despises a particular *Simpsons* episode where the Australians are portrayed as lying, thieving, incoherent simpletons, which, obviously, they are not.

Australians are proud of their continued hardy existence in a country where it's relatively easy to get yourself killed. The environment can be inhospitable, the animals/birds/reptiles bite, the waves threaten to drag you to a watery grave. Nowhere is their pride in self-reliance better illustrated to me than when the Steve Irwin scandal breaks. Irwin, the now sadly deceased Crocodile Hunter, decides to hand-feed a large crocodile in front of a crowd while holding his infant son. Some Australians and the appalled American media condemn his behavior, likening it to Michael Jackson dangling his baby over a balcony, but Carly's friends adamantly express an opposing attitude. "If there's one thing that guy knows, it's crocs," they say, or "He's been wrestling crocs since he was nine years old!" Carly has often claimed Irwin is a caricature of an Australian, but even she joins in the chorus supporting him. He is fearless and capable, just like the twentysomethings who surround me in Sydney.

Australia, unlike the U.S., doesn't sugarcoat the inherent dangers of being a human being, of inhabiting a vulnerable body. Australia is your tipsy blunt uncle who tells it like it is. There is danger. You are not immune. The world is not a fair place. Life is precarious and fleeting, but what's the point of letting these obvious facts get you down? Better to be out catching an ocean wave, or diving headfirst from an airplane, or whatever you do to enjoy yourself in the here and now (Australians do different things than most for enjoyment because they are bad-asses, but you get the idea).

"Did you know," Carly asks me one day, "that Australians invented the lawn mower, the revolving outdoor clothesline, *and* wine in a box?"

"Umm...no, wow, I didn't realize that," I say. This trinity of innovation, unlike her jests about the drop bears and hoop snakes, is true. It's a strange assortment, to say the least, but one that swells Carly's national feathers like a peacock's.

I come to learn certain other fascinating things about my new country. When it comes to fashion, Aussies are firmly and proudly stuck in the eighties. Mullets still reign supreme. So do fluorescent (fluoro) shirts with the collars up and Jane Fonda–esque off-the-shoulder T-shirts. Another piece of trivia: prostitution is legal and regulated. And another: Australian citizens are required by law to vote. Politics here are far more entertaining because people say whatever the hell they want. During my stay, the head of the Labor Party was quoted calling John Howard (the prime minister) an "arselicker." Another high government official told a reporter a new bill was "a load of frigging crap paperwork." These examples illustrate what I think are some of the fundamental qualities of Australians: they are practical (prostitution is the world's oldest profession, after all), blunt (just imagine Nancy Pelosi calling George W. Bush an "arselicker," if you will), and above all, they don't take themselves too seriously (mullets— business in the front, party in the back). And then there is their unflagging friendliness. Any time I try to sneak a look at my Sydney map, lost for the dozenth time that hour, the nearest Australian pops his head over my shoulder to ask: "Are you right?"

My favorite piece of Australiana is an indie movie called *The Castle.* Its hero, Darryl Kerrigan, lives with his family in a rundown but proud abode so close to the airport that the planes sound like they're in the living room. Though his "castle" is clearly no castle, the family resides there contentedly until one day the government threatens to take it all away by forcing the family to relocate so the airport can expand. Darryl takes his case all the way to Australia's high court. When asked what law he is basing his appeal on, he shouts: "The law of bloody common sense!," which, for me, pretty much sums up Australia.

After Carly pops out the DVD, I open my journal to add it to the list of my various Sydney experiences. Carly leans over me. "You make a lot of lists," she says.

"How else will I keep track of everything?"

"Why do you need to keep track of everything? The *doing* part of it is the fun part, not the preparing to do it and then crossing it off the list once you've done it."

"Well, yeah, sure," I respond, not totally convinced.

"I used to keep journals, too, Rach," Pete chimes in. "Should I pull them out?"

Carly says, "Dad, no, please, so boring" while I say, "Yes! I'd love to see them."

He disappears into the hall closet and reemerges with a dusty stack of brown leather journals. "Here we go. Take a look at this. This is good stuff."

Page after page recounts his mundane routine when he was an assistant in an accounting firm, before he traveled the world with Muriel, long before Carly.

> January 10, 1975
> Picked up a paper and went for coffee. Rain.
>
> January 11, 1975
> Picked up the paper and ran errands for Mr. Jones.
> Sunshine.
>
> January 12, 1975
> Woke up late. Went to work. Sunshine.

Carly raises her eyebrows at me, like, Now do you see what you're up to? But I don't care. I want to keep a record of all this, being in a foreign land with a foreign family, down to the evening's DVD. Writing has always been a way for me to make sense of the world, even if the most important changes happening to me abroad—many of which are imperceptible until years later—are nowhere to be found on those pages.

My Irish friend Dee has been living in Australia for close to a year. She's one of the masses of English, Irish, and Canadians here for their gap year. She planned to return to Ireland two months ago but fell for an Australian man a few months after arriving in Sydney. Now she's applying for de facto residency, a type of visa program based on the fact that you are dating (but not engaged or married to) an Australian citizen or permanent resident. Nothing comparable exists in the U.S. In order to get the visa, you have to live with your partner for a certain number of months, so Dee has moved into John's tiny Bondi Beach apartment. I take the bus from the city center to visit her, and we lounge around sipping tea and nattering on her couch—John yelling questions at Dee from the bedroom, or slinking off to work after an awkward hello. He doesn't seem particularly fond of the idea of Dee having friends, and the one time they come out to Forestville for a Dawson barbecue, he sulks and shifts and avoids all attempts at conversation until Dee excuses herself and leaves with him after half an hour. But she seems happy, she wants to stay here, and after a few visits, he warms up enough to accompany us to the beach, clad in his signature blue board shorts and wraparound shades that completely obscure his eyes.

Bondi is the closest ocean beach to Sydney's city center. Carly's dad spent his early childhood here before it became a popular hub for surfies and backpackers, back when it was a cheap settling place for a large group of Jewish and Italian immigrants, though Pete's ancestors hail from England and Wales. His father was a moody, thoughtful veteran who had no interest in talking about the war, or much of anything else. He had received medals for his service as a gunner, and the family lore is that one day while they were at the market, he deftly pinned them on a pumpkin and kept on walking. Pete's mum was a redheaded cafeteria cook and every bit as theatrical and outgoing as his father was reserved. She pretty much let her offspring run wild. The streets were ablaze with kids back then.

Bondi is still home to a large population of Jews and Italians, but now it's also a gathering site for the hordes of backpackers and tourists who arrive in Australia all year round but pack in tightest in the summer months. Flip-flops, backpacks, discarded clothes, and beer-filled eskys (the Australian term for coolers) cover the sand around crisping sunbathers while volunteer lifesavers in red and yellow uniforms and paid lifeguards in blue patrol the area. The beach is only one kilometer long, and it's body to body in the summer months, a blanket of exposed pale European skin ignoring the omnipresent warnings about skin cancer. The locals soak up the sun more judiciously but are still several shades darker. A shark net dives eight meters below the water and extends a hundred and fifty meters out, though there have been no shark fatalities since 1937. Red and yellow flags designate swimming areas, which change according to surf conditions. The northern end and the center of the beach are typically the safest, though sweltering tourists at the southern tip are renowned for heading into rougher waters instead of taking the short walk, their impatience sometimes rewarded with a lifeguard rescue. The ocean is lukewarm, barely cool enough to keep the heat at bay. On Christmas Day, the beach swarms with girls in bikinis and Santa hats, boys in red swim trunks. As with almost everywhere in Australia, it is perfectly acceptable to walk into local shops and restaurants barefoot. Carly thinks our American NO SHIRT, NO SHOES, NO SERVICE signs are a punch line to some unfunny joke.

When it's too hot for the beach or Dee's baking apartment, we head into downtown Sydney and spend $3.50 to ride the air-conditioned monorail around in circles, Chinatown to Darling Harbour to the long-standing Paddy's Markets, selling everything from exotic fruits and veggies to the koala souvenir key chains I buy in bulk and never end up giving to anyone back home. It's funny to meet up so far away from our homes.

Dee misses Ireland. She wishes she could fly back to visit—her sister's birthday is coming up—but the visa process makes it impossible. Does she picture herself here forever? She scrunches up her nose at the thought. No. Does she picture herself with John forever? Yes. Where that leaves them is not a question I ask, nor one that she offers to answer. Whenever you're traveling, you have these thoughts of home. At what point will you have been away so long that it will no longer be recognizable—or you won't be?

*   *   *

One afternoon I open an email from Erica saying she's gotten a job at Deutsche Bank that starts in June, soon after she graduates. It's a definitive move in the opposite direction from the low-wage art world. Like Tara and Jen, she's headed to New York City. Her brother already works at Deutsche Bank. He tells her every day, "You're going to *hate* this job," but she takes it anyway.

I can't picture her there, among the cubicles and traders, happily plugging away at a job that equals all money and no time or creativity. This is the same girl who convinced me to let her take naked photos of me at two A.M. on Locust Walk, a cobblestone drag in the center of campus, for her big junior-year photography assignment. In them, I have two accessories: my glasses and an empty corduroy book bag, as though I'm on my way to a fantasy class in a nightmare. She's blurred one of the pictures so that my body looks like it's in motion, my head turned to face the camera, smiling at the danger of getting caught.

Then again, maybe Erica has the right idea, or at least the practical one. I have infinite time and no money, a reverse equation. I can picture myself doing the same thing she is back home, convincing myself that it's only a few shitty years of time-sucking monotony. In the meantime, I'd save a bunch of money, then do what I *really* want, whatever that is. Her email reminds me I, too, have to figure something out, and why should I be any different than my friends, paying dues at jobs that soon will seem like their past and their future—stretching in all directions but the present. What's the right way to go about this time in our lives? Should you do what you love, what's outrageous and unpredictable, and worry about the future later, or plug away at a steady job first and go off and have your fun when you retire?

In five years, when we analyze our post-college lives over numerous glasses of sauvignon blanc, Erica will confess that she's unclear how she ended up here: "here" being an apartment on Central Park West and another, higher-paying finance job, still slaving seven to nine most days.

"It was, like, momentum," she'll say, as though her life had a force of its own and she was along for the ride.

Here in Sydney, it's impossible to imagine myself in a high-powered job, much less in a suit. Just thinking about polyester makes me shift uncomfortably in my seat, as though I am not in fact wearing a sarong and tank top, no shoes, a few minutes from an afternoon dip in the pool.

I know Carly would never dream of working in finance or in an office. "What kind of career do you want?" I asked her a few weeks ago, and she looked at me like I had requested a definition of the space/time continuum. The Brazilian rain forest, Prague on a rainy day, ancient Chinese temples, this is her language. For now she works as a bartender at the Manly Wharf Hotel, a sleek, modern version of the traditional seaside pub. Her only goal is short-term: make enough money for the next trip.

Like healthcare or student loans, rent isn't an issue for Carly—whereas moving in with parents after graduation is seen among my friends at home as failing to make it in the real world. Carly also has the advantage of coming home after each of her journeys. Although it's typical for Australians to reside with their parents during university, the way the Dawsons have opened their home indefinitely to Carly is pretty unique. They've never funded any of her trips (that's up to her and the handful of jobs she has at any given time), but she is always welcome to return to the family residence. Her room remains untouched, all the snapshots of her and her high school friends still tacked to the same spot above the dresser.

One night at dinner, Muriel tells me about the magpie problem they had when Carly, Mike, and Steve were in grammar school.

Australian magpies are black and white birds that resemble crows, with beady red eyes and long, pointy black beaks. They're extremely territorial, especially during breeding season. They've been known to swoop threateningly close to intruders (like any human coming too close to their nests), sometimes pecking the person in the ears, neck, or eyes or, worst-case scenario, dive-bombing and pounding the person's head with its chest, WWF-style. In response, Pete and Muriel and the other neighborhood parents made the kids wear empty ice-cream containers with eyes and a mouth drawn on the backs as a decoy. The bus stop was apparently ground zero for the attacks because it was right under a magpie nest, so every day was a mad dash to get the kids safely to and from the bus, their plastic helmets bobbing, magpies buzzing menacingly all around like a dark cloud.

The Dawsons are nonchalant about such incidents, though it's difficult for me to imagine a world in which walking to the bus stop was fraught with anything greater than whether or not the rowdy boy down the street had a crush on me, too. Maybe this is because there have been other incidents, par for the course in Australia but which make Carly's youth sound like an episode of *Survivor*. For example, on one family trip, hours and hours into a dry, deserted landscape, they happened upon a mob of emus. Emus are Australia's largest birds; they're flightless and resemble ostriches. Pete screeched to a halt. "Go on, kids," he encouraged. "Get out and chase them! See how fast they can run!"

Carly and her brothers excitedly jumped out. Carly turned back pretty quickly after getting spooked by a decapitated kangaroo carcass, but Mike and Steve kept up the chase. Soon they came upon a wire fence cordoning off some property. All the emus started awkwardly scrambling over it, but a young one couldn't make it. Steve and Mike were getting closer, and the little guy started to get agitated. That was when Papa Emu got pissed. He eyed the boys, and they stared back, as in an old-western duel. And then the chase reversed, the enormous

bird in hot pursuit of the boys, who sprinted back to the car, terrified.

There are other, similar family tales, though poor Steve seems
to have weathered a disproportionate number of these encounters, like when hungry dingoes surrounded him on Fraser Island
one summer. I discovered only recently that a dingo is a dog and
not, as I thought for reasons unclear to me now, a specific type of
kangaroo.

"Maybe a dingo ate your baby!" I shout at dinner one night,
performing my butchered Australian accent after Pete has dis-
played an American accent that sounds like a Texan swallowing
a Bostonian, every sentence ending with "you guys." My Australian accent still inexplicably resembles Eliza Doolittle's, like
the Irish one before it, though this time it's mixed with Crocodile
Dundee. Since I don't know the next line, I improvise: "Maybe it
put it in its pouch and ran away with it."

Everyone laughs, but then what I've said registers with
Muriel. "Wait—what's that, Rach? What's the last thing you just
said?"

"Maybe it put it in its pouch and—"

"Put it in its pouch?" Muriel repeats. All three of them lean
toward me with curious expressions. "Rach. What exactly do you
think a dingo is?"

When I tell them it's a really mean-tempered kangaroo, they
erupt with laughter. Carly is practically in tears. "It's—it's a wild
dog, you idiot," she says once she catches her breath.

"Crikey dick," Muriel exclaims, one of my favorite expressions,
beat only perhaps by "throwing a wobbly" (having a tantrum)
and "up and down and in her lady's chamber" (having looked all
over for something) and Pete's "strewth" (as in an exasperated
"honestly" or an agreeing "ain't that the truth, sister?"). Crikey
dick, technically a New Zealand expression left over from
Muriel's upbringing there, is an expression of surprise that translates to something like "for heaven's sake."

"Ohhhh," I respond thoughtfully. I try to picture a thin, raggedy mean-streets dog (this gets easier when I see one a few months later), but as hard as I try, all I see is a hopping-mad kangaroo, teeth bared, claws gleaming, with a little baby bundle in its pouch.

The Dawsons' colorful wildlife encounters do not comprise even a sliver of the myriad differences between Carly's childhood and my own. Family vacations for the Dawsons typically involved road trips and camping in the bush. The five of them would pile into the car and head up or down the coast a few hundred miles, then pull over with their big yellow tent and gear and settle in for a few days of what Darryl Hannigan from *The Castle* calls "the serenity." My parents did not camp. My dad likes to joke that "roughing it in my book is a hotel with three stars." My mother appreciated nature as an activity, but not as somewhere one might hunker down and remain among the elements once the sun set, a cozy bed disappointingly replaced by the hard earth below your sleeping bag.

Carly's parents took the kids on a few extended trips when they were growing up, once pulling them out of school for six weeks to visit Europe, Egypt, Thailand, Canada, and the United States. It was unfathomable that my parents would take me out of school for anything less than emergency surgery (and even then we'd surely try our best to coordinate with a long holiday weekend) much less to head off on an extended cross-continental adventure. When I was little, travel was something we did as a family. Later, when my parents' marriage was disintegrating, we took separate vacations. I remember being pleased about being let off on my own, like a grown-up, at eleven or twelve, off to music camp or a week with a friend's family or a visit to my brother out in California. I felt tremendously independent and pushed aside any darker thoughts about the fragmenting of my family. I'm jealous of all the memories the Dawsons have together that extend up to the present.

Carly had stability waiting for her after living a travel life in flux for however many months. My life lacked this. My childhood home was sold. My dad had moved to Chicago with his new wife, into a condo where they converted the second bedroom into an office. And no matter how hard my mother attempted to make one of her spare rooms comfortable for me, I was still a guest. Maybe this was partly why I found the Dawsons' intact family so appealing, and appreciated the space I occupied in their lives so much, a space without any past to complicate it.

# [ 10 ]

*Our heroine and her trusty guide consider life, adrift in waters neither deep nor treacherous, with many adult beverages to guide their meandering trains of thought. Our heroine questions happiness and the means by which one might obtain it.*

Life at the Dawsons' ticks along at one's self-appointed pace, and even though there are many new activities to occupy my time, Carly and I spend what feels like years' worth of yawning, lazy afternoons in the backyard pool. We make mojitos and spread ourselves across blue inflatable rafts. I spend a lot of time floating belly-up, *The Graduate*–style, pondering what I want in life. The answer is like a piece of candy with the wrapper still on. I know there is something delicious in there, something I really, really want, but I can't get to it through all the damn plastic that is formed by the myriad other voices in my head. Other times I consider nothing more profound than the warmth of the pool water or the swaying clothes drying on the line. But it's not like my wall-staring time senior year of college. In Sydney, I feel like a toy winding down as its battery runs out, a slowing accompanied by spurts of incandescent thoughts when it feels like there is time enough for everything. The Dawsons provide a kind of sanctuary I didn't even realize I needed.

What exactly did my sister's "Welcome to the real world" toast mean? People back home were offering up these kinds of expressions for months before graduation, warnings that implied everything up until then was a wonderful dream from which you eventually have to wake. Is my time abroad a part of this dream? Who decides the parameters of this real world, where the initiation seems like self-sacrifice? Give up your personal vision of happiness in exchange for a collective vision: work hard, get married, buy a house, have a kid or two, diversify your portfolio, retire comfortably without burdening your children, die. For my generation of women, who have inherited the benefits of our mothers' and grandmothers' feminism, we're supposed to want it all and to excel in each area of our life. Our opportunities are exhilarating and overwhelming, though my father's new wife, a pediatric cardiologist, offered me her own piece of hard-earned life wisdom at that same graduation dinner: "Career, relationship, kids—now pick two."

I share these conflicting messages with Carly.

"Fuck expectations," she summarizes.

We clink our mojito glasses, the ice already melted in the burning afternoon sun.

Much later on, when she has let her college degree dangle unfinished for over five years, Carly's parents will urge her to finish it up and be done with it. But here, we're only twenty-two, and they don't push any particular time line on her. It's not that Carly's life is entirely free of pressures. It's just that she has a totally different relationship to her parents' approval. She wants to please them, but it's not the all-encompassing stressor it is for me, and she would never dream of giving up her own desires to make them happy. Pete jokes that he hopes she'll become an accountant so he can rename his firm Daddy and Daughter, but the idea is so beyond laughable that even he knows it. Pete and

Muriel often tell Carly, "We want you to do what makes you happy." Although my own parents provided me the best education, the highest-quality music lessons, and an abundance of financial support, I never heard them utter these exact words. It is in Australia that I realize I will have to garner the strength to speak them to myself.

I have been keeping a secret from my parents—my acceptance to a master's program in theater studies at Trinity College Dublin. I have a vague notion of wanting to write plays, though I've never written one. I applied for a spot at the end of my senior year, before I decided to come to Australia, when I saw no way to leave the country again without a purpose that would satisfy them. Trinity has let me defer my spot until the fall. I packed the letter in my suitcase. I showed it to Carly a few days ago. "What are you going to do with that?" she asked me. I didn't know if she meant the piece of paper or the degree, but it didn't matter, since I've been asking myself both questions.

I have always loved the validation that an acceptance letter brings, but when I received this one, I felt only emptiness. I think of my friend Adam, off at UCLA, pursuing his Ph.D. Whenever he finished an exam, he put all his textbooks in the freezer for a week. It was his way of saying, "Astronomy 101, you no longer rule my life." (He wanted to sell the books back to the bookstore, so he refrained from anything more drastic.) I put the letter in the Dawsons' freezer to see how I felt, but still it called out to me. I threw it under the bed with one of Mike's dusty, forgotten socks. But I retrieved it a few hours later. I don't know what I'm going to do with that letter, any more than I know what I'm going to do with the spot reserved for me, or this pressure I always feel to continually achieve certain goals that appeal to my parents more than they do to me.

Back in high school, Carly developed an interest in speed walking. The story goes that she picked it up and something like three seconds later had placed nationally in a competition. A few

months after that, she dropped the hobby altogether, returning
to her normal ambling pace, never looking back. It did not haunt
her, like music did me. No one expected anything more of
Carly—nor did she of herself—than to do what worked for her
in the moment. And the fact that she had natural abilities in this
and many other things did not make her feel beholden to them.
Her parents supported her. They gave her opportunities. And she
appreciated all of it without the intense pressure to please them
that I'd always felt. It was in Australia that I started seriously
considering my own private destiny as I witnessed Carly un-
apologetically pursuing hers at full speed.

"Hey." Carly interrupts my thoughts by splashing some water
in my direction. "Do you want to go to South America together
when your visa expires?"

"Why South America?"

"Why not?"

"Let's do it," I say, just like that, because that guttural voice
I've been coaxing out as I examine my options in Australia is
shouting "yes!" so loudly that it's the only word getting through.


I find Carly's life philosophies incredibly alluring and her
mother's experiences unceasingly fascinating, especially because
the early events of Muriel's life are in many ways similar to my
own mother's, yet the outcomes are so different. In 1966 Muriel
left home. She was eighteen, like my mother was when she ran
off, and three years younger than Carly and I when we met in
Ireland, similarly determined to break free of our lives. Up until
then Muriel had been biding her time in Te Puke, a small country town in New Zealand. Muriel calls it a "little tinpot farming
town." I imagine it's not all that different from where my mother
spent her childhood in upstate New York.

Muriel always wanted to leave home. "My two sisters were
rushed down the aisle at nineteen, like many girls in small towns

in the 1960s, pre-Pill days. I knew I didn't want that. My mother didn't, either."

Muriel's mother had always wanted to travel, something she finally got to do later in life, after many unhappy years in tiny Te Puke. Some of this unhappiness must have rubbed off on Muriel, and maybe something like wanderlust was inscribed in her makeup, since not everyone who is unhappy walks away, and not everyone who walks away goes to another country. My mother made it only as far as Ohio for a few years before winding up back in New York, an hour's drive from her troubled childhood home. But Muriel crossed an ocean. She boarded a boat to Australia the April after her eighteenth birthday and arrived on the shores of Sydney three days later with fifty dollars and a large cardboard suitcase. It was only at that moment, as she looked over the harbor to the nearly completed Opera House, where the half-finished sails that formed the roof were reflecting the afternoon sun—at least this is how I imagine the moment—that the full force of her current situation hit her: she was on her own.

She spent a few petrified nights at the local Salvation Army, lying awake on the other side of the three-quarter wall from the snoring hoboes they let in at night. After two weary days wandering the city alone, she went to the railway station and departed for Adelaide, seven hundred miles south. The British had precisely plotted Adelaide in a grid, the boxy, appealing inner city surrounded on all sides by green parks. It was orderly and precise, not like back in New Zealand, where it seemed like everyone had shown up and cobbled together their new lives.

The ticket cost Muriel most of the thirty dollars she had left, but there were distant relatives at the other end who offered to take her in. They had a daughter around her age, Joy, and as soon as Muriel had made a little money, the two of them journeyed up to Darwin, a young city at the top of Australia in the sparsely populated Northern Territory. Here they picked mangoes, rock melon, and tomatoes, depending on the season. Soon they looked like laborers—callused hands, tanned, strong thighs. They liked how they felt doing that work. When they left, it was simply because they were sick of the routine, ready for something new.

Muriel returned to New Zealand for her twenty-first birthday. Her sisters threw her a small party. One of them had given birth two more times by then, a baby on each knee and a toddler running through people's legs as Muriel blew out the candles on her fruitcake. Her mother stood alone at the edge of the group, watching her daughter. Muriel glanced up at her and felt something akin to pity but not entirely unrelated to annoyance. Everything in Te Puke was the same, but Muriel was different. Or maybe everything had changed and Muriel had, too, but in unrelated, incompatible ways. Whatever it was, she knew she was leaving New Zealand again, maybe this time for good.

Norfolk Island, located between Australia and New Zealand, seemed like a good place to start. The tiny piece of land, an eroded remnant of a basaltic volcano, had fewer than two thousand residents. One of them was Dan, a carpenter who adored fishing and took his small boat out into the choppy Pacific whenever he had the chance. Muriel had planned to stay on the island for a few months to earn some money for a big move to Canada, but instead she married Dan. Soon she was pregnant. She was twenty-four and working as a hairdresser on the island, feathering all the women's hair. Her water broke early one morning. There were complications. The baby only lived a few days. A few weeks later, when she thought she had already lost everything, she lost Dan, too, proving there is always something more that can be taken away. He was trying to help a friend out to sea when his boat overturned. It was dark and Dan, fully dressed when it capsized, disappeared into the sea.

Muriel stayed on the island for one more year. She took a job as a dental assistant; her customers were quieter than women who needed their bangs trimmed—they couldn't jabber nonstop with all that metal in their mouth. The days stretched out before her. Once again, she felt she had nowhere to go. She could see the future—how the lives of those around her might play out—but could not picture her place within it. One day she left because the pain of staying would not retreat. First she holidayed in Fiji with her sister-in-law for a few weeks, holed up in a bungalow where the outdoor shower required you to hold the chain with your teeth in order to keep water flowing while you scrubbed the ocean salt off your skin. Then she returned to Darwin—for once longing for something familiar—to start over. And then, amazingly, she lost everything again.

The day before Christmas Eve in 1974, Muriel drove into the bush to camp with some friends. It was midsummer. The heat was oppressive, and they couldn't swim in the ocean because of the jellyfish. They lounged atop thin mats and sleeping bags with their legs apart, drinking warm beer and trying not to move. They told stories and waited for the storm that was thankfully coming to cool them down. When it arrived the following afternoon, they hunkered down inside their truck while rain slapped the windows. Heavy unrelenting winds rocked the vehicle from side to side. "Something isn't right," they whispered.

When they rode back into Darwin the next day, it was destroyed. "Everything was gone," she told me. "Try to imagine being totally isolated in a town that was flattened. It just kept raining—no birds, leaves, trees, or clean water. It was as if an atomic bomb had gone off. Darwin was getting on its feet, and the cyclone blew all that away. It blew away all that past." The gauge at Darwin Airport officially recorded winds of 217 km/h (135 mph) before being blown away itself.

Because of her dental training, Muriel was deemed essential personnel and required to stay behind to care for the injured. Everyone who didn't serve a function in the new Darwin— mainly those needing medical attention or offering it—were rushed out on planes. Then came the lootings, which lasted for a few days, but after that the town settled. It seemed to hit everyone at once that all they had left were their lives. This changed people, some temporarily and some forever. Here is what Muriel learned: "I am strong. I survived."

Again.

And she let go. By that I mean she no longer thought she had control over anything.

"If this is what life is going to be," she said to me one night across the kitchen table, and to herself back then when she laid eyes on Darwin after the cyclone hit, "then bugger it."

She traveled all over the world, on her own most of the time, and eventually found her way to Sydney. She had just turned thirty. When she met Pete in a pub she was as unencumbered as the day she left Darwin. Since she forsook Te Puke, she had experienced loss on many levels, in contrast to my own mother, who had been acquiring men, debt, degrees, and children during those same years.

I carefully observe Carly's parents together while I'm living with them. I examine their faces for signs of a woman who is still restless or a man exhausted by the effort of trying to settle down with someone who once lived for roaming the earth. But they appear genuinely happy and, an even more slippery acquisition, content. Because my parents' marriage and so many of those I grew up around lacked these traits, Pete and Muriel's relationship is a mystery I'm dying to solve. "Tell me how you met," I beg them. "Start from the beginning. Don't leave anything out."

And even though they repeat the story again and again for me, I cannot figure it out. I cannot pinpoint the forks in the road. I cannot see anything at all but coincidence and Muriel's tragedies piling up one after another. And then Pete. And her kids. And her house in Sydney. And happiness. And contentment. Maybe there is no formula at all, just luck and perseverance.

* * *

It's late at night on Boxing Day, the day after my first Australian Christmas. The Dawsons' annual barbecue is over. We've thrown all the prawn shells in the trash and collected all the paper plates and cups strewn about the deck. Earlier in the evening, Muriel and her friends uncorked a bottle of wine and challenged me to a game of Scrabble that ended when one bottle became three and Muriel knocked some of the pieces off the board with her elbow as she was bending down to give Sebby a scrap of chicken. Now I hear her in the kitchen dumping the last letters into the cardboard box. I'm cross-legged in bed, reading a guidebook. Tomorrow Carly and I leave for a ten-day road trip. After that, I'm backpacking alone for three weeks up the east coast. And then Carly and I will abandon Australia for South America.

When Muriel enters my room, she is crying fat, silent tears. She sits beside me on the edge of the bed. There is a small rip in the blue sheets, and she picks at it distractedly. "I used to play Scrabble with my sisters every Christmas," she tells me. She inhales deeply, as if she can't get enough air.

I put my arm around her. I don't think I've ever had a moment like this with my own mother; never before have I sat beside her while she revealed something so simple yet so intimate and then reached out to offer comfort, asking nothing in return. We've grown further and further apart over the years. Her happiness has always relied on my successful display of daughterly duties. Do I love her enough and in the right ways? Do I appreciate her? Am I sufficiently grateful? No on all accounts, not by a long shot. For as long as I can remember, I have disappointed her, so I have put a wall between us in an effort to protect myself. In my anger, I've never taken the time to know my mother or really see her, and this hits me now that I'm with Muriel, with whom I have a relationship uncomplicated by history.

Both Muriel and my mother left unhappy homes. Both had a difficult, bullying parent. Neither had much money or opportunity. They were pretty much on their own. But whereas Muriel

seemed like a trailblazer, my mother's existence appeared to revolve around the series of men who supported her and my half
siblings. I judged this narrative of my mother's life with the easy
scorn of someone who has never physically feared her own parent or been forced to run away. But here with Muriel, it looks
more like my mother was a woman doing the best she could to
stay afloat. I feel myself softening the distance between us a little, even if we are an ocean away.

The house is quiet apart from Carly's wheezing in the next
room. She's coming down with something. Mike has returned
from Europe, so I'm in the guest room with the pullout couch
that Sebby always pees on when he's displeased. Steve is off at a
friend's. Pete is upstairs, drifting off to sleep.

"It's okay," I say to Muriel. And then, because I don't know
what else to offer her: "I'm sorry."

Even the homes we leave on purpose, the families we break
away from to be ourselves or someone else, call us back again and
again, to a place that has long since ceased to be home yet still
holds power over us. I know this myself now that I have left this
place behind and have not yet created anything to replace it, if
such a thing is even possible.

# [ 11 ]

*Our heroine, her trusty guide, and a goateed suitor depart*
*the sunny suburbs of Sydney and journey south. The trio*
*encounters malformed birds and cities, strange prostheses*
*and mysterious landscapes. They welcome in the*
*Year of Our Lord two thousand and four.*

At the end of December, Carly and I leave for a road trip down south, winding our way along the coast to Melbourne and planning to spend New Year's Eve at a nearby music festival. Carly wants her boyfriend, Michal, to come, an addition I grudgingly accept because he's offered his car for the journey and Carly's beat-up Barina has been breaking down with increasing frequency. Michal is originally from Poland. He moved to Australia in his teens, and he and Carly met at university a few months ago when Carly dipped back into her undergraduate studies. She's technically a senior, I think, but our plans to travel around South America in a month will extend her degree indefinitely.

Michal is a cultivated eccentric who craves attention. He shouts random phrases like "bleeding cows!" and "berry deliciousness" when we're in the middle of dinner and everyone else is discussing movies or rugby. Carly's brother Steve, a straightforward, macho Aussie bloke, regards him with the mild disdain one might a piece of lint stuck to his collar, while Muriel smiles politely and Pete asks, "What's that now, Michael?" perpetually mispronouncing his name. Michal responds by stroking his wiry goatee with two fingers and staring off into space.

To be fair, Michal is an artist, a talented musician, among other things. He plays guitar and writes quirky but compelling tunes about things like ingesting rotten lemons. Or he'll ask you a serious question, guitar strapped to his back, and right when you're considering your response, he'll whip the guitar around and start jamming his punk-rock tune "Concentration." This song involves shouting the word "concentration" a few times while bullying an angry riff of chords, his pick flying off the strings. If you get annoyed and walk away, he'll follow, still playing. Your only option is to wait it out until he gets bored and moves on to someone else.

Carly thinks Michal is a hilarious genius, and regardless, "It's nothing serious."

Well, then, I think, what's the point, especially with someone who is so much work to be around, who takes up the whole room with his mad melodies, Tourette's-like shouting, and squeaking balloon animals? Carly has no problem dating casually, while I, as with everything else, treat love with heartbreaking seriousness. It's got to be desperate, soul-searching movie love or nothing at all.

Michal and I share a lot of interests, music being the most obvious one. Even though I haven't touched my viola in months, I love a guitar-accompanied sing-along, and Michal is always up for that. But I childishly regard him the same way Sebby did me when I arrived at the Dawsons—as an unwanted intrusion. I'm jealous of him taking up Carly's time, and the fact that I find his personality insufferable is written all over my face, which puts Carly in a rather awkward position between us. Still, I resolve to be as tolerant of Michal's antics as possible on the road trip (no doubt he gives himself a similar pep talk regarding me), and off we go in his white Ford Falcon packed with his guitar, a four-person tent, our backpacks, and an esky full of turkey and cheese sandwiches, me curled in the backseat with the window rolled down and my bare arm stuck outside to feel the wind.

Our first stop is seaside Kiama, two hours from Sydney, famous for its blowhole that shoots water up to eighty feet and, as Carly announces when we pull in to a parking lot, "home of the infamous no-legged seagull."

I lean forward and poke my head between their seats. "Sorry, what?"

"I can't remember exactly what happened," she says, "but the last time I was here, I choked and there was a no-legged seagull somehow involved."

"Involved how?"

She shrugs, unconcerned with the details, while I imagine all the many strange ways a deformed seagull might cause someone to asphyxiate.

The blowhole is just that, a big geyser of water that shoots through a hole in some craggy rocks every three minutes or so with a loud whoomp, all the Japanese tourists whispering "ooohhh" each time and snapping innumerable photos. "This is a blowhole, not a bomb!" Michal shouts nonsensically into the rocks, and they inch cautiously away from us.

Carly and Michal don't want to stop in Canberra, but I insist. The two of them are up front with the maps, deciding our route as we go, and I can see if I don't put my foot down early on, I'm going to be the feckless kid whose parents drag her along to every blowhole from here to Melbourne.

"Fine," Carly sighs. "But it's in the middle of nowhere, and there is nothing to do. I know—I've been there."

Michal sings, "Oh, capital, oh, capital, we hate your gleaming politics!"

I ask them just what kind of crap-ass Australians we would be if we didn't make time for Canberra.

"Well, you're American, Michal's Polish, and I'm half-Kiwi," Carly says, "so it's a pretty irrelevant question."

"You're bossy," I mutter.

Either she doesn't hear me or doesn't want to get into it five hours into a ten-day trip, but she doesn't respond.

"They should make cars out of chocolate so you can eat a piece of it while you're driving!" Michal shouts.

Canberra is four hours from Sydney and a good six or seven from Melbourne. It was the source of much past contention and controversy. Both Sydney and Melbourne vied for the position of Capital Territory. For the sake of Australian fairness, it was ulti-mately agreed that the capital be built between the two cities. The plans for Canberra were laid by Walter Burley Griffin, an American architect. Griffin worked for Frank Lloyd Wright be-fore the two parted ways after a falling-out. The crux of their disagreement apparently centered on Wright's attempt to pay Griffin in Japanese prints for some design work, which does seem pretty bloody insulting.

Today Canberra professes to be a lively government town, boasting the sort of perfectly planned tree-lined neighborhoods that would make the Stepford wives proud. Canberra is so green and orderly and manicured, the streets nearly empty of human life, that it's almost eerie. As we drive along looking for our campsite, a lone woman waits at a pristine, oddly shaped bus stop. Instead of the usual rectangular shelter, this stop is a half-dome gleaming in the sun, looking like it might return to its mother ship at any moment. Twenty minutes later, when we realize we're headed in the wrong direction and have to make a U-turn, we pass the woman again, still sitting perfectly postured in the same spot, the wind lightly blowing her magazine-perfect updo.

Despite the distressing proportion of trees to people, I'm determined to show Carly and Michal Canberra's exciting side, since I'm the one who insisted we come.

"First stop: the National Museum of Erotica," I tell them. "The guidebook says it has a small collection of artwork, that it's low-key and not at all sleazy."

We pull over on Northbourne Avenue and file up a narrow flight of stairs. At the top is a small room where dildos of every imaginable size, shape, and color are tacked to the walls. In one corner, a forlorn blow-up doll sits with her mouth in a perpetual expression of surprise. In another is a curled-edged poster featuring a bare-breasted woman on a horse. The artwork?

Behind a small counter, a balding man in a black sweater is hunched over a magazine. I ask him if we are in the National Museum of Erotica, and he responds affably that no such place exists and that we are in fact in Club X, which is, as we have all suspected since having to go through both a door and a black rubber curtain to get inside, a porn shop. Oh, and are we interested in buying the blow-up doll?

"Half price because she's got a small leak somewhere and deflates if you press on her too hard."

"Blowhole!" Michal shouts at the plastic woman.

I have to admit Canberra only gets weirder. We head off to Questacon, the National Science and Technology Centre. After placing our heads in a fake guillotine and feeling the terrifying whoosh of air as the ax swings down, we decide to attend a short presentation on circus physics. It's led by an American in a floral Hawaiian shirt and plaid shorts, with crimped, stringy hair. He's demonstrating some principle that involves balancing on a plank that rests atop a ball. His major effort at humor during this act is to call up a hefty bald man who is asked to don a pink tutu and be his assistant. The bald guy's kid hops up onstage, too.

The performer is rocking back and forth, telling us something about balance and weight or whatever, picking up speed as he goes, when, *wham,* he flies off the plank and hits the floor. Fifty pairs of little hands smack their cheeks, *Home Alone*–style.

"That's got to be part of the performance, right?" I whisper to Carly and Michal, who are sitting there dumbfounded as the performer bounces up like a spring.

"I don't think the blood's for the kiddies," Michal observes. He's right. The guy is bleeding profusely from the ankle. It's soaking through his white cotton sock.

The kid onstage cries out, "You're bleeding!"

"It's all part of the act, children," Circus Jack assures them. He yanks his sock up higher.

"I can still see it!" the kid yells.

A Greek chorus of other youngsters echoes the sentiment. The youngest kids are distressed, crying and pointing, while this nut job is back up on that damn plank, rocking like a maniac while the blood drips like an IV onto the floor.

"Time to go," Carly declares.

"Well, that sure was something," I say outside, trying to stay positive.

"Now can we get out of here?" she asks, triumphant.

"Fine, whatever. I guess I'll just miss the coin museum." It's all I can come up with on the spot to make my case.

"I guess you will," Carly says.

Although we are ready to leave Canberra, the city is not ready for us to go. Back at the car, someone (ahem, Michal) has left an interior light on, and the battery is dead. By the time a tow truck arrives with jumper cables, it's quite late, and we decide to spend the night at a nearby campsite. No one is manning the camp's entrance, so we drive in undetected. We push off at four A.M. to avoid having to pay on the way out.

"For the record, I think we should leave what we owe. This is against the rules," I huff to Carly and Michal.

"You're a real outlaw now, Rach," Carly says. She grins at me in the rearview mirror.

Australia is full of little towns where, as in little towns every-where, life has slowed to an amble. A recent wildfire has whipped through tiny Jervis Bay, leaving behind patches of singed trees. We stop in Corryong, where the coffee is stale and the large Australian woman running the café is reprimanding her bored-looking teenage daughter for forgetting "the fucking eggs." The headline in the local newspaper is 2003'S MOST POPULAR DOG NAMES. We pass through Tarangatta, a place whose welcome sign proudly announces their major accomplishment: THE TOWN THAT MOVED IN THE 1950S.

We stop at a pizza place for dinner somewhere along the way. It's a family joint with red checkered tables and paper tablecloths being manhandled by ankle-biters with crayons. It's been a long, hot day without a decent cup of coffee, and we're famished. No sooner have we walked through the door than we discover it's open-mike night, and two seconds later, Michal is up on the stage with his guitar. He starts off with a relaxed melody, some wistful chords, while staring mournfully at his audience. He sighs heav-ily and pauses dramatically as the last few strummed notes re-cede into the acousticless dining room. And then, with far fewer but no less interested child eyes observing him than the bleeding American at Questacon, he proceeds to belt out "The Suicide Song."

*We come to the shops not for the shopping, but for plastic bags*
*We put 'em on our heads why, oh uhghmnguhmnd*

*Suicide, suicide,*
*do the homicide*
*Suicide, suicide*
*you need to die now,*
*die die die....*

And on and on and on and *on.* I put my head in my hands, mortified, while Carly sings along.

Ned Kelly was an Irish-Australian bushranger (a term originally used to denote escaped convicts but which now identifies the Australian equivalent of Wild West outlaws, à la Jesse James), and he looms large in the Australian psyche. He's an iconic folk hero: self-educated, articulate, and a loyal family man. For some he's a mere criminal, and for others he's a Robin Hood–type figure of national pride.

In photos, he looks a bit like Heath Ledger, who played him in the 2003 movie version. It's all in the eyes. Ledger eerily captured their squinty intensity, though even right before Kelly's death, those eyes retained a certain Irish mirth, a "well, that's life, now somebody pass me a pint" attitude that the two nationalities share.

Today's Glenrowan, where we spend the next morning, would be entirely unfamiliar to Ned Kelly. Now the whole place revolves around Ned Kelly and the famous showdown that took place here, in the way that small towns with big histories sometimes evolve. It reminds me of Chittenango, New York, about twenty miles from my hometown, renowned for its yellow brick road (technically a sidewalk). The yellow brick road existed prior to *The Wizard of Oz*—supposedly, it was Frank Baum's muse—but it's been refurbished, and themed businesses have sprouted alongside it, like the Emerald City grill and Oz ice cream.

Glenrowan even has a Disneyland-like computerized robot

display of Ned Kelly's final stand, though this being Australia and not the U.S., everything is proportionately smaller and less glitzy. The best part of Glenrowan is the six-meter statue of Kelly. Underneath it, I make Carly pretend she's being held up while I peep mischievously up Kelly's iron-armor skirt. Michal snaps photos and wonders out loud whether one might successfully climb up Ned Kelly with a guitar and perform a tribute song or ten.

When we reach the music festival on day five, it is a mess of tents packed tight in a valley. We set up ours, Carly briskly designating where and how as Michal and I lazily stick the ends into the baked earth. It's so blazing hot by seven A.M. that you want to curl up and cry, and so confusingly cold by eight P.M. that you want to do the same. The flies stick to your face as if they've got nowhere else to be but right there on your sweaty upper lip or, in Carly's case, on her glistening silver nose ring. It's too hot to do much of anything but sit around and wait for the music to start. Michal makes himself a sandwich of bread and chips and declares, "It's not a cookie, but it's almost as good as a cookie." We pour copious vodka and Cokes. In the afternoon, when we can't stand it anymore, we catch one of the packed buses into nearby Lorne, swim in the ocean for a few hours, then head back to camp with renewed supplies of dripping ice.

The festival is reminiscent of the Phish concerts I used to love so much in high school. Michael Franti comes onstage, talks about the war, and sings "you can bomb the world to pieces but you can't bomb it into peace." He's got long dreads and bare feet. Xavier Rudd, an Australian singer, comes out with his didgeridoo, a wind instrument developed by Aboriginals. It's a hollow eucalyptus branch that he blows into to produce long, low notes. There are girls with patchwork dresses and long-haired boys with guitars, everyone smoking pot and feeling the love. We throw our arms around each other, even Michal and I, and ring in 2004.

After a stretch along the picturesque Great Ocean Road, our last tourist stop on the way back to Sydney is Hanging Rock. A well-known Australian novel and, later, a film by Peter Weir tells the story of two girls and a teacher who disappeared here during their school Valentine's Day picnic in 1900. Carly and I rented it my first week in Sydney, and I had nightmares for days after. The film, with its supremely creepy choral-music soundtrack accompanying whispering young girls with ribbons, white dresses, and feathery hair, climaxes with a haunting image of the lost girls disappearing inside the rock. It summons them like a siren, and they simply climb higher and higher, gloveless because the afternoon sun is warm, holding hands.

There is no evidence that this is a true story, but many cling to its veracity. Something about the place supports this narrative; plus, there is the cryptic Aboriginal belief that the rock has "unfinished business" and thus is best avoided. It was formed six million years ago when lava squeezed through a narrow vent in the earth. From a distance, it's an unusually shaped rocky outcrop encased by a ring of trees and shrubbery. Up close, it is a maze of nooks and crannies. Carly dives into them, wiggling herself into crevices, while I have daymares about her disappearing. She gives the psychic energy of the place no credence, or assumes it is no match for her own will.

I'm feeling bolder these days, more and more confident in my new Australian surroundings, ready for my upcoming solo backpacking excursion—my first ever. Still, I walk gingerly atop the rocks, declining to insert my limbs into any small spaces. I don't wish to tempt fate or mess with things I don't understand, though it seems like I've been doing a lot of both lately.

# [ 12 ]

*Our heroine musters her rawest courage and lightest bottle of
shampoo for a solo jaunt up the east coast of this fine country.
The path is rife with backpackers, a camel-like species with
belongings like humps on their weary backs. Relates to readers
some history of Australia, though not much, for this book
is not meant to boreth but rather to exciteth.*

I'll be traveling by bus on my three-week excursion up the east
coast of Australia, one of those hop-on-hop-off deals, and I don't
have any set plans other than arriving in Darwin by a certain
date in order to catch my flight back to Sydney. Until then it's up
to me. I haven't even booked hostels. "You don't know how long
you'll want to stay someplace until you get there," Carly instructs.

Not so long ago, this lack of planning would have seriously
freaked me out, but I find I'm excited by the idea of roaming the
countryside at will, seeing where I'll land.

My first stop is Newcastle, a huge coal exporter where hefty
ships queue for hours en route to Sydney. I read that this is where
the penal colony's most nefarious criminals were once sentenced
to work in the mines. I had planned to spend my five-hour lay-

over trekking around the city, but the train's luggage hold closes at five P.M., and it's just after that when I arrive. I thought I had made a valiant effort packing, since I was able to easily zip my backpack, as opposed to when I prepared for the Outback and, after having sneaked in some extra clothes when Carly left the room, had to sit on it until the contents sufficiently flattened. But now, when I hoist my gear onto my back, I make it only eight blocks before dropping like a sack on the nearest bench. So instead of sightseeing, I heave-ho back to the bus station to park myself on the room-sized brown rocks that dot the nearby shoreline and wait for the sun to set, always a worthy pursuit in Australia, where the sky is as changeable as the landscape. Tonight's is cloudy streaks on a pink-flamingo backdrop. Dinner is Nutella on crackers. Parked around me, teenagers blast music from open-windowed cars, well-dressed women stroll along the water, and sweating bodies jog with their dogs. Two passersby strike up conversations with me, both about the current freezing temperatures in New York once they hear I'm from there.

"I couldn't get out of bed in weather like that," one guy says. He shakes his head sadly.

"Can't wear those in the snow," the other announces proudly, pointing to my flip-flops.

Home is so far away, mentally and geographically, that I'm starting to feel like I'm not even from there anymore.

My first overnight bus is a lesson in discomfort. I take my assigned seat next to a German sprawled out like we're in yoga class. Around two A.M., he groggily inquires if I'm carrying "something sharp—like a knife" in my pocket. He claims something is poking him, and it's "very, very irritating," he informs me, promptly elbowing me with a gangly limb as he settles back into sleep.

"Umm, no, I'm not carrying a knife," I mutter, but I sure wish I were. I can't sleep. I am in an aisle seat, and I try lying back against the headrest, but really I don't understand how anyone sleeps sitting up. On planes, I normally unlock my food tray and bend myself over it, making a pillow out of my folded arms and drifting off happily, or lean against the side when I have a window seat. But I have nothing to rest on here, and sleep is just not happening, so I shut my eyes and wait for daylight to come.

Six hours later, before dawn, I'm dropped off at a desolate bus stop in Coffs Harbour with a spiky-haired British girl. We quickly realize we're headed to the same hostel. A minivan is supposed to pick us up, but when it doesn't arrive, we consult our vague guidebook maps and shove off into town. Carrie studied law at university before a summer in France led to a year there, working for a charity. That led to a year abroad in Australia. She's obsessed with Bruce Willis and is remarkably adept at inserting him into seemingly unrelated sentences, as in: "Isn't this just like in [fill-in-the-blank movie] when Bruce Willis did/said/ thought/wore...?"

Carrie and I drop our stuff at the hostel and, after two cups of strong coffee, head straight to the Big Banana together—an homage to Coffs Harbour's number one export. The whole country is chock-full of these kitschy "big things" (the big prawn, the big gum boot, the big Captain Cook, the big *poo*), and it all started with the Big Banana. Why did Australia construct all these magnificent gaudy sculptures? I can understand the regional and historical ties of some, but the big poo? Whatever their reasons, they punctuate many a childhood memory of family road trips, a fact I am sorely jealous of.

The Big Banana is just what you'd expect. We stand outside it, snap a photo, then stroke it phallically like everyone else does. Inside is a haphazard exhibit. The lead photograph, with the caption SPECTACULAR VIEW OF THE BIG BANANA, is missing the corresponding photo. We peruse the abundant stuffed-banana souvenirs and sidestep the unnerving number of kids chin-deep in drippy chocolate-covered fruit. Outside the Big Banana are trike rides, since no Australian tourism is complete unless it requires a helmet and the possibility of hurting yourself at least a little.

Carrie wants to visit the botanic gardens, but I want to see Mutton Bird Island, so we go our separate ways, with plans to meet up later at the hostel. I'm used to traveling with Carly, each of us with definitive ideas about where to go and what to see, with Carly usually winning the debate, so it's strange to disengage from someone I've spent the afternoon with. It's freeing to do my own thing. I walk along the coast to Mutton Bird Island, kicking the sand along Park Beach. When I get there, I notice lots of scuttling crabs in the mud, and a distressing amount of mutton bird poop, but no actual birds. Behind me on the walk is an Irish family, parents and two kids.

"Well, I saw the birds, so now you have to see the airport," says Dad.

"But why would you want to see an airport?" the confused mom asks. I want to know, too, but I lose his reply in the wind.

Mutton Bird Island is associated with one of the Aboriginal communities' dreamtime myths, the creation stories that explain their origins. Before Westerners arrived, only elders were allowed to visit the sacred island. The mutton bird's real name is wedge-tailed shearwater; it was given its current moniker after early settlers tasted its fatty, muttonlike flesh. The bird's migration patterns are astounding. They cover about fifteen thousand kilometers in two months, pursuing an endless summer across the Pacific. The trip commences in mid-April. All the chicks are left behind until, desperate with starvation, they set off after the adults, somehow managing to trace the unfamiliar migratory route. In the first year, only about half those leaving the nest survive, but still they are compelled to try and make it on their own, like most of us are.

* * *

After Coffs Harbour comes Byron Bay. If Sydney and its north-
ern-beach environs took me mere hours to fall for, then Byron
Bay is love at first sight. The streets are a bustling mix of cheap
eats, art galleries, spas, yoga centers, and little shops selling flow-
ery dresses. Its new age laid-back persona ohms through the
whole town, and I can feel my whole body adjust to the new relaxed rhythm. Even the waves are serene; they curdle toward the
shore with languid indifference.

My hostel is full of murals and mess, the walls and furniture
all varying shades of ocean blue. Two backpackers lounge in a
cream-colored hammock out on the balcony, flipping through
tattered magazines, legs tangled together. Nearby picnic tables
are packed with shirtless guys and girls. Bare feet abound, as
usual.

"Breakfast is free, and dinner is four dollars," says the tattooed
hipster who checks me in.

The dorms rooms are typical—six bunk beds wedged in and
not much else. I throw my stuff on one, then head off to catch the
shuttle inland to Nimbin, a nearby town in the North Hinter-
lands I've wanted to visit since reading about its otherworldli-
ness in my guidebook. I've got plenty of time to explore Byron
when I get back. I've already decided to stay here at least a few
days.

Nimbin was a quiet, struggling dairy town until the 1973
Aquarius Festival, a convergence of college kids, hippies, and
alternative-lifestyles adherents. After the party ended, many at-
tendees stayed on, some forming communes. Soon enough, other
creative types found their way here, as did environmentalists
and people interested in permaculture.

The main drag has an unexpected frontier feel, low wooden
buildings with jutting roofs offering needed shade. But unlike
an old western town, the roofs sport psychedelic paintings—
rainbows and dreamy lizards, dolphins in the sun and radiating
stars. People smoke pot everywhere, blatantly and without pre-

tense. Every few steps I'm offered cannabis or Nimbin cakes, the local equivalent of pot brownies.

The shuttle offers an optional tour that leaves an hour after letting us loose to explore the city center. After scarfing down a veggie burger at the Rainbow Café and traversing the length of the teeny town three times, there isn't much left to do, so I grate-fully hop back on the air-conditioned vehicle. The driver is a transplanted Londoner, Ed, who has lived in Nimbin for nearly twenty years. He tells us all about how Nimbin (Nimbinji to the Aboriginals) used to be a place where the old men of the tribes headed when they became too feeble for the nomadic lifestyle. They'd come here and chill with the other wise old dudes. There was plenty of bush tucker (foods native to Australia), so they didn't have to hunt every day, and periodically the young mem-bers of the tribes who showed particular promise would stay with them for a stretch to learn about the history of their people.

Ed describes Nimbin's annual Hemp Olympics, where, he tells us, "getting a green medal gives you a whole different kind of high." Events include joint rolling in the dark (if you make it to the second round, they turn on a fan) and bong throwing.

Ed is eager to prove there is more than this to Nimbin, how-ever. After visiting several permaculture communes, we check out a company that develops and produces alternative-energy sources. It was started by a man called Peter Pedals, who at first simply pedaled a bike to charge a battery for his electricity. Then he hooked up the bike to do his laundry. Then, just for shits and giggles, I guess, he rigged it to a juicer and pedaled around town selling his homemade concoction. Now they make items like solar-powered flashlights, water-powered fans, and plant-based air-conditioning systems.

On the shuttle bus back to Byron Bay, I strike up a conversa-tion with an American girl. She attended Berkeley, came out here to travel Australia the summer after graduation, and was about as far along in her journey as I am now when she hit Byron Bay.

That was nine months ago. Now she unrolls a thick blanket each morning near the beach to sell her homemade jewelry. She shows me a beautiful necklace, transparent blue beads on a silver chain.

"How long are you staying?" I ask her.

"Probably forever," she replies dreamily.

Back in Byron, I stroll along the sand. There's a juggler performing. His head is shaved minus a small circle in the back where a dreadlocked ponytail sticks out like a cactus in the middle of the desert. I'm not sure he's technically juggling, actually, since the oversize clear orbs are always in contact with his body. They flow up and down his arms one after another, over his smooth skull, then back down his arched stomach. I keep expecting them to drop, wondering if they'll shatter on the sandy sidewalk, but they never do. Around him struts a woman on stilts, her dreadlocked hair in pigtails, her abnormally long blue pants a shade darker than the ocean behind her. It's hypnotic here, the dying waves, the soft sand, the promise of all the days to come on the road. Unlike in Ireland, I feel completely alone but not at all lonely.

# [ 13 ]

*Our heroine dives into the depths of the briny sea, then
launches herself from great heights. Survives the crocodile's lair
and a particularly strong current, is rewarded with
some small insights.*

Heed this warning: four and a half hours in Surfers Paradise is four hours too long. From seductive, sleepy Byron, I arrive in the land of gaudy skyscrapers and shopping centers. I've left New South Wales for Queensland, and this is the last stop on the Gold Coast, a stretch of beach where the overzealous tourism has a commercialized, theme-park feel. Along the Esplanade, elderly men stroll with pretty, young Asian girls on their arms. A crazy-haired woman scrutinizes the sand with a metal detector. Coming across a Hard Rock Cafe is the final straw. The only indication that this is still the Australia I love is a prominent sign at the beach cautioning: DANGER, MARINE STINGS, yet two swimmers happily splash away.

While I'm lying down on a bench waiting for the minutes to rattle by until my train arrives, two creepy young men approach me, doubling the number of creepy men who have approached me since I arrived in Australia over three months ago. The first guy wears smudged sunglasses and asks if he can have my plastic water bottle when I finish. He's rambling somewhat incoherently, but from what I gather his current plastic bottle has a hole in it and needs replacing. My bottle is still three quarters full, and I tell him I won't be done for quite a while, but he shrugs and stands there. After ten minutes, he finally gets the hint and starts to walk away. Then he turns back. "You're a very pretty girl."

"Thanks."

"I wish someone would say that about me."

"What—that you're a very pretty girl?"

He shakes his head sadly.

The second guy towers over me, blocking the sun. He makes Romeo #1 look like the picture of good health, he is so abundantly drunk and dirty in ripped shorts and bare chest.

"Hey, babe."

"Don't talk to me."

"Baaaaabe," he pleads.

"Go," I command in the same tone I used to employ with my West Highland terrier.

"I could have taken you out. A good Australian bloke. It's really too bad," he says, like I have just made the biggest mistake of my life.

I take this second interference as a sign and head to the station to wait for my nine P.M. train. When it hasn't come by nine-thirty, I call Greyhound only to be informed there is a one-hour time difference in Queensland, a fact I feel the government should swiftly and decisively remedy so no one is ever unwittingly stuck in Surfers Paradise again.

I reach Brisbane, my next destination, late at night, but the hostel's owners have left me a key in an envelope outside the entrance. This place's best years are long past. It has a sinking roof and overgrown brush everywhere, as if the house itself is one more root. Inside, the kitchen is a mess. Unlike other hostels, where everyone tidies up after themselves, here, abandoned, crusty pots and dirty silverware overflow the sink and counter-tops. Hair clogs the shower-stall drains. The beds smell like they have been doused in insecticide. I chose the place based on its proximity to the station and city center and, as always, its price—twenty-three dollars—but instantly I'm glad I'm staying only one night. It's the kind of hostel that makes you consider scrapping the whole consciousness-raising backpacking thing and checking yourself immediately in to the nearest Quality Inn, which would feel like the Four Seasons at this point. In general, though, Australian hostels are pretty great, and they're ubiquitous. Some nine hundred thousand backpackers wandered through Australia in 2003, spending around $2.7 billion.

I'm out the door by eight-thirty A.M. to explore Brisbane before catching a four P.M. bus. It feels like 100 degrees already. I've been in Sydney for three summer months, but the Brisbane heat is a new beast to be reckoned with. A few times I buckle against the nearest tree, swooning and fanning myself like a lady-in-waiting. I spend much of my day lazing through the botanic gardens, walking along the raised bridges where the mangrove roots disappear below brackish water. When I have longer stretches in places later on in my travels, I'll wander like this for many days, luxuriating in the little surprises around every corner. It won't be anything like our speedy family trip through Europe when I slept (slept!) through the Alps. It will be slow and meandering. It's so counterintuitive for me to absorb my surroundings instead of studying the regional culture, history, and exports as though preparing for an exam. In scorching Brisbane, I discover one of my favorite ways to see a new city even if it's not hot as Hades: walk without purpose, pausing every hour or so for an iced coffee or an inviting park bench to people-watch or strike up a conversation with some willing locals, but never entering any of the myriad galleries, government buildings, or museums on offer. In Brisbane I'm my own tour guide.

The next day I land in Hervey Bay, a do-nothing town that occupies itself mainly with setting up tourists on trips to Fraser Island. Here I happily fork over ten dollars to patronize the gruesome, kitschy Vic Hislop's Great White Shark and Whale Expo. Vic, a strong-armed, sandy-haired shark hunter, is a self-proclaimed Australian icon. He perpetuates numerous conspiracy theories, like many shark-attack deaths are covered up as drownings, and whales who beach themselves are often shark-attack victims that, even after humans push them back in, will stubbornly rebeach, terrified of what awaits them in the water. The entrance is an open-jawed shark, and inside, three frozen great whites hold court over the crowds. "Call me Vic," I say under my breath.

I've booked an eighteen-dollar-a-night hostel in the heart of the Hervey Bay backpacker action. I make friends with a perky Canadian girl, and we go out for a few drinks. She's a nurse who's come to Australia to travel for a few months, then find work somewhere in the country for a few more months. Her boyfriend was supposed to come with her, but they broke up two weeks before the trip, so she is here on her own.

"He still has his ticket," she says. "I don't know if he's over here or what, but if I run into him, I'm cutting his balls off." She mimes a snipping motion.

"Cheers to that!" I toast a little too loudly. We've known each other for a grand total of two hours, but I'm connecting at inexplicable speed with other lone backpackers. We have no past and most often no future together, so we let it all hang out—our body odor, our raw emotions. It's intoxicating to strip away the excess: it's just me, my backpack, and the world.

*   *   *

The next morning I'm back on a bus for a day tour of Fraser Island. While we're waiting to depart, I watch two picnicking families outside the window. Each has a little girl around five, and the two are eyeing each other from neighboring tables. As if in some silent accord, they hop off their benches in unison and approach each other. A flurry of animated conversation ensues, but soon one family has finished and packed up and is ready to push off. A distracted-looking mom turns to tell her daughter to say goodbye to her new friend, and she vigorously embraces her while the other girl pats her back motheringly, as though assuring her they will meet again, though it saddens her that it might not be for a very long time.

Fraser Island is one big sandbar created by thousands of years of long-shore drift. Our bus driver, George, tells us this and much more, his voice so even and low that I drift off to sleep several times. Though his monotone never reveals any hint of pleasure, he does end each sentence (in typical Aussie good-natured boasting fashion and also because it's usually true) with the phrase "in the world." "This is the largest sand island in the world." "These are the only trees of this kind in the world." "The dingoes on this island are the purest breed in the world." He also treats the tour like it's a spelling bee: "Those are coffee trees—C, O, double F, double E. Coffee trees." Finally, every time we get off the bus, he specifies exactly how long we have within a five-minute time range. We'll be there for "fifty to fifty-five minutes" or "thirty to thirty-five," but never the unforgivably vague ten to twenty minutes, say. He checks his watch while we reboard the bus, counting the seconds until someone is officially late and he can sigh disappointedly into his hairy wrist.

He invites passengers to sit up front with him for a stretch, and I, perpetual pleaser, dutifully make my way up there after lunch. He tells me how all the proceeds from the tourist camping tax are *supposed* to go toward the maintenance of the island. He raises an eyebrow and looks meaningfully at me for longer than someone off-roading in a massive four-wheel-drive bus should. When I don't inquire further, he moves on to more benign subjects like the various reptiles found on the island: frogs, snakes, skinks, and my least favorite—the stout, crocodile-tailed way-too-freaking-big-to-be-a-lizard goanna with its old-woman-neck wattle. I nod with feigned enthusiasm.

We stop to swim at Eli Creek (no going out in the shark-infested ocean here). I plop down beside a British couple and their teenage daughter. "I do not want to hear about or see any spiders," she's telling them.

"Right, love," the mother says, then takes off in an all-spandex ensemble to run laps around the shallow creek. The husband warbles off to the knee-deep water in swimming trunks pulled up to his nipples.

At lunch I meet Sabrina and Rupert from Austria. They're off together on a one-year excursion: a month in New Zealand, two in Australia, and the rest of the time in Mexico. We have a little language barrier—their English is above average, and my Austrian is nonexistent—but we get on instantly. By the time Rupert's coffee slips through his suntan-lotioned fingers and splashes all over his knees, we are cackling away like old friends. When we separate later that evening, I want to hug them fiercely like those little girls I saw. Maybe this is what travel gives you—or gives you back, in most cases—that childlike sense of wonder, and with it a kid-style openness where you want to finger-paint with anyone and everyone who shows up. Maybe it's because people are in such an open state, on the road ready to absorb all the experiences and strangers that come their way, like we did when we were little. Some are fleeting, like the Canadian girl in Hervey Bay, but some you hope to see again, even though you know you might not.

I've never been scuba diving, and Carly has assured me that there is no better place ("in the world!") to give it a go than the Great

Barrier Reef. Lindsay, our guide, helps us put on our gear: flippers, mask, and oxygen tank. We practice equalizing and clearing our masks. Then he tells us to drop beneath the water's surface and breathe in and out through our mouths. I flail about and hold my breath because I cannot wrap my brain around the counterintuitive notion that inhaling will not end in lungs full of salt water. Lindsay parks himself directly in my eye line. He nods encouragingly, his underwater ringlets bobbing in slow motion.

Down the five of us go, along the sweeping reef that stretches farther than any other in the world. It is the largest structure made by living organisms, minute polyps that pile themselves atop one another, some dead and some living. I float along like a ghost, pausing to examine a brilliant blue starfish or to let a school of zebra fish pass. I often fall behind, distracted and wide-eyed, and at one point Lindsay simply grips my belt and pulls me alongside him like a lollygagging child.

Despite how awkward breathing underwater feels, I am at home, as I always have been in the water. I was one of those infants you see parents tossing back and forth in the lake long before they can swim, then one of those little girls her mother calls a fish and has to bribe out of the neighbor's pool. But I have never been down this deep or seen what lives this far below the surface, where the sun and the sounds of people eating their shrimp lunches back on the boat are a million miles away. I can feel myself getting bolder and braver.


I'm staying the night at a hostel on Magnetic Island, one of the oldest island resorts in Australia. It must have been lively once, but the recent move of the terminal to Nelly Bay has slowed the place down. Though everything is neat and tidy, the rooms have an air of neglect. The bathroom tiles are gaudy and mismatched; the striped rug in the lobby is fraying. On the walk to my dorm room, a turkey waddles after me, its skinny neck weaving back and forth.

"What's with the turkey?" I ask the girl in skintight short shorts leading the way. It is a testament to Australia's kooky wildlife that I now regard this familiar yet totally out of place bird with nonchalance.

"He lives here." She shrugs her bony shoulders and glares menacingly back at the turkey until he hobbles away.

My new roommate is brushing her wet golden hair in front of a round mirror. "Hey," she greets me. "I'm Stephanie. Don't let that fucking turkey anywhere near this room, okay? He already ate another girl's toothbrush."

Stephanie is from Calgary, Canada. She recently finished high school and is on a one-year working holiday before figuring out if she wants to go to college. "It's not for everyone, you know?"

"Of course not," I agree, not quite believing myself. Increasingly, I'm stranded between the Byron Bay–esque, laid-back traveler me and the old me who still thinks things like higher education are as necessary as breathing.

Stephanie and I stir-fry chicken and broccoli for dinner. Georgette, another Canadian roommate, joins us. She doesn't look a minute over twenty-five, and my eyebrows jump when she reveals she's forty. She beams. "Travel keeps me fit." She's here to dive the reef for six weeks.

"How can you take so much time off work?" I ask.

"What do you mean?" she says. "It's my vacation time."

"You must have been at your company for a long time."

"No, not really, two years."

"Then how do you have so much time?" I'm suspicious now. My friends back home have ten days of vacation, tops, which they're all afraid to use.

"It's what we're given. We need this time to recuperate, don't you think?"

Actually, I do think, though I've never considered it before. Another reason Americans don't travel for long periods, I suspect.

I had intended to stay on Maggie Island for another day but it's so sweltering the next morning that I decide to return to Townsville, a little city port, and spend the day at the beach with Stephanie. She's booked a room above the transit center, and I can leave my pack with her until my twelve-thirty A.M. overnight bus departs for Cairns.

It's a sauna back on the mainland. One might stand the 90-plus-degree temperature if the humidity didn't hover between 70 and 90 percent. We're constantly soaked in sweat, every pore dripping. Even when we stop for ice cream, the relief lasts only as long as it takes to sloppily consume the melting mess. At the beach, Stephanie sets herself up in the shade while I mad-dash across the burning sand to the disappointingly warm water. I float on my back, still perspiring. Even so, a rush of gratitude overwhelms me: not just that I am lucky enough to come from a country where enough money can be saved up waitressing to traverse the globe, but I'm also palpably thankful to be alive, to feel the water and sun and wind. I have always been a person who volleys between the past and the future, never able to fully partake of the pleasures of the present. Until now.

I go a little bit crazy in Cairns, an adventurer's paradise in the far north. First I jump out of a tiny green plane holding steady at ten thousand feet. Rod, my instructor, takes me through the steps on the ground. He instructs me to cross my arms against my chest and keep my head back until he taps me on the shoulder, the signal to let my arms fly loose at my sides. I'm supposed to keep my knees tucked up when we land so I don't trip him.

"It's about twenty seconds of free fall," he tells me. "Get

ready." How does one prepare for such a thing? I think back to that moment on the plane in Dublin, when I was so terrified of the figurative free fall I was facing after graduation. Now here I am, literally throwing myself into it.

All of Rod's directions exit my brain as he scoots me toward the open door of the plane. He's strapped behind me. As one body, we tip over the edge, out into the clouds.

"Ahhhhhh!" My jaw seems to unhinge as I scream through the first few seconds; after that it's a silent Munch scream. We're plummeting so fast it feels like the earth should bash into us at any moment, but for the longest time, it's only specks of white rooftops and the faraway rain forest. As we tumble through space, more space is created for us, like when Alice drops down the rabbit hole. Then Rod pulls the parachute, and we're jerked briefly upward. We drift down like a feather after that.

Back on the ground, a series of bodily sensations that were suspended in the sky return: blood pumps in my ears, my arms tingle from the harness, my jaw aches a little from screaming bloody murder.

Rod smiles calmly, just another day at the office for him. "How was that?"

"Whoa," I breathe.

"Bloody oath," he agrees.

Some molecular shift occurs in Cairns. I'm certain of it. Otherwise, why would I decide that the best way to top off this particular day is to bungee jump? Bungee jumping is even more terrifying and satisfying than skydiving because I have to jump myself. No one is attached to me, making the decision. It's just me on a fifty-meter platform in the dense rain forest I saw from a surreal distance while skydiving. A glorified piece of rubber binds my ankles like cuffs. I need to give my weight in order to calibrate the rope, and I wonder if the five pounds I instinctively fudged off mine is going to make a fatal difference. The rubber device feels flimsy, as if I'm being lowered down the edge of a cliff with floss around my waist, not anything that will prevent me from smashing into the lake and rocks below.

Two slinky New Zealanders are running the show. One of them keeps rattling on about losing my "bunginity." The other creeps right up behind me and whispers, "Just let go. It's going to be so good."

In order to jump, I do have to let go. I know that—of my fears, my anxieties, my ego. To fling yourself out into the abyss requires shutting off the analytic part of your brain, which wants to discuss the few pros and many cons in paralyzing detail—otherwise, you can't jump. If you're doing any talking to yourself up there, it's talking yourself out of it. Besides, I'm tired of playing it safe.

So I let go. I curl my toes around the edge of the platform and fall forward. My stomach lurches. The water reaches out for me, and I brush it with my fingertips. Then I'm back up, down, up, down, slower and slower until I'm suspended inert upside down. A question appears before me as the adrenaline drains from my body: Have I ever been truly present at any moment in my life before now?

Back at the hostel, I meet two friendly Japanese girls who are here studying English. They're headed down to the restaurant next door for dinner, and I join them. They introduce me to our fourth roommate, half-German and half-Thai Jasmin. She's aloof and keeps her eyes on her food. The next night I run into her again, and after a few quiet drinks, she explains her current depressed state. She came to Australia with a good friend who for some reason ended up renting a car with a mutual friend. Jasmin and her buddy originally had plans to tour the Outback, but her friends changed their minds without consulting Jasmin. She spent a miserable, blistering week in the unair-conditioned car with the two of them, pulling over on the side of the road every night to sleep in order to save money on accommodations. Eventually, the lack of showering and annoyance at her friend's completely changing a month's worth of plans was too much, and she had them drop her in Cairns.

"I wasn't supposed to be here alone," she says. "I can't get used to it."

"What are you going to do?"

"I'm going home ten days early. I already changed my flight. But first I am seeing that big red rock. That's why I am here."

"Good for you!" I say enthusiastically, reminding myself of jubilant Pedro back in Dublin. Usually, I have the tendency to absorb the energy of whomever I'm around, but I am determinedly keeping her depressing vacuum at a distance. "You know what you should do? You should go bungee jumping."

She frowns. "Definitely no."

I shrug understandingly, happy anyway to have a temporary friend after a long day alone. We order another beer. Tomorrow Jasmin is off to Uluru, and I fly to Darwin, a city that looms large in my imagination because of Muriel's stories.

It rains hard my entire first day in Darwin, so I take the owner up on his offer to let me stay a free night in exchange for helping him paint the common room blue. He offers me thirty dollars to put some stickers on promotional pamphlets, so I do that, too. A number of backpackers are performing odd jobs around the place, including cleaning, which probably explains why the bedsheets are always slightly askew and why a girl claimed she saw a cockroach in the kitchen this morning. But I don't care because the place has infinite free pancakes for breakfast and a large pool I plan to swim in as soon as the lightning stops.

Try as I might, I cannot get a good feel for Darwin. The Darwin of Muriel's youth was flattened by Cyclone Tracy, and now it's mostly modern buildings with trendy restaurants unaffordable on my backpacker's budget. I walk the stone remnants of the Old Town Hall many times, trying to imagine the force of winds capable of uprooting the sturdy Victorian structure. I visit the art museum, where you can hear an eerie recording from the cyclone and see pictures of the devastation. But the city itself seems to have moved on, and I feel like I'm looking for something that has been lost.

I've made a mistake by choosing to stay in Darwin for eight days. Muriel warned me—"you'll see it all and then some in four or five hours"—but I wanted to plant myself in this distant city at the top end of a distant country, as Muriel did two decades before. I wanted to inhabit her life somehow, from when she was my age, as though this would offer some great insight. But all I get is long hours wandering back and forth along the esplanade. From the vantage point of Survivors' Lookout, at the southeast end of the city, I read about the 1942 bombings on Darwin by the Japanese. These were the worst wartime attacks in Australia, and large portions of the city, as after the cyclone, needed to be rebuilt. It's a strange thing, cities like this that recover over and over after tragedies, phoenixes rising from the ashes, some choosing to replicate what was lost while others using the opportunity to reinvent.

I am reinventing myself, too.


I book a three-day Kakadu National Park four-wheel-drive excursion to break up the endless afternoons in Darwin. Our guide, James, is twenty-five. In sunglasses, he's an attractive, tanned guy, but when he removes his shades, I notice that his eyebrows are situated below the brow bone in a way that throws off the whole symmetry of his face. James brags about never acquiescing to the pretty girls who try to pick him up on the tours, then makes sure I understand that heaps of pretty girls do try.

James first takes us on a jumping-crocodile cruise. Our group boards a catamaran on which a lanky, bush-hardened guide dangles bloody meat tied to a pole over the water, then yanks it up while the deadly saltwater crocodiles jump for it in vain. The "salties" personify stealth, coasting partially beneath the water for long, slow stretches before seizing their prey with a burst of energy. Often they drag the doomed animal (or human) back underneath the water, where it drowns, if the croc's powerful jaws haven't killed it already. This particular breed of crocodiles is the largest in the world; they are thick, lumbering things, with square scaly ridges all along their back. Compared to the massive torso, the crocodile's feet look shrunken and mismatched. When the jaw opens, two rows of uneven teeth reveal themselves like an ancient torture device. Their dark, scheming eyes terrify me.

The guide knows all the crocodiles along this stretch of water. Some of them have been gliding out to greet him for over a decade, yet even the most familiar, seemingly agreeable croc is not to be trusted—ever. "Give her a chance," he says about a female circling the boat, "and she'll rip you limb from limb." With that, he rewards the croc with a piece of raw steak. She sinks like a submarine with her prize, beady eyes the last to disappear.

I recently read about a group of three guys racing around on motorcycles in a flooded area somewhere nearby when one was picked off by a scheming crocodile. The croc quickly buried the body, then came back for the other two guys, who were by then hiding up in a tree. The croc stalked them for three days, menacingly circling the trunk, though they eventually escaped. The fear of being ambushed by a crocodile haunts me our entire three days in Kakadu. I think about it as we walk through the cathedrals of Aboriginal rock art, where we witness the pelicans and storks bowlegged on the rocks and point out to one another the silver barramundis whirling the water around like it's being flushed. Water holes that are baked land in the dry season abound now that it's the wet season, though many of them are off limits because of lurking crocs. The only stream James offers to let us swim in is surprisingly fast-moving. On one side is a flat bank where we strip off our sticky hiking gear, on the other is a rock cave big enough for five or six bodies to climb up into.

"Are there crocodiles here?" I ask nervously.

"Shouldn't be," James says. "But you can never be one hundred percent positive." The real worry, he tells us, is the current. In order to reach the rock cave, we'll have to swim upstream against the water at a pretty quick clip. Otherwise, we risk being washed away to some unknown destination. James makes it clear it is not in his job description to go after us. "So who's keen?" he wants to know.

The two Irish girls who choose to pair miniskirts with chunky boots to hike each day are. So is Eva, the German girl who, while we're washing dishes one night after dinner, can't think of the English word for "pruney" so points to her hand and announces poetically, "I get old." One of the boys will cross, but the other two won't. James jumps in first, then the others heave themselves in one at a time to his outstretched hand. When it appears no one else is crossing, James makes a move to follow the others up into the rock cave.

"Wait!" I yell.

I dive into the cold water, immediately feeling the current drag me. My arms beat the water like a windmill. My legs flutter wildly. I beg all my years of middle-school swim lessons not to desert me. I forget my fears of crocodiles. I forget everything except my body in motion, its strength and determination and the feel of James's calloused hand just as I am starting to slow.

He grins, then hoists me up onto the rock. "Welcome to the other side."

* * *

I like backpacker me. She is easygoing. She talks less, listens more. She doesn't wear a watch. She doesn't have anyone to answer to because she is far, far away. She is freer than ever.

In Ireland, I was pleasantly depressed, surrounded by friends and Guinness. In Australia, I am relaxed, a new experience altogether. Being so close to the ocean has somehow slowed me down, and Australians' constant "no worries" philosophy has rubbed off on me like a fake tan. I have shelved my worries, large and small, like preserved jams. Who will I be in South America? Will I shed these former selves like snakeskin? Or perhaps it's more about perspective, the right angle. It's like trying to see your entire body at once. Even with wall-to-wall mirrors, it's impossible. You have to turn your head to view each part, so you constantly exchange one view for another.

# [ 14 ]

*Our heroine reluctantly returns to the bosom of Saint Diego
and to her family, who express concern over her future
misadventures. A stranger insists she cannot go to Brazil,
though her ticket sayeth otherwise; thus, she prepares to
depart for the Paris of the South instead.*

Carly takes off for Sweden, Denmark, and Thailand a week before I arrive in Sydney for my final night in Australia. We're set
to meet in Rio de Janeiro, Brazil, after I return to San Diego for a
quick visit with my half-brother, Marc. My dad is flying out to
meet us. Muriel drives me to the airport, and we shift uncomfortably in the hard plastic seats and try not to cry. I'm not ready to
leave Sydney. Or the Dawsons. But my visa has expired, like Ireland's before it, and it is time to move on, a fact I'm slowly starting to accept about Australia—and about life.

In San Diego, my father tells me flat-out that I should not go to
South America. Ireland and Australia, okay. Developed countries
where they speak English. But two young women traveling by
themselves all over South America? "Not a great idea," he says.

"Two young women!" I throw my hands into the air. "Oh, how

the mighty feminist has fallen! I doubt that if Marc ran off to Mexico with a buddy, it would be any cause for concern." I recount how I have already successfully negotiated two new continents. "I'll have no part of your convenient double standards!" Then I storm out.

Two minutes later, I slither back to his side. "Umm...so it looks like I need a yellow-fever shot."

Bam! Just like that, I'm fourteen again (though the dramatic storming out was already pretty teen-tastic), dreamy and careless, book-smart but absentminded. All my time away, the maturation I felt occurring, does not exist. I appear to my family ill-prepared for the chores of adulthood, such as getting a lifesaving vaccine before traveling to a foreign country. I slip back into familial neverland. My father spends the rest of the afternoon helping me track down a doctor who will take me on such short notice. In the waiting room, I slouch between him and my brother. "Why does this always happen?" I mutter to myself.

"You don't like change," my brother responds loudly.

I'm in no mood for a lecture. "Then why am I traveling all over the world?"

He thinks for a moment, then revises his theory. "Okay. You like it, you are compelled by it, but it scares you, so you make a plan to leave or start something new, but you don't take care of any of the details because subconsciously you don't actually want to go."

Is this true? Do I have two struggling selves? Does one part of me wish to move forward while the other half of me wants to stand still? I think about all the dorm rooms I've left unpacked until the morning of a move. Although in other matters I'm compulsively organized, I am forever letting my mom show up to a place overflowing with half-filled boxes. "Right," she'll exhale, readying herself. She knows by now to bring her own packing tape. I never, ever have tape.

"Is that your diagnosis, Freud?" I challenge my brother. "Even if you're right, people change. I've changed."

"People don't change," he says nonchalantly. "Not really. Not deep down."

"How can you possibly believe that?"

He shrugs and turns back to an ancient copy of *National Geographic*.

The nurse calls my name. While I wait for the doctor, I examine myself in the full-length mirror. What I had always interpreted as an adorable crop of freckles that sprouted on my nose in Sydney now looks more like dirt. I rub my nose to see if any come off. Nothing.

The doctor injects me and hands over a box of malaria tablets, another item I did not realize I needed. Incidentally, the bill for this visit—about sixty dollars—will float through the mail system for the next three years trying to find me, lost amid all my forwarding addresses, ultimately locating me via a collection agency, a small indiscretion that punishes my credit rating for a dishearteningly long time.

In an effort to prove my brother wrong, I call the airline when we get home to confirm my flight to Rio de Janeiro. The attendant tells me cheerfully that everything is on time, but flights typically aren't delayed forty-eight hours in advance. She asks me if there is anything else she can help me with, then reminds me to bring my passport and Brazilian visa.

"Right," I say, doodling on a Chinese menu. "Passport and Brazilian vi—" Wait. "Excuse me. What do you mean by 'Brazilian visa'?"

"You need to have a visa to get into Brazil. It should be stamped into your passport."

Remain calm.

"Hmm. No, I don't seem to have that." As though I've misplaced a sock. "I'll just get one in Brazil."

A moment of silence passes during which I can almost hear the viscous sound of eyes rolling.

"No, that's not possible. You must have it before you enter

Brazil, and it takes three to four weeks to obtain from the embassy."

"Well, surely if I explain the situation…" The explanation being that I had no clue I needed a visa.

"No, I'm sorry. Even if they allow you on the plane, you are sure to be sent back once you reach Brazil. I suggest you allow me to change your flight. There aren't any flights into São Paulo for another two weeks because of Carnival."

Ho. Ly. Shit.

My timing is terrible. Last month Brazil began requiring American citizens to be photographed and fingerprinted. These new security measures match the U.S.'s own changing policies for Brazilian visitors. The increasingly complex process of entering has become a sore spot between the two nations, and I am stuck in the middle of it. If I had been keeping up regularly with the news while traveling up the east coast of Australia (a much lower priority on the road than at the Dawsons' breakfast table), I would have read about two Americans who were recently arrested for expressing their annoyance at Brazil's new procedures in the form of an apparently internationally recognized hand gesture. Understandably, this did not improve the tense relations.

I look back at my family playing Scrabble. My poor unsuspecting brother and his new wife are about to have an unexpected (i.e., uninvited) houseguest for ten more days. I think of Carly, who is thirty thousand feet in the air, sleeping peacefully on a red-eye to Brazil, where she plans to spend a day with friends before I meet her in Rio.

The airline agent clears her throat.

"I'm not sure what to do," I whisper. I don't want my brother to overhear before I can come up with a proper defense against his prophecy.

More silence.

"Where else can I go?"

"I can get you on a flight to Buenos Aires in five days," she says.

Buenos Aires: Borges, Evita, tango, economic collapse—these scant details are all that leap into my brain. I take a deep breath. "Okay, let's do that." She exchanges the ticket, and I throw the hundred-dollar change fee onto my credit card with all the other charges piling up.

Carly ends up waiting for me at the airport for three hours before checking her email and finding my frantic, apologetic message. We make a plan to meet a week after I arrive in Buenos Aires. She'll head west through Brazil. I'll travel north up Argentina, and we'll reconvene somewhere in Bolivia, a country that conjures up even fewer details than Argentina. In the meantime, I'll have to land alone in South America. Despite my recent successes as a solo traveler in Australia, it's a daunting proposition. Looks like I've got ten days to learn Spanish.

# Part Three

# South America

# [ 15 ]

*Our heroine arrives in Buenos Aires, city of tango and turmoil
and of much delicious food and drink. She takes up with a
merry band of backpackers. Consciously determines to meet up
with her trusty guide but unconsciously procrastinates.*

When the airport's nether regions have borne their last piece of
luggage through the black rubber curtain that divides us, I am
empty-handed. The woman next to me asks someone in a uniform: *"¿Nada más?"* I repeat the phrase hesitantly, pretty sure it
means I'll be wearing the same underwear for the next twenty-
four hours. I carefully print the address of my hostel on the
missing-baggage form. When I called there a few days ago from
San Diego, the Argentinean woman on the phone chuckled a little when she took my name, saying, "You are very planned." It
didn't sound like a compliment. Now, however, I'm glad I made
the booking, even though in under twelve hours, this same
woman (who has by then met me in person) will swear up and
down that I am not a guest, nonchalantly turning away my precious backpack like a scorned lover.

The airline agent hands me U.S. $50, a small fortune at this
juncture in my financial life. I plan to stretch it for several days.

I possess under two thousand dollars for this three-month trip, leftover Australian earnings and unused American tips. Even with favorable exchange rates, it's a paltry sum. Luckily, Carly and I are the perfect monetary match: she is cheap, and I am always broke. A few steps away is a *cambio,* a currency-exchange kiosk. It is a silent exchange, with *hola* and *gracias* bookends. Not knowing much of the language has added a new dimension to my arrival disorientation. Obtaining a bus ticket to the right area of the city now seems like a monumental task.

"*Hola,*" I exhale. I struggle through two sentences, pointing to my guidebook map and smiling like an idiot before one of the two women at the information desk holds up her hand as though stopping traffic.

"Let me explain what you must do," she responds in perfect English. "It is very simple, yes?"

An hour later, a bus deposits me on a narrow street across from a dilapidated grocery store. A few laughing backpackers clamor out of the hostel, holding the door open for me as they go. I wander up a dark staircase. At the top is a sunny yellow room. Two girls my age are chatting animatedly. They are beautiful, short and slim, with caramel skin and auburn hair.

"*Hola,*" they greet me.

"*Hola,*" I respond, and then we stare at one another for a few calculating seconds.

"*¿Inglés?*" the shorter girl inquires.

I nod helplessly, an infant waiting to be attended to.

She fans her face while she counts my pesos then shows me to my dorm room. It's full of blue bunk beds and yellow curtains, and it will soon be the setting for a lesson in the advantages of earplugs after I am kept awake all night by the honking city traffic. I choose a top bunk, just like I did at summer camp, based on the same logic as when I was twelve, which is that there is a greater chance of being crushed to death by a top bunkmate if the unit collapses than of tossing and turning in my sleep so much that I roll off the bed and onto the hard floor. It's entirely faulty reasoning, since while I have never seen anyone squashed, I have been woken up by a crying girl lying bewildered and bruised on the floor, one leg stretched unnaturally behind her ear. Regardless, I throw first my small bag and then my body up onto the bed. I loosen the money belt chafing at my belly and let out the gigantic sigh of someone who is contemplating letting her exhaustion fully take over. But just outside my window, Buenos Aires is waiting, unwilling to be ignored in exchange for a nap.

Buenos Aires has the air of a dazzling but crumbling European city, of better times not so far in the past that they are forgotten. Its marble neoclassical façades, grand balconies, and imposing columned structures are chipped remnants of a wealthier time before the recent economic collapse. The peso used to be almost equal to the dollar, but now it's worth a third of it. You can dine like a king here at an all-you-can-eat buffet, where the meat is so tender it yields to a butter knife, for under five U.S. dollars. The city is abuzz during the day with perpetually packed cafés and bookstores and at night with clubs that pulse with sensual bodies.

I burst out onto the chaotic streets, some so narrow you could reach your hand through the open windows of the compact cars that clog them. I think back to my hesitant arrival in Dublin, how uneasy and unsure of myself I was, and can't believe it is the same girl who stomps through this new foreign city, ready to explore.

I turn left once, again, and then stop short at the edge of the busiest and broadest street I have ever encountered. Avenida 9 de Julio is a monster of a road, with twelve huge lanes stretching across it. It makes California's Highway 5 look like a park trail. Down one end of the avenue is the huge white Obelisk, one of Buenos Aires's most well-known landmarks and the place where parades and celebrations often begin or end. Several sets of lights line the pedestrian intersection, and people appear to be crossing the road in phases, stranded on islands every few feet, the wind of the racing cars and buses blowing up hair and skirts. I watch for several minutes, but no one succeeds in negotiating it in one go, although one sprinting man nearly gets flattened as he momentarily considers braving the last little section of concrete before changing his mind and jumping back. I stalk an unsuspecting woman, letting her guide me to the other side in three heart-stopping takes. She's wearing a colorful suit and fantastic pink stilettos. I'm sporting my Aussie-uniform flip-flops, and the grimy streets have already stained my exposed toes.

As is my new first-day-in-a-foreign-city custom, I do absolutely nothing other than walk aimlessly and stop at bustling cafés to sip café cortados and gobble *alfajores* (cookies layered with dulce de leche that I can already tell will be my Argentinean substitute for Tim Tams). The Spanish spoken in Buenos Aires— by *porteños,* as the local residents are called—has a distinct Italian accent, due to the vast numbers of Italian immigrants who settled here in the nineteenth and twentieth centuries. I studied Italian for two years in college, so when I first hear conversations flying about, I am disoriented by the unfamiliar wrapped in the familiar, like a present packaged in a box from another store. People say the transition from Italian to Spanish is easy, but I think this is the case only if you are fluent in one of the languages before switching to the other. I catch just the most basic words drifting by: *café, bueno, gracias, mucho.* My ears need some time to adjust to the pace of the language. If Sydney's English moves as unhurriedly as island life, eliding certain words, disregarding some consonants altogether, then Buenos Aires's Spanish is as fluid yet precise as tango. At first I try desperately to keep up, but soon I find it's easier to let go and allow the words to wash over me. There is a certain bliss to being in a foreign place with a foreign tongue. It leaves you free to wander about and take it all in experientially, without language as one more barrier to meaning.

I walk without intention. I have no place to be. There is only the decision to turn left or right, to stop or keep going. All that exists is the "what now?" of the present moment in Buenos Aires. I get lost several times and ask for directions in tentative Spanish. One hunched, becapped man points me south, but soon I realize he is mistaken, and I ask a passing woman who duly points me west; a third local points me south once again, and I am no closer to my destination. This is the beginning of a common experience in Buenos Aires. No one ever says, "Sorry, I'm not sure where that is"; it's perfectly acceptable to point in the general vicinity of where you *think* something might be rather than admit you don't know. Maybe there is a tell that gives away those who know from those who are bluffing, but each direction-giver is monumentally confident, so I always totter off gratefully, getting where I need to go about 50 percent of the time. It doesn't matter. I'm not scared of getting lost the way I used to be. At dusk, I meander back to my hostel. I announce myself at the door to be buzzed in, yet again confusing the same girl who checked me in and later turned away my luggage and who appears to have a mental block against my very existence.

That night I make friends with two German girls who are in Buenos Aires to learn Spanish. After a cheese-and-crackers dinner, we sit at the kitchen table, notebooks, textbooks, and in my case, heavily illustrated children's books in Spanish spread out like it is the night before finals. We practice our new language—they have a dialogue in which one girl pretends she is the waiter and the other is a customer while I helpfully interject Rain Man non sequiturs such as "I like brown cats!" or "I don't like brown cats!" Like all beginning language students, I am reduced to simplistic phrases. I like. I dislike. I want. I don't want. Nuance is elusive. Eventually, I leave the faux meal, announcing my departure with "I want no more food. It is the night." They smile encouragingly while I walk the mere two steps into my dorm room. Inside, the walls are so thin I can still hear their every word.

It would be nice to take a shower, although I don't have any fresh clothes or a towel. By now I have heard about my rejected backpack, so I'm stuck in sticky jeans and a black tank top for another twelve hours, at least. But I did splurge on a toothbrush and toothpaste with my airline inheritance, so at least I can remove the day's grime from my teeth.

A tall, broad-shouldered girl unpacking on the bed across from mine turns around to face me. "Hey, I'm Samantha," she says. "Do you have any books you want to trade?"

She's got something waterlogged and true-crime-looking and a copy of *The House of the Spirits.* I pass on the former but trade her my copy of Nick Hornby's *How to Be Good* for the Allende. I don't yet know Allende is an epidemic among female backpackers in South America—every third girl is carrying *The House of the Spirits,* and it takes me four days of peddling to get something new from a Canadian girl who just arrived in Argentina and doesn't know any better. Since backpacking requires carrying all your possessions, there is not enough room for more than one or two books. Extra cash is lacking for luxuries like new novels, so trading is a vital means of reading survival. And because transportation in South America is often a days-long affair, you learn to take into account not only content but how long a given text can last you. I write my name and location in each book before I trade it away, hoping these pieces of myself will be carried to the remotest corners of the earth.

Samantha is a little older, in her late twenties. She's recently had what I've begun to think of as a "this can't really be my life" epiphany—a variation of a common enough travel storyline. Samantha lives in Seattle. Up until a few months ago, she worked for Amazon.com. One morning, for no apparent reason, she awoke feeling bored and useless. The state persisted for several days until she recognized it was not a mere phase but, quite possibly, a permanent condition, so she sold her comfortable condo, put her possessions in storage, packed her blue backpack, and flew to Sucre, Bolivia. She planned to immerse herself in intensive Spanish classes for one week before beginning five months of travel in South America. On her first day of class, she strolled down the tree-lined lane where she was staying with a Bolivian family to the small school in town and sat down in front of another student, Jap—pronounced "yap," like a dog's bark. At this point, Samantha takes out her digital camera and shows me his photo. Jap is several giant leaps above attractive. He is the Dutch version of Jude Law, with those same chiseled cheekbones and wavy dirty-blond hair. I try not to exhibit surprise, which is difficult to hide post–jaw drop, because Samantha is rather plain, though lovely and smart and funny. One week with Jap turns into five, and Samantha sees more of Sucre, Bolivia, than any person should be subjected to in a lifetime. They finally part ways to continue their own travels, Samantha through Ecuador and Peru and now to Buenos Aires, while he heads off to other parts of Bolivia. She is in Argentina until next month, when she and Jude Law plan to reunite in Chile. "This is the real thing," she says.

"That's wonderful," I coo.

Normally, I would be skeptical of this type of definitive pronouncement, having seen many relationships fail with far less to overcome than being from different countries, but everything seems so possible and optimistic when you're traveling that I believe in them immediately. I form a neat mental picture of their future, rocking on a porch swing in the Netherlands, where they occupy a tidy two-bedroom house surrounded by yellow tulips.

The next morning Samantha and I meet two other girls staying in the room. Ivana is also in Buenos Aires by herself. She is an adorable, small blond Slovakian girl with a husky accent who attends Boston University. She says "fuck" every third word and is traveling with a suitcase that nearly rivals Big Red. It is secured with a heavy silver padlock. "My fucking camera got fucking stolen in Chile," she explains. "All my pictures—fucking gone."

Ivana recently quit her job and decided to take a break from school to travel, spurred on by her own traveler epiphany, the one I call a "relationship" epiphany. She recently found out her Brazilian boyfriend of three years was cheating on her for, oh, around the past three years.

Jenny, a Czech girl, rounds out our group of temporary best friends. She's here because of an "epiphany of purpose." She has decided that what she desires more than anything is to own a vineyard in Argentina. She can't do it yet. You need money first and foremost. But this trip gets her one step closer. Her feet are on Argentine soil. In a week she will walk into a vineyard in Mendoza, take off her sandals, and squish grapes beneath her toes.

We have all left something behind—Samantha her cubicle, Jenny her go-nowhere bartending job, Ivana her adulterous boyfriend, and me, the expected version of my future, the future I do not want but do not know how to dismiss, like a dinner guest who won't get the hint that the wine has run out and it's really time to go. And the accompanying mystery: What is it that I *do* want for myself?

Friendships in hostels are instantaneous and intense, jumping over several intermediary steps straight to comfortable intimacy, as happens when you live with someone—when you sleep close enough to hear him or her breathing. The four of us form a happy clique and roam Buenos Aires as if we've known one another forever. We take long meals together in cheap restaurants or join the makeshift *asados* the hostel hosts on the rooftop—barbecues where row after row of supple grilled meats are slid onto our plates.

It is on the roof that I learn the ritual of *maté*, a national drink that tastes similar to green tea. One gourdful passes around a circle of friends, and if you accept the *maté,* you must drink the entire cup yourself. Then you pass it back to the host, who refills the gourd and passes it to the next person. If you say *"Nada más"* when the gourd reaches you again, you are saying you are entirely finished with the *maté,* and you'll be passed over the next time around.

Late at night on that roof, we reveal intimate details of our current lives. Samantha talks about the guy she was afraid to leave behind because he might meet someone else, and now she is afraid to return because she has. Jenny fears she'll never quit her job. Ivana worries she'll be alone forever. I say that I am scared to go home and face my life. Our confessions wind up toward the night sky like cigarette smoke, a cloud of revelations mixing together above our heads. We are all far from home and think (know?) we will never see one another again after we leave Buenos Aires. Our secrets have never been so safe.

My romanticized image of Buenos Aires as a place where residents tango in the streets, red roses between their teeth, is not terribly off base due to the lucky timing of my arrival with the annual tango festival. Locals and professionals dance for audiences in the plaza during the day and for themselves in the parks at night, cloaked in darkness and so close it's difficult to distinguish which arms and legs belong to which body.

One night we attend a performance at the famous Teatro Colón, the city's magnificent opera house. As with so many of the buildings in Buenos Aires, certain sections are in desperate need of repair, but inside, the main theater is magnificent. It holds some three thousand people in swirling layers delineated by tiny chandeliers every few seats. The king chandelier dangles like icicles from the domed, frescoed ceiling.

Buenos Aires is a city of protests; each day seems to bring another rally of bodies, many focused on the high unemployment and the financial crises. People here harbor a great deal of anger toward the banks that closed after the crash, leaving many without access to their life savings. They were given tickets and told they could cash them in eventually, with no word on exactly when that would be. Meanwhile, the wealthier customers were alerted of impending trouble and retrieved their funds before the meltdown. The Argentineans' fury is illustrated by the graffiti scrawled all over the boarded-up financial institutions and when they take to the streets.

My first encounter with a protest occurs on my second night in the city, when I wander into what I naïvely assume is some sort of parade or festival. People drum pots and pans while sidewalk vendors sell cheap diced meat. It is only when I am spat out on the other side of the masses that a police officer informs me what I have just skipped blithely through. If I saw these rallies on the news back home, they would make me fear Buenos Aires. Yet here, in its midst, I don't feel scared. Mainly, I want to understand what it all means.

On Sunday the girls and I drift through the outdoor artisans' markets that snake around a park in a fashionable neighborhood called Recoleta. They're filled with handmade jewelry and clothing. I buy a pair of impractical white linen pants that tie like an apron behind my waist and then again at my belly button. Every time a breeze blows, I have to untangle them from around my ankles. We visit the adjacent cemetery filled with massive marble mausoleums, where Evita's grave is stuffed with notes and flowers and where stray skinny cats dart around the cavernous corners. I spend one whole day alternating solely between book- and shoe stores, both of which are plentiful in Argentina. I scrutinize the simplest texts with my handy dictionary, then reward myself by trying on cheap, beautiful high heels. Another day I wander from one tango demonstration to another, stopping in all the parks and plazas in between. I visit La Casa Rosada, the striking pink structure where Evita famously addressed the Argentines and where, much to the dismay of many residents, Madonna embodied her in the 1990s film version. La Casa Rosada sits on the eastern edge of the Plaza de Mayo, where a women's group called the Mothers of the Plaza de Mayo gather every week to acknowledge their missing sons and daughters abducted during the Dirty War of the late 1970s and 1980s and to pressure the government for answers. Many of the missing were tortured and killed; many are still unaccounted for. The women march counterclockwise in a symbolic gesture of turning back time.

Since Carly and I parted before my three-week trip up Australia's east coast, she has been off having her own adventures. She bought an around-the-world ticket for $2,500 Australian because it was cheaper than going straight to South America and because, really, why not? The tickets stipulate you move in one direction—no backtracking—so she has gone from Sydney to Bangkok to London to Stockholm to Copenhagen then to Rio, where we were supposed to meet.

She immediately regretted her decision to spend a few weeks in Scandinavia. It was the middle of February and blistering cold, and her backpack was full of light South America summer gear. In Copenhagen, she stayed in a massive hostel—a converted factory—with beds for two hundred, though only around ten people were there at the time, all of them seasonal workers. Carly was the sole tourist. On the third day, a film crew came looking for backpackers for a documentary, and they filmed Carly walking around the deserted, frozen city. She was convinced the name of the program translated to something like "People Who Are Stupid Enough to Visit Copenhagen in February, and What the Fuck Do They Do All Day?"

Rio is the first place Carly ever backpacked, half a year before we met in Galway. When she arrived at her hostel back then, the other guests were understandably on edge because the previous afternoon four armed men charged in and robbed everyone. Though it's hard for me to imagine, Carly was nervous those first few days in Rio. She was nineteen, and it was her first trip alone. The hostel was in a bad area (obviously), and the local men aggressively leered at her on the streets. After a day she departed for the countryside to stay with Brazilian friends she had met in Australia. And that was where, outside congested, frenetic Rio, she fell in love with Brazil.

When I don't show up, Carly is stuck in Rio alone again, in another shady hostel. Like the last time, she quickly shoves off to find her old mates. She also meets up with an acquaintance from an earlier trip who makes the mistake of declaring his undying love for her, prompting her to drop him immediately. "He was one of those guys who gets all scared to go off on his own. I swear, guys are the worst for that," she tells me later.

Carly is a magnet for clingy men. Every few months she acquires a story about some dude she had to ditch like a bandit in the middle of the night. Once an American guy she thought she'd successfully unloaded glimpsed her smoking on her hostel balcony in a city she claimed she'd departed several days earlier. "I'll be right down!" she shouted, feigning excitement at their unexpected reunion. "Wait there."

Then she hastily stuffed all her gear in her backpack, paid her hostel bill, and sneaked out a back door and down an alley while he waited for who knows how long below her empty room.

While we're apart, Carly spends some time in the Pantanal—the Brazilian wetlands—piranha fishing and horseback riding. She meets two German guys around our age and takes a train with them to Santa Cruz. There she develops a bronchial infection that lasts several days, forcing her to bed rest. The concerned Germans deliver food and medicine and diligently look after her. The one tourist sight she manages in Santa Cruz is a glimpse of the renowned sloth family that lives in the main plaza, and there is very little Carly hates more than being out of commission in a brand-new city.

Once she is well enough, the group heads west to Potosí, the highest city in the world, to see the city's famous silver mines. "I'm glad I saw it, but I would never do it again. Never," she tells me when we reunite.

The tour guide is a former mine worker, but he had to quit after falling ten meters down a mine shaft and breaking his leg. After that, he learned English and got into tourism. He tells the small group that he thanks God every day for his injuries, because he no longer has to work in the dreaded underground, where safety precautions are nonexistent. The life expectancy is around thirty-five. Superstitions about how to strike it rich run rampant. One way is to bury a llama fetus. When Carly was there, a disturbing rumor was circulating that a newly wealthy miner had sacrificed a baby a few weeks before his big find.

To enter the mine, they squeeze through a few body-sized holes. They walk the entire way, down three levels. There are no carts, as she imagined. No equipment. No one is wearing helmets except the tourists. Every now and then the unnerving bang of dynamite startles the group.

Carly was recovering from her bronchial infection when she arrived in Potosí, and between that and the extreme altitude, she never felt 100 percent herself. She couldn't get her equilibrium. She'd be walking in the musty streets and suddenly just fall over, like she was in a fun-house wheel. The Germans had to place themselves on either side of her like crutches. After two days, the group left for Uyuni—which is where I am supposed to meet her.

My plan was to leave Buenos Aires after two days, take a bus to Córdoba for a look around, then head farther north to reunite with Carly. But two days pass, and then two more, and then another two, and I remain in Buenos Aires. I start imagining my

own itinerary, studying Spanish here for a few weeks, then drifting around the Argentine countryside. Each morning I wake up
and think, Just one more day.

Carly is annoyed by my delays. She's already missed Carnival
because of my Brazilian visa mishap, an event she was looking
forward to for many months. She's used to traveling on her own,
not compromising or waiting for someone else. Carly had already
been living in Galway for a few months when I showed up. Australia was her home turf. So Buenos Aires constitutes the first
real traveling I've done without her or that doesn't carry the imprint of her experiences. It feels like my own little secret. So
while I want to begin my adventures with Carly, a part of me is
thrilled to occupy this new space on my own. I'm racked with
guilt, both because I've screwed up our itineraries and because I
feel like I'm keeping some wonderful delicacy hidden from the
person who taught me to cook in the first place. I'm not consciously putting her off, but looking back, I realize I was prick-
ling at the idea of Carly being the guide on these travels, as she
was so often before. I was unconsciously asserting my burgeoning independence.

# [ 16 ]

*Our heroine is coughed up in Tilcara, a small locale with many
fine crafts and hippies. The effects of altitude are gravely
endured until she is cured by a native medicine known for its
darker properties. Departs for Bolivia in the company of a
love-struck Australian and a travel-struck Swiss.*

Eventually I extract myself from the clutches of beautiful Buenos
Aires. As in Sydney, I feel like I've drifted into a city I could call
home. I wouldn't have been at all surprised to run into some alternate version of myself happily living out her Argentine existence. (Of course, I haven't fully considered the ramifications of
surviving here on pesos as opposed to U.S. dollars, few of even
those as I have.)

Because I overstayed in Buenos Aires, I skip Córdoba and head
straight up on a twenty-hour bus ride to Salta, a welcoming little
colonial town at the base of the Andes. A day after that, I journey
to Tilcara, a tiny Andean town in northwest Argentina. On the
ride from Salta, green trees become brown shrubs as we climb
higher and higher. The road gradually narrows and the mountains rise up around us. The pulsing avenues of Buenos Aires slip
away like a dream as we disappear inside the land. Even though
my guidebook map indicates only a few marked towns along the

way, the bus halts several times in desolate spots where I have to squint to see a house or two in the distance. Once it slows to a crawl and I see nothing, not a soul or dwelling anywhere. Like a ghost, a man brushes past me and out the door, shuffling off into the vast emptiness.

The people landscape changes, too. With my dark hair and eyes and leftover Sydney tan, I could almost pass as a local in Buenos Aires, populated by various European-influenced complexions, provided I didn't actually say anything. But the middle-aged man next to me on the bus to Tilcara has darker skin and eyes whose pupils and irises melt together into singular blackness. Some of the women wear long black braids and thick, colorful skirts. Belongings are stuffed between their feet in crinkly, checkered plastic bags. The bus is way past its prime. Most of the rubber lining the windows has fallen off. Stuffing juts out of the seats.

I'm coughed up at the Tilcara bus station, in front of a small ticket booth and groups of patiently waiting families who stare straight ahead. There is no shuffling about or straining, like back home. No one looks at her watch or complains about the deplorable conditions of travel these days. It doesn't seem like they are waiting for anything particular to happen—or not happen—they're just waiting out the day. At one point a black car pulls up and five people cram themselves into the backseat, defying all laws of physics.

I remove my backpack from beneath the bus. Even though there are lots of bags below, mine is the only one that looks like it's been rolled around in flour. It looks so grimy and abused that I consider the possibility that maybe it somehow fell out and has been dragging behind the bus for the last few hours. I swat at it, then strap it on my back, wheezing and light-headed, and consult my map. As the bus pulls away, the wheels ignite a thick cloud of dust that blows all over me.

Disoriented and coughing, I careen from side to side like a

character in some romantic comedy about to drop a four-tiered wedding cake that has improbably wound up in her arms. I manage to remain upright, barely. I look back at the crowd, ready to make eye contact to show them that all is okay and have a group laugh over my gracelessness. I might even spin one finger around at the side of my temple, the international sign for crazy, and mouth, *"Loca Americana!"* But no one meets my gaze, making me now actually feel a little nuts. A lone little girl is giggling, a tiny hand covering a small mouth that is not emitting any sound. When she notices me smiling back, she buries her face shyly in her mother's skirt.

"Hostel Malka?" I ask the agent in the ticket booth. Tilcara is so tiny that my guidebook doesn't offer a map of the city center, and now that I'm here, I realize how silly it was to assume there might be tourist maps on offer or even a waiting cab. The sun is setting quickly, and I have no idea where to go. The agent answers me in Spanish no longer draped in an Italian accent, and I don't understand a word. *"¿Qúe?"* I say helplessly.

He points toward a desolate road behind me, the kind that might plausibly lead into town or some place that is decidedly *not* town. But his tired gesture is all I've got, and my head is starting to throb. I feel like the moisture has been wrung out of me, like I need not only a long, cool drink of water but also to submerge my entire body in liquid. I'll have to trust the directions. I'm starting to realize my utter dependence on strangers here in South America.

After a short walk, I enter what looks like the city center. I'm amazed at the unexpected spurts of joy I feel in South America at something as simple as ending up in the right place. Tiny accomplishments fill each day: finding my way to a hostel, eating something delicious that my stomach doesn't reject three hours later, successfully conversing with a local using an eclectic set of nouns, verbs, and charade-like hand gestures.

Adobe houses and stone walls line the street. A few places

have signs hanging outside, as if they might be shops, but the doors are all closed except one. It leads to a small white room that is the tourist bureau. Inside, I am profusely welcomed by a diminutive, friendly man with the look of someone who has not had a visitor in a long time. He leads me to the large map of Tilcara that covers the back wall, traces my route with his finger, then taps three points on the map—*"museo, pucará, iglesia."* Words I know. Museum; *pucará* is the pre-Hispanic hilltop fortress I've just read about in my guidebook; church. He's show-ing me the tourist attractions.

My guide walks me to the edge of the road to point me in the direction of my hostel, then sends me off with an encouraging nod. I cut directly through the center of a plaza filled with ven-dors, an oasis of green grass and plump trees resembling old pho-tos I've seen of 1970s San Francisco street markets. Some of the women are older and have the darker skin and hair of Andean peoples, but there are also young people with dreadlocks and tie-dyed T-shirts who look like they just finished touring with the Grateful Dead. Many of them are knitting or painting in their stalls. Few people seem to be shopping, though; there are far more sellers than buyers.

At the other end of the plaza, I take a left onto a deserted street minus a Scraps-scrawny dog who limps hopefully after me. It's as if all the color in Tilcara has been drained into the center plaza, leaving the surrounding houses pale and dusty. Row after row of faded pink, white, and beige little abodes populate the quiet street that ends in a short but steep ascent up to my hostel. I huff and pant. I suck in big, greedy mouthfuls of thin air. Halfway up the hill, I drop my pack onto the dirt and collapse atop it. Just sitting there is an effort. It feels like a weight is press-ing down on my chest; a hand is squeezing my throbbing lungs.

By the time I reach my room, my burgeoning headache is so overpowering that I have to lie down. The top bunk is free, al-though I would have chosen a lower one this time because the mattress is only a few inches from the ceiling. I slither across the covers, scraping my shoulder on the wall. I cover my face with a sweatshirt and hum softly, trying not to consider whether I am having an aneurysm.

When I open my eyes a few minutes later, there is another person in the room. For some reason, the hostel has decided to put two single beds in this room, along with one bunk bed, so he is sitting comfortably upright across from me, reading a book.

"Oh, hi," I say.

"Hi to you," he says.

I imagine how I must have looked in my coffin/bed, prostrate and humming. Assuming he might understandably be concerned about sleeping in the same room as a crazy person, I attempt an explanation. "I'm Rachel. I don't normally lie down in the middle of the day and sing, but I have this terrible headache."

He grins deeply, three layers of smile lines bunching outward toward each ear. He looks strikingly like the Grinch who stole Christmas. He's not green, and he isn't bad-looking either, but his wide face is definitely grooved and sly.

"I'm Hans," he says, clearly more interested in whatever he is reading. Then he glances up, as if he's decided that I deserve a few more minutes of his time. "If you have this headache, it could be from the height. You should get some coca from the woman who runs the hostel."

"Thanks," I say gratefully, realizing that I am being introduced to altitude sickness at the rather wimpy height of 2,461 meters (about eight thousand feet). I walk to the main office cradling my throbbing head.

Inside is a bookcase with a "two-for-one" sign. This is often how the book-bartering system works in hostels, sometimes insisting on a trade of three or even four books for a measly one in return, but I'm in too much pain to be annoyed about it. I ring a bell. The owner appears, and I point to my temple and explain my situation through gritted teeth.

"*Hola. Estoy enferma. Aquí. Por favor.*" This impressive linguistic feat translates as: "Hi. I'm sick. Here. Please."

"You need coca," she pronounces. She pats my shoulder and hands me a bagful of green leaves. I look around nervously. Since it doesn't look like a setup (not that I have any real idea what a setup looks like, other than from watching cop shows on TV), I let her steer me toward the kitchen, where I am instructed to put the leaves in hot water. "Drink," she commands. "All of it."

Half-blind, I stumble back across the grounds. In a heap on the hallway floor, I sip my tea, and within minutes my headache vanishes completely. With it, a heavy fog lifts from my brain and body—similar to the effect of my morning cup of coffee. I can breathe again. I marvel at the magical green dregs at the bottom of my cup.

I assumed I had misheard Hans when he suggested the coca. I expected to be handed some Tylenol or laughed at and told no one gets sick at this piddling altitude. But coca leaves really exist. They jump from the description in my guidebook into my hands. Historically, the relationship between Andean people and coca was a straightforward one. It's presently complicated by the creation of cocaine, whose biggest customer is the United States, but coca leaves have been consumed by South Americans for thousands of years. They combat altitude sickness, increase blood circulation (crucial at heights), and lower cholesterol. They were once traded as currency and are still used in social exchanges. Two men might greet each other by offering their coca pouches, exchanging leaves as a gesture of goodwill.

Once I feel well enough, I walk back down the hill to investigate Tilcara. The whole place is still eerily deserted. Even the plaza vendors have packed up and left for the day. I plot out the route to the Pucará ruins but am diverted by the sound of horns and drums growing louder and then the sudden sight of what must be the entire absent town parading down the street. In the center of the crowd, several young men in bright red garb are dancing and tossing around what looks like a giant doll made of cornhusks. I stand near the back of the revelers, hoping to remain unnoticed, but two young boys instantly swoop down on me as I'm sneaking a photograph of the foreign scene. I recoil in confusion, assuming they are after my camera. It is only when they are right up against me that I am embarrassed to realize all they are interested in is the package of cookies I'm holding. They widen their eyes and point shyly to the bag. I hand it over. Without another word, they fly from me, and lacking further allure, I sink into the background. I follow the procession as it winds back to the center of town, then part ways near my hostel. Pucará will have to wait until tomorrow.

When I ask the hostel owner what I've witnessed, she tells me the party is part of the local Carnival festivities. Tilcara's festival lasts nine days and is dedicated to *il diablo*—the devil. The doll bandied about was a devil effigy, which is buried the rest of the year in a rocky lair; the boys in red dressed as devils are the envied leaders of the procession.

Back at the hostel, my headache returns with a vengeance, so I pour myself more coca tea and take a seat at the stone table outside the dorm rooms. Two children from an expiring barbecue a few feet away approach and ask my name. Where am I from? How old am I? Their questions stretch the limits of my novice Spanish, but they seem happy enough to endure replies with no prepositions or conjunctions. After a few minutes, I run out of words, so they run back to their family, undoubtedly announcing that they have just had a conversation with a very simple girl.

After that, I sit in silence and watch Tilcara fade into darkness. I feel palpably remote, lost in the landscape. I *want* to be lost in it. Like I did in Buenos Aires, I start imagining my Tilcara life. I could learn how to knit and take up a stall in the square. Maybe the hostel would let me stay on in exchange for some sort of labor. More and more, quicker and quicker, the places I travel draw me in like a spell.

I haven't emailed Erica since I arrived in South America, and she feels even farther away now than she did when I was in Australia. Her life and mine, so intimately intertwined at college, feel like they've started down two diverging paths. Watching the sun set behind the Andes has no quantifiable value, like my friends' burgeoning careers, but I know that I am gaining something that is as important. I don't know how to define this period of my life, but I don't know how to define myself at the moment, either. I'm no longer a student. I'm nobody's employee or girlfriend. Thankfully, I still have my parents, but I'm no longer defined in relationship to them, either. I'm in a space that defies these traditional categories, one I have carved out that is just for me.

Hans is in the kitchen stirring rice when I come indoors. A wispy-haired girl hovers beside him, intently observing him add spices. She is so enthralled that she doesn't notice me until Hans turns to say hello.

"Would you like some rice?" he asks me. "We are about to eat."

The girl's smile vanishes. Her eyes are daggers, and when I shake her hand, it's vampire-cold. I have to say I'm intrigued, since before this moment no one has ever despised me so wholeheartedly so immediately. It's easy to tell her iciness revolves around Hans and the meant-to-be romantic dinner I have interrupted. I glance at my pathetic packet of soup and decide to take my chances with my new nemesis because the smells coming from that pot are way more delectable than anything I have a shot at concocting.

Cassie is Australian, so I try to impress her by revealing that I'm on my way to meet an Australian friend, as if to say: "See, we're not so different. You're Australian, and I have an Australian friend. And I'm not trying to steal the Grinch—just his rice, which I think we *both* agree looks delicious." It does not appear to have any tenderizing effect on her, so I shift tactics. "How long have you two been traveling?"

This gives her the chance to tell me about their recent romance, which cheers her up considerably. I learn that Hans is from Switzerland, the French-speaking part. He's a true vagabond, returning home only in the winter tourist season to work and save money to spend the second half of the year traveling abroad. He has no interest in a career. His lifelong pursuit is seeing the world, and he has no intention of slowing down until he has ingested all of it. He is in his early thirties, and Cassie is a few years younger. She has taken work leave to travel for five months, and she tells us how much she misses Melbourne, looking longingly at Hans. He nods thoughtfully. "I've been there," he says, and I can tell he's crossing it off his mental map, though Cassie's sigh indicates a different interpretation. I pull out my ultimate bonding card and tell Cassie that I've just come from four months living and working in Australia, and she becomes almost tolerant of me.

"Are you crossing the border alone?" Hans asks as I'm drying the dishes.

"Yeah."

He frowns. "This is not a good idea."

He doesn't elaborate, but in Salta I did hear some rumors about corrupt Bolivian officials who bribe and harass.

"We're crossing tomorrow to Tupiza," he says, but it is Cassie, in a miraculous change of heart, who extends the offer for me to travel with them into Bolivia. It means missing the Pucará ruins, but I gratefully accept their invitation. We head back to our shared room, where I knock myself nearly unconscious climbing into my bunk and drift happily to sleep.

We rise at five A.M., load our packs, and walk off into the still-dark Tilcara morning. I have learned to like being up before dawn (minus my stressful stint at the Sydney café), whereas in college, I would have scratched your eyes out for even suggesting such a thing. Backpacker me is perky as a blond gym bunny at this hour, though I need my daily dose of caffeine to carry on an intelligible conversation. South American coffee is dark and bitter. It laughs right in the face of yuppie Starbucks brew like some scrappy city kid.

The morning is so cold I can see my breath, and I know for certain I have not brought proper Andean clothing. Hans's and Cassie's backpacks are much bigger than mine. After Hans's gourmet meal, I have come to think he might have an entire kitchen packed in there. The spices he sprinkled in the rice came from a small pouch that hangs off one side of his pack; off the other, salt and pepper shakers rattle against each other. I pretend we are bandits stealing across the border in the dead of night, and it takes severe willpower not to break out in the *Mission: Impossible* theme song. When we get to the bus station, the ticket window is shuttered, and I'm a little worried, since Cassie and Hans already have tickets. I don't yet realize that Andean buses are magical creatures that stretch to fit anyone willing to pay the fare. Although the bus that arrives is barely full and I easily find a seat, there will be many times in the near future when I stand or sit in aisles for hours, bumping and banging against the strangers next to me.

Hans is afraid of knots. Not of tying them but of untying them. I learn this fact three hours into the four-hour drive to the border. Somehow (and we must have exhausted a wide range of topics before winding up at this one), we find ourselves discussing his unusual fear.

"I cannot get near them." He shivers a little. "My skin feels like, ah, bugs are under it."

"Crawling," I say.

He nods.

This must be a misunderstanding. I try to recap. "So you can tie knots." I mime the act, one hand rolling over the other, then pulling two pieces of invisible thread away from each other. "But you can't…"

"Unknot them. No."

"What about your shoes?"

He's wearing sandals. His sneakers turn out to have Velcro straps. I think of other things that need tying. "Presents? What about unwrapping presents that have bows?"

"If the bows are tied, this is not possible."

"Did something happen to you?" I ask. I want to crack a joke, maybe throw out some sort of pun about him being knot quite right in the head, but I can't tell if we have a sense of humor about this slight eccentricity or we're dealing with some sort of PTSD. Did someone close to him die in a knot-related accident?

"Nothing that I remember." He shrugs, then unzips his hefty pack to retrieve his sunglasses. He's been camping on and off while traveling through South America, so in addition to the usual array of clothes and guidebooks, he has pots and packets of instant soup, a sleeping bag, and a blue tarp. He strikes me as a guy prepared for anything, who fears nothing other than knots and a bland, sedentary existence where he cannot make his way through one foreign country after the next.

Travel takes hold of some people, like a virus. Carly's "bug" has been long-nurtured, but mine is just starting to show its strength, which is understandable since I've only recently un-earthed the traveler within me. I consider all the places Hans has been where I want to go: Greece, Tibet, Russia, Thailand; the list goes on and on. My father has told me that he will "really start to worry" if I am still wandering around in another year. My mom is concerned, too. But right now it feels like a year is not nearly enough time to see everything.

# [ 17 ]

*Our heroine boards a crowded and not entirely pleasant-*
*smelling vehicle for Tupiza, alongside her two temporary*
*companions. The threesome is soon joined by two more, and*
*the five begin an excursion both cursed and blessed by fickle*
*Mother Nature, who maketh both thunder and hail,*
*pink flamingos and salt flats.*

Our predawn excursion to Tilcara's bus station turns out to be
the most excitement of the day. In La Quiaca we pay a taxi driver
three pesos each to take us to the border, a fee he seems to pull
out of thin air after appraising us. The Bolivian border agent has
a unibrow and treats us like unwanted vagabonds who have arrived to use up all his hot water and toilet paper, two things
there are never enough of in Bolivia. He wields his passport
stamp like a gavel and announces, *"Treinta dias"* like a prison sentence. We leave Argentina and shuffle over an uninspiring concrete walkway into Villazón, a bustling border town of rickety
stalls that looks patched together by people who live, or wish to
live, somewhere else.

Bolivia has the most indigenous population in South America.

Over half of the people here claim pure Amerindian blood. Quechua and Aymara speakers form the biggest bloc. Unlike Tilcara, which has a mix of physical appearances, everyone in Villazón has the darker skin and hair and shorter stature of the indigenous people. The women wear thick, elaborate skirts, layers upon layers expanding outward from an invisible waist. Two braids of abundant black hair meet at their backs, the ends held together with a piece of string. Their feet are protected by chunky clogs. The young girls have tiny waists and luminous skin, while the older women's cheeks are chafed from years in the harsh Andean cold, and their bodies have expanded significantly in womanhood; or it may just be the skirts that give the illusion of endless hips. The women all carry black bundles on their backs packed with clothes, food, or a small child who is never crying, just sleeping peacefully or calmly watching the world go by. The Bolivian women walk purposefully past me on the streets, short and strong, slightly bent forward. The men stroll along at a more leisurely pace, exchanging extended greetings; they never seem to be lugging anything or going anywhere in particular.

Cassie, Hans, and I find a tiny restaurant selling beef and chicken empanadas and settle in at one of three rickety tables. We take turns in the bathroom, which has no seat cover or toilet paper. I hover precariously over the hole, gripping the roll of toilet paper I bought in town with one hand and holding the broken latch closed with the other, all while trying not to make any noise, since our table is directly on the other side of the door. It's clear I'm going to have to let go of some hangups pretty fast in Bolivia.

Our bus to Tupiza doesn't leave for two hours, so after lunch we walk over to the park to kill some time. A young boy is dragging around a large scale, the kind you might see at a carnival where people let a stranger guess their weight. I wonder if he is earning money predicting people's measurements or simply charging them to step on the scale and see how much they weigh, obligingly subtracting twenty pounds for the women's skirts, I hope.

Although we're the only foreigners, we are blissfully ignored. I was expecting the usual stares and comments—most of them thankfully indecipherable—that have increased in frequency since I left Buenos Aires. I don't realize until I head off alone to an Internet café that it is Hans's presence that has thus far allowed me to stride unimpeded through the streets of Bolivia. Without a man at my side, I am once again subjected to a splattering of lascivious whispers and whistles. The abrupt shift is jarring, as if I'm suddenly walking around in someone else's body. I can see how a man and woman might come away with entirely different impressions of South America. I wonder what it's like to travel in a man's relatively inviolate body, to claim enough power that people ignore you and let you go about your traveler business. As a white woman backpacker here, I'm an automatic spectacle.

Our bus to Tupiza looks old but not nearly as tragic as the dinosaur beside it. (While men load and tie luggage to the top of our neighbor, several rusty parts fall from underneath and clang against the ground.) The eager crowd surges onto the bus to illustrate a phrase that must have originated in Bolivia—"hurry up and wait"—since even after everyone is loaded, we remain at the terminal another half hour for no apparent reason. When all of the seats are filled, more passengers squeeze down the aisle, sucking up any remaining precious oxygen. They stand body to body for the entire ride.

The windows don't open, and the searing sun feels like it's burning a hole in my chest. My soaked tank top is swimming beneath my purple sweatshirt. My own sour scent mixes with the others perfuming the sweaty air. We climb higher and higher into the mountains, and I hear the concrete turn to gravel below our wheels. I survey all the people tucked into every crevice of the bus and try not to imagine collisions and toppling, crunched bodies.

Four hours later, we shoot through a series of tunnels and are reborn in Tupiza—a southwestern-looking, dry, mountainous landscape. At the bus station, two small Bolivian boys in Nike sweatshirts slither expertly through the emerging passengers. In an instant, they spot the three "gringos" awkwardly extracting their packs from the aged bus's grimy underbelly and appear grinning at our sides. Our backpacks are not only dusty, like after the trip to Tilcara, but also wet—so wet that several layers of my clothing are damp and all of my belongings emit a mild mildew aroma. Several other boys (none look older than eleven) have caught up with the first two, and all are passionately delivering their sales pitches.

"Cheap rooms, lady!" they exclaim in carefully pronounced English. "Hot water, yes?" They unfold colorful pamphlets to illustrate their wares. "This way. This way." We allow ourselves to be led away by the two who reached us first, following their outstretched arms down the road, a reverse Pied Piper scene.

A woman stands to greet us when we enter the hostel. Her black hair is pulled back in a ponytail with two thick strands hanging down on either side of her face like open curtains. She drops a few coins into our young guides' palms, and they sink contentedly into one of the lobby chairs. We hand her our passports as identification and, because it is cheapest and we are all on strict budgets, book one room with two beds for the three of us. It's eighteen bolivianos a night—under three U.S. dollars.

"I'm a very light sleeper," I warn Hans, and am rewarded with a Grinchy grin.

We leave our wet clothes with the laundry service and are told they'll be ready in two days. I assume the duration is a courtesy to the employees until I see my underwear hanging from the stairway rails a few hours later. As in Ireland, nothing ever really dries here.

There is no dormitory-style accommodation in Bolivia; this place is more a hostel/hotel hybrid, with private rooms and a shared kitchen and common areas. Two guys in the TV room are watching *Butch Cassidy and the Sundance Kid*. Supposedly, the infamous outlaws hid out here shortly before their deaths, and the connection with Tupiza is big tourist fodder. The woman who checked us in encouraged us to watch this video—for a small fee, of course. In the kitchen, I meet a man from San Francisco. He's bone-thin with greasy shoulder-length blond hair. His sandals are coming apart at the seams. A cigarette hangs lazily out of the corner of his mouth as he stirs soup. He's been in Tupiza for five months, four of them at this hostel, an unusually permanent fixture in a transient space. "I'm never leaving South America," he says.

"How are you supporting yourself?" This question is a pressing one for me, try as I might to reconcile the material goods-lacking bohemian I'm growing into with the future-looking part of me wondering how I'll make some sort of living.

"I teach English. Every six months, I leave and find another teaching job when I get somewhere I like."

I don't miss the possessions I'm increasingly discarding. I can't even remember the stuff I left back home; none of it seems important now, anyway. What I'm attached to instead are people and places and experiences and this new version of myself I'm cultivating on the road. I think it might be my true self—or at least the person I'm determined to be, even after I go home. I can definitely see the appeal in continuing on in a minimalist way like this guy is doing, though I'd probably opt to shower a bit more frequently.

Tupiza is my introduction to the striking beauty of Bolivia. It's surrounded by the Cordillera de Chicas, which stretch around it in a halo of hills, mountains, and canyons. Its dusty vastness is breathtaking. It's easy to see why Butch Cassidy and the Sundance Kid came here to escape, because it feels like a place that could easily envelop you. Although those bandits are likely the most famous celebrities among Western tourists, the artwork around town reveals the locals' favorite: Ernesto Che Guevara, the legendary leader of the people, spent time in Bolivia encouraging the working class, like those in Tupiza, to rise up against a government that kept them impoverished. His image is everywhere, usually in his signature red beret and green tunic.

Tupiza is a quiet spot with few tourists, and for once no men call out to me. It's afternoon when we arrive, so I spend the last remaining daylight hours exploring the town. I head to the local labyrinthine markets, where open stalls sell hand-knitted sweaters, cheap sandals, and greasy fried bread. As is the custom throughout South America, the siesta is observed for several hours in the afternoon, salespeople simply dozing in and out of consciousness amid their wares. As the sun sets on Plaza Independencia, uniformed schoolchildren stroll hand in hand, revolving in slow circles around the main square. In the gazebo, a small band strums guitars while the church bells chime in the harmony. The road back to my hostel is quiet except for one blaring television, a dozen adults and children gathered around its illuminated screen. I stare out into the shadows to the endless desert, which seems to lead everywhere and nowhere all at once.

Our two dark-haired guides magically reappear that night when Cassie, Hans, and I leave the hostel in search of dinner. Once again they lead the way to our destination. This time it is a bare-walled room with four folding chairs and tables with a battered sign on the front door to identify it as a restaurant. We are the only customers. When I order a pasta dish from the menu, our waitress looks distressed. When I see her return with groceries, I realize I have chosen a meal they did not have the ingredients to prepare.

Hans fearlessly munches away on a salad, dismissing any possibility that the lettuce might not have been washed in boiled water. Cassie and I, more cautious, start with a hearty vegetable soup. I still have a dull altitude headache and not much of an appetite, but the cooks have clearly gone to such trouble to prepare my dinner that I make sure to finish everything on my plate. Though the boys decline our offer to order them full meals, we buy them sodas, and they giddily slurp at the table next to us. When we've finished, they dutifully escort us back to the hostel and disappear into the night.

I have one more day in amiable Tupiza before a four-day jeep tour of Bolivia's famous salt flats that finishes in Uyuni, where I'm meeting Carly. For sixty bolivianos (about eight U.S. dollars), I hire a guide and horse for a three-hour trek through the mountains. An older man who works in the hostel loans me a large cowboy hat and helps me into the saddle. My guide is a soft-spoken nineteen-year-old. He instructs my sedate horse in a secret language, and I follow him through the small town up into the jagged Cordillera de Chicas, passing a straight-backed Bolivian woman in a black bowler hat watching over a herd of cows along the way.

This is only my second time on a horse other than the depressed, circling ponies at the apple farm my parents used to take me to every autumn when I was a kid. The first horse I mounted that didn't look suicidal was in Australia. Carly's family took me to Hidden Valley, the co-op where Carly spent much of her youth riding horses, including her latest, Destiny. I was excited about the idea of riding but a little uneasy about Carly leading the expedition through the woods. I worried because she knew how to ride and I did not, but even more because she lacked the chemical that triggers fear in normal human beings. And I did not. The ride began pleasantly enough. The path was flat and my horse very Zen. I was just getting comfortable when Carly veered off to the right and disappeared down a steep hill.

"Umm…" I called out.

"Mate, come on down. The horse knows what it's doing."

The horse slid down the rocky slope practically on her knees, while I clung on, trying not to fall nose over heels into the dirt. At least this is how I exaggerated my triumph to Carly's parents later that afternoon while she rolled her eyes. "Good on ya, Rach!" Pete declared, clapping me on the back enthusiastically and uncorking another bottle of wine.

My current guide leads me on a less treacherous route, pausing every few minutes to point out a rock formation and tell me the name. He speaks little English and I try my best to communicate in Spanish, but neither of us fully understands the other. I scan each Spanish sentence through a mental word bank with very little currency. Each glimmer of understanding frustratingly disappears into the murky water of context.

We stop below a large rock. "Climb up to the water," he instructs me. He will stay with the horses. *"Cuidado"*—be careful.

I scramble up the rocks to a plateau, where little puddles have collected in sunken pockets of stone floor. I thought he said something about a waterfall. I'm not sure if I'm supposed to go higher, but I don't see anywhere else to climb except a slippery rock face a few feet away. Surely *cuidado* is not the extent of a warning given before tackling something so steep I'll have to will my way to the top. We are in the desert, after all, a place where any water is cause for celebration, so I head back down and give him two enthusiastic thumbs up when I reach the bottom.

When we don't speak, there is only the plod of horse hoofs on the dry, cracked earth.

"Why do you come here?" he asks me.

"To see Bolivia. To see how Bolivians live."

"But why?" he asks again, as though there must be an underlying purpose of greater importance.

Because I can, I guess is the honest answer—because I am able to buy a plane ticket and because Bolivia is cheap and exotic and because it is exciting to come all this way and talk with you.

"I have lived here all my life," he says, and then the path narrows and he pulls in front of me to lead the way.

When we descend out of the mountains and reach the long stretch of wide, open road leading back to the hostel, he asks if I want to go faster. He picks up speed to illustrate his question, then circles back around to my side. I nod, not quite sure I do, then grip the horse's reins with both hands. The guide makes a clicking noise, and off we gallop into town. I bounce roughly in my seat, hair whipping in the breeze.


Hans and Cassie have booked the salt flats jeep tour with me, but I'm happy to see another couple waiting at the pickup spot, too. I have been the third wheel with these two long enough, and it's getting uncomfortable watching Cassie engage with her fantasy Hans—the one who will give up his life of travel to settle down with her—as opposed to the real Hans, who gives her not the slightest encouragement to this effect. Danny and Hermine are from Belgium. They have recently quit their corporate jobs to travel for nine months in Latin America, though their bosses have promised to rehire them upon their return if there are open positions, a piece of luck that seems unheard of in the U.S.

Danny and Hermine are married and emanate the relaxed energy of a pair who have spent many happy years together. Somewhere in my suburban childhood, I developed the idea that I better get all of my "living" out of the way before settling into marriage, at which point a switch would flip and I would cease to be an interesting person and instead be someone captivated by things like paint swatches and casual Fridays. I saw marriage as a type of prison sentence in which both people felt they had sacrificed something vital in order to be with the other person and so must eventually grow to resent them. But Hermine and Danny seem like a well-functioning partnership. They have traveled all over the world together and have plans to see more, not less, of it in the days to come. As with Pete and Muriel before them, I'm collecting these examples of happy lives wherever I go, hoping I can somehow pick and choose the best parts to apply to my own existence.

Our silver jeep fits the five of us plus our driver, Simón, and our guide/cook, Loli. The gear is strapped up top beneath a beat-up tarp. The exterior of the jeep is shiny and spotless. It's the newest-looking vehicle I've seen in Bolivia, giving no indication of the treacherous trip to come.

We drive seven hours the first day. The scenery is breathtaking—snowcapped mountains in the distance with greener, rockier terrain on either side of us, populated by the occasional shaggy llama. We top 4,300 meters (14,000 feet), then descend back down to 3,000 to sleep that night. By the end it's difficult to enjoy because I'm nauseated from the altitude and the painful indigestion that knots my stomach. After forcing down Loli's painstakingly prepared dinner of vegetable soup, chicken, rice, and fried potatoes, I head straight to bed. Clutching my stomach, I hear only the pounding rain and the throbbing blood between my temples.

We're staying on someone's property. It's not any sort of hostel or hotel but just a big, bare room with ten beds. We arrived here after dark, and the whole town was black. No one but us seems to have electricity, and we've got only a few bare bulbs dangling from the ceiling. The one toilet is a few feet off to the right. Instead of the automatic flushing mechanism, there is a large barrel filled with water and several plastic pitchers so the user can dump liquid down into the dark water to flush. There is no light in the bathroom. I have never seen this level of poverty, and we have the best accommodation in town.

Around two A.M. I'm roused by my riotous insides. No matter how hard I try to ignore them and fall back asleep, I cannot will

away the pain. I find my flashlight but then remember I gave my
toilet paper to Hans before we went to bed. I take a dirty pair of
pants with me in order to have something to place between me
and the foreign toilet seat and pray that someone has left paper
inside the stall. They haven't—not that I can relax enough to go
anyway. The hiss of my urine is the sole soundtrack filling the
night air, and I'm too self-conscious to hazard emitting any other
bodily noises, so I stumble back to my bed doubled over in agony.
I swallow an ibuprofen and drift off for another hour or two.

We're on the road by 5:45 A.M. to visit Pueblo Fantasmagoría—
a forgotten village about thirty minutes from the town receding
in the predawn distance. The place was abandoned many years
ago, after residents started seeing ghosts. It's creepy and beautiful, now only the crumbling stone half structures of abandoned
houses and an old church at the center. It's made otherworldly by
the light layer of snow dusting it.

Our route was plotted based on dry-season conditions, but the
unusually heavy rains last night have turned everything to mud.
Our jeep is no match for the thick stuff, inches deep. We get
stuck, our back wheel spinning helplessly while Simón twists the
steering wheel back and forth. The rest of us tumble out, still
bleary-eyed and shivering in the cold mountain air, to prod the
vehicle forward.

"Bloody hell," Cassie mutters.

With a few grunting pushes, the jeep is back on its way. It
speeds ahead of us, and we run to catch up with it. This happens
every fifteen minutes or so for the next hour. By the end, our
clothes are speckled with mud as if we're a bunch of Jackson Pol-
lack paintings.

Next we hit snow. Perched high in the Andes, we inch our
way along icy trails no wider than the jeep, roads not meant to be
traveled in these conditions. The car is quiet, a collectively held
breath. Even fearless Hans grips his camera with white knuckles.
I think for the first time in Bolivia but not nearly the last that

there is a very good chance I am going to die. All it will take is one slipping tire and over the edge we'll go, crashing down hundreds of feet to our rocky demise. Bolivian adventure is nothing like American adventure, which is peppered with permission slips and legal waivers and the promise that someone will pay if an accident occurs. Even Australian adventure felt designed more to make you pee yourself than lose your life. When I skydived, I was confident the instructor would take care of me. The challenge with bungee jumping was more psychological than physical. But here in Bolivia, I feel like anything could happen, like I'm no longer playing at adventure. And that is scary.

In Buenos Aires, I made acquaintance with a chain-smoking Argentinean at the hostel. One evening we found ourselves in a heated discussion that began with his demanding I refer to myself as a United Statesian instead of an American, since he was an American, too, and ended with him laughing at my culturally inherited notions of invincibility and optimism.

"That's what's so funny about you *Americans*," he scoffed. "You always assume the best, while the rest of us know to expect the worst to happen."

I once thought the world was a fair and secure place, but that faith has been shaken of late, and I'm not sure that's a bad thing. When we make it across in the jeep, I consider it no more than a stroke of good luck and not the inevitable security of my continued existence, as I once would have.

"I really thought I was going to die that time," travel-wizened Hans admits when we stop for hot coffee and stale bread smothered in dulce de leche, and we all laugh nervously.

A few hours later, we approach what appears to be a deep river cutting off the road. Two vehicles are parked, defeated, on the other side; their occupants lounge with the doors open and music blasting, waiting for I don't know what. We are prepared to stop, too, all signs pointing to the fact that the water is impassable, but Simón plows straight into it without a moment's hesitation. Smack in the center of the stream, the car dies. A range of emotions whips through the backseats like we're one organism as we watch freezing-cold water slowly seep in through the doors. First, silent shock. Then we get annoyed, marked by Cassie shouting, "This is just fucking stupid" half a dozen times. But soon, as we realize we must jump ship, a kind of manic hilarity takes over. We know if we cross in our shoes and pants, we'll freeze the rest of the afternoon. So we strip. Off come the boots, the three layers of socks, and the two pairs of pants. In our underwear, we gingerly hop into the chilly water and wade toward the shore, clothes held above our heads, much to the amusement of the locals on the other side.

The jeep miraculously roars to life once the guys prod it onto dry land. By then we have all made peace in our different ways with the fact that today is going to be a series of the unexpected. Soon enough, black storm clouds gather, and we're engulfed by a downpour that lets up only long enough for us to pull off the road to check out the rows of pink flamingos lining the edge of a pristine lake. It is here that we're nearly struck by lightning. The bolt strikes so close that everyone drops to the ground in panic. Except me. For some reason, my twisted instinct is to jump *up* in fear. We race back to the relative safety of the car and skid through a terrible snow/hail storm for the next hour. As though to add to the delightfulness of Mother Nature's tantrum, Simón believes using the windshield wipers depletes the car's battery, so he uses them only when an inch of snow has completely obstructed the front window and we're skidding blindly into the abyss. Then he lets them flap once, barely clearing the obstruction, before shutting off the device again.

When we arrive at the salt flats the next day, we've earned it. At four-thirty A.M. we're up racing along in the dark. The sunrise is a hundred different shades of orange, and the water atop the salt plain makes it seem like we're gliding along a lake. It also reflects the sky, so the mountains and clouds are both above and below us. The salt plains themselves stretch for twelve thousand square kilometers. The area used to be part of a prehistoric lake that almost completely covered southwestern Bolivia. The lake dried up, leaving behind a few small bodies of water and these salt pans, of which Salar de Uyuni is the largest. From our final vantage point, there is nothing in any direction except endless salt and sky. We are insignificant specks in the middle of nowhere. Embracing the full force of that truth is liberating.

# [ 18 ]

*Our heroine and her trusty guide reunite. The two make haste
to La Paz, where misfortunes beset the heroine, who must
question herself and her fears and attempt to make
some sense of the tricky pair.*

Carly and I reunite in Uyuni. When she appears in front of me
decked out in camouflage, I can't help joke, "Have you joined the
Bolivian army?" (Not that it's totally out of the realm of Carly
possibility, really.)

"Hilarious," she says. "I've been waiting for you in this crap
town for so long I might just be desperate enough to do it."

Our annoyances (hers at being stuck in the middle of
nowhere waiting for me and mine at feeling pressured to rush up
and meet her) dissipate in our excitement over being together
again. We buy train tickets for the next day—the earliest we can
get away—and settle in for a tedious thirty-six hours in Uyuni.
At the local market Carly buys some yarn. She's taken up cro-
cheting in South America, and in her customary way, she's already pretty good. She presents me with a slightly lopsided but
attractive blue-and-white-striped hat. She herself is wrapped in
a newly made scarf. Carly attempts several times to teach me

what for her is a soothing ritual, but I can never get into it. When I relax, I want to be transported mentally by a film or book, whereas she prefers the trancelike momentum of physical repetition.

At the markets, a wrinkled man listening to a beat-up radio tells us that yesterday several trains in Madrid were bombed. Instantly, we think of Portu, who returned home soon after I left Ireland, but we never feel the impact of the event because after our encounter with the old man, we don't see or hear anything more about the bombings. Outside of large cities, the Internet in Bolivia is unreliable and expensive. We log on every few weeks to send a mass email to friends and family, but otherwise we avoid it. So the important piece of information drifts easily away from us, as though it happened on another planet. We're so connected with the all-encompassing realities of South America, and with ourselves, yet we've dropped far enough off the grid that we're somewhat detached from the rest of the world.

The overnight train ride from Uyuni to Oruro sets the bar for extreme discomfort. Carly and I take turns in the window seat, where there is at least the hard glass to lean on, but neither of us gets any sleep. When we depart in the early morning, our bodies ache and crack as if we're eighty. The Oruro station is an excited mob of passengers elbowing their way to their luggage. A Bolivian woman smacks me in the gut with her huge blanket stuffed with what feels like bricks, but I'm too groggy to register it as anything other than one more bodily pain. Once we've gathered our packs, we trudge straight to the bus station to get tickets for La Paz. It is no less chaotic. Representatives from each company brandish brightly colored signs and enthusiastically yell out their prices and locations. We're both so exhausted that we're actually looking forward to another bus ride. No matter how uncomfortable, we're so weary that nothing will be able to prevent us from passing out.

* * *

While we wait to leave the station, skinny kids shout, "Empanadas!" into the windows and do business with the outstretched hands motioning to them. A family of three is crammed awkwardly into the two seats next to us. The young son perches precariously atop his parents' thighs, resting his bony elbows on his knees. As we leave the terminal, he shifts his weight a little and drops his head onto his mother's thin shoulder, their deep-black hair colliding.

The bus ambles along without incident minus two small delays. First a flat tire keeps us lopsided in the road for a little over an hour. Carly is asleep, but I watch the male passengers depart, smoke, circle the dead wheel, and linger in the cold sun, chatting with one another while they keep an eye on the slow repairs. An hour after the bus starts up again, we are stopped at a checkpoint. Two tight-lipped men in black board and dig through the luggage piled in the nets overhead. Tense, silent minutes pass punctuated only by the rustle of mistreated belongings. Although for an extra five U.S. dollars, we could have booked roomy, reclining seats on one of the luxury buses that backpackers often splurge on in South America, Carly and I opted for the cheaper transport because the trip was only supposed to take three hours, which have now stretched into six. We are also determined to travel like the locals do. We firmly believe this is the most authentic, consciousness-raising way to travel, but some days in Bolivia are more physical and practical than enlightening. We spend a lot of time simply trying to get from one place to the next in one piece.

What are they even looking for?

"*Drogas,*" a man behind me whispers, as if he is reading my mind.

The dour-faced men motion for two couples to follow them. Both the women look our age. Their male companions grab their bags and silently descend the bus's three beige steps and depart into the fading sunlight. It is only when I catch a fleeting glimpse of one of the women crossing the road to a small hut that I notice she is crying. Maybe I misunderstood the man behind me, because they don't look like drug dealers. They look like us, some kids on a trip. I want to turn around and attempt to ask him to explain what happened, but an imposing silence permeates the air, so I keep quiet. The bus hobbles off without them, their empty seats offering no answers.

In La Paz, we push through the crowds and out into the cool afternoon to grab a taxi. A handful of relaxed drivers lean against their cars puffing cigarettes, but when they see us, they jump into action. The quickest whips open his door and ushers us into the faded leather seats. As we descend, I notice how the city climbs like ivy up the sides of the canyon surrounding it. A film of dust seems to have settled on the bleak houses and steep streets we spiral down. I try to relax and take in my new surroundings, but I cannot help feeling anxious, because a few weeks ago I met a pair of girls in Buenos Aires who were robbed on this very route. Halfway to their hostel, two men opened the back doors of their cab and climbed in on either side. Claiming to be government officials, they demanded a "tourist tax"—the price of which was hastily determined to be the full contents of their wallets. The driver said nothing during this exchange, and when the men finally departed, he dropped his terrified passengers at their destination without a word.

But Carly and I have no such bad luck. Our driver is an amiable guy chewing coca leaves who chats away first in clunky English and then in rapid Spanish. He leaves us in town with a smile and some directions I don't understand. On either side of us, dusty stalls packed with mysterious bottles and supplies fill the narrow streets. Only later, when I'm studying the folded map in my guidebook, do I realize this area is an infamous witches' market and those are unfamiliar potion ingredients like llama embryos, frog powder, and armadillos' bodies. Carly confidently leads us to what seems to be a cheap, clean hotel. When I ask her how she knew about this place, she laughs and says, "I was just walking, mate."

Inside, a heavyset woman takes our bolivianos and hands us a key. She nods in the direction of the stairs. At the top, we open the door to a room containing two narrow beds with scratchy blankets and stained sheets. I unbuckle my heavy pack from around my waist. It sags below my hips, and I slide it off with a quick shrugging motion. Inside this bag—plus the clothes and worn sneakers I'm currently wearing—is the sum total of my belongings: three T-shirts, two sweaters, a few pairs of pants, socks, ten pairs of underwear, bug spray, sunscreen, malaria tablets, some blue and green necklaces I picked up as presents, a guidebook with pages torn out, my journal, camera, a Michael Moore book I traded for a copy of *The Lovely Bones* a few days ago in one of the many hostels where we have gotten a few hours' rest before heading back out on the road, and some fraying bits of red yarn left from Carly's unsuccessful attempt to teach me to crochet. It's enough to make my back ache on days like today. Carly's pack is wet where her rice bag failed to protect it from the damp bus. It smells faintly, or we do. I can't tell. We both desperately need showers, but the woman at the front desk has already warned us that there is no hot water. Since we are too cold to contemplate our third icy shower this week, we head downstairs to make some hot tea and attempt to warm ourselves up.

In the common area, a long-legged girl is draped over a bulky leather easy chair. "Have you done the Death Road?" she asks us in greeting.

I watch in horror as Carly's eyes begin to glow. "No," she says, leaning in. "What is it?"

The girl shuts her book and tucks her spider legs beneath her. "Well, the road from La Paz to Coroico is called the Death Road because apparently one vehicle goes over the edge every two weeks!" she tells us with what can only be described as sheer delight. "It's the most deadly road in the world." She pauses to let this sink in before bestowing her final piece of information upon us. "They take tourists mountain biking down it. You drop four thousand meters in four hours, and it's sheer adrenaline the whole way. It's so cold your arms and butt go completely numb and you feel like throwing up from the altitude." This last bit seals the deal for Carly, although, truthfully, the girl had her at "Death Road."

A glance in my guidebook confirms this tale and continues: "So, if you're up to an adrenaline rush, you'll be in your element, but if you're unnerved by unsurfaced roads just wide enough for one vehicle, sheer one-thousand-meter drops, hulking rock overhangs and waterfalls that spill across and erode the highway, your best bet is either to walk to Coroico or to bury your head and don't look until it's over."

Back in our room, I read this page out loud to Carly and tell her that I'm flexible: I'm open to either walking to Coroico or burying my head until it's over.

"Oh, mate, come on. How many times do you get to bike the Death Road?"

Umm, zero, if I have my way, I think. I don't. We have already decided to go into the jungle, a deal I made with Carly in exchange for visiting a Chilean observatory, a much more civilized expedition, in a few weeks. Unless we fly there, which we have already agreed is too expensive for my rapidly receding funds and Carly's determined thriftiness, the Death Road is our only option.

There is a bravado among backpackers, especially the ones who have flung themselves into the more impoverished, off-the-beaten-path nations of the world. Stories of near-death experiences are the currency among this group, and in South America, many of the bragging rights come from getting somewhere spectacular through nontraditional means. Have you rafted to the Igauzu Falls? Hang glided over the Rio beaches? Hiked twenty-six miles through the Andes to reach Machu Picchu? Biked the world's most dangerous road? Like a group of scouts sitting around a bonfire, we regale each other with tales of near-misses, and respect is bestowed in direct proportion to the level of danger, planned or not. Carly, as competitive as an Olympic athlete, is vying—might be vying for the rest of her life, in fact—for the boldest, baddest adventures that can be had. Me, well, I could feed the flames of my travel legend indefinitely off the terror-fest that was my jeep tour a few weeks ago. Hell, I think I should get three hundred gold stars just for setting foot in Bolivia in the first place. But Carly won't rest until we've trapezed our way through South America with one arm tied behind our backs. This was part of what drew me to her, as I was looking for a way to test myself, too, though I had no idea how in over my head I was about to be.

The guy who sells us our "Death Road packages" has dozens of photos tacked to his wall displaying various red-faced riders giving the thumbs-up as they straddle their bikes or grinning broadly as they admire the awesome views. This will not be me. Carly, sure, but I've never even mountain biked before.

"One ticket for the last day of my life," I tell the salesman. Carly rolls her eyes, then pries a credit card from my clutches.

The Death Road does have one advantage, however. It will get me out of La Paz, a city I am desperate to depart, a city that almost compels me to quit South America altogether. La Paz is Bolivia's de facto capital (the government is here), although the second capital, Sucre, remains the judicial center. In La Paz, indigenous skirts mix with business suits, black bowler hats with briefcases. It's frigid here, thanks to an altitude of 3,632 meters. And it's even harder to breathe than in Tilcara, though we're starting to get used to it.

Carly and I spend much of our time juice-stall-hopping in the crowded markets. We start to forgo meals altogether in favor of the thick, fresh, pulpy drinks with muesli and seeds mixed in. Women in white lab coats and chef hats serve us while we perch on bar stools among the papayas, mangoes, watermelons, and pineapple. One day we pop into a store selling musical instruments, and the blind owner shows me how to play the *zampoña* (the panpipes). Carly snaps a picture of us, him in a thick red jacket with black stripes and me in my gray poncho, a row of guitars and *charangos* (similar to a ukulele) hanging from the ceiling above us. Next door a girl no older than eight bargains with us for a pair of alpaca gloves.

Gone are the friendly, easygoing locals of Bolivia's countryside. As in any major city, they have been replaced by greater extremes of humanity: the poor, crazy, and ambitious all crowd in together, vying for space and clean air. We shuffle along with them, trying to keep out of the way. One afternoon when we are leaving the markets, something wet smacks my neck. Instinctively, I touch it. The crowd around me seems to get tighter, and I am sucked into the vortex. *"Arriba, arriba!"* people are shouting at me. Hands dig into my back and shoulders, shoving me forward.

I lose sight of Carly, who is up ahead and has not yet noticed I am no longer a step behind. When the crowd parts, I am somehow next to her again, disoriented, until I notice the zipper of my money belt is open. My wallet and camera have been stolen. I realize the locals shouting at me were trying to help. They understood what was happening and were trying to get me to run away. But it happened too fast; it was over in seconds. The most frustrating part of getting robbed is that I read about this exact scam in the Bolivia section of my guidebook. Someone spits on you or—and I don't know if this second option is more or less appealing—dumps liquid down your back. Distracted, you stop to examine yourself. While you're wondering what the hell kind of bird poops orange soda, the thief swoops in and nicks your stuff. Easy.

Reading about something doesn't mean you're prepared for it, though. Luckily, I had stuffed the five hundred bolivianos I had just gotten from an ATM inside my bra and left two of my three credit cards in the hostel. I lost my driver's license but not my passport, a roll of film, a little bit of American cash, plus a few traveler's checks I'll have to cancel and have no idea how to replace while in Bolivia.

Back in the hostel, Carly and I lie side by side on my bed, me wallowing in self-pity and berating myself for not having synapses that fire quick enough.

"Don't worry, it happens," Carly says.

What I want her to say is "It could have happened to either of us." But we both know this isn't true. And Carly is nothing if not honest. Sure, she might fib to me about something trivial to lift my spirits, like when I came across a picture of myself taken my last week in Sydney, my stomach spilling in rolls over my struggling bikini. "Uggh, I'm huge," I grumbled.

"Don't be ridiculous," she said, laughing. Then, to make me forget about my chubbiness, she pointed at the photo and said, "Look how tan you are, mate!"

But something that matters, something like being the kind of person who gets robbed versus the kind of person who doesn't, is something she would never gloss over. Carly always looks like she belongs, like she's in control. I'm jealous of the way nothing ever seems to faze her. I haven't yet realized that this is a misperception on my part—just because she reacts differently does not mean she is wholly unaffected—or that it would be much better to accept who I am, different as it is from Carly, and give myself credit for doing the best I can.

I call American Express. "Have you filed a police report?" the woman asks.

"Lady," I reply, world-weary all of a sudden and running low in the optimism department, "have you ever been to Bolivia?"

I pull out of my funk by the afternoon, in time to walk out into the streets of La Paz and get groped. As a tall, angry-looking man and his companion pass us, he reaches between my legs and grabs me hard. Then he just keeps walking. I'm filled with such intense anger and shock that my body feels like it's on fire. I scream at him, something in unintelligible half-Spanish, and he turns around to face me. His face tightens. I do not look away. But then, fingers curling into fists, he begins to walk toward us again. On his face is the expression of someone who wishes to do real harm, someone who feels it is his right to touch women in the street, or maybe just foreign women. There are others nearby but no one comes to our rescue. No one seems to notice or care. What can we do? We run. We sprint two blocks to the hostel, where I collapse on my bed in tears, robbed, violated, and angry at the whole city of La Paz, angry at Carly for making me come here, angry at myself for agreeing.

"Why does it have to be like this?"

"It's harder," Carly agrees. "But that's how it is."

"Do you ever wish you were a man?"

"No," she says, which is of course the truth. Carly never wishes to be anyone but herself, whereas I am constantly imagining my life as a different person. I think of the women in *On the Road*. What is their role? They're around to be screwed, to be divorced, to be punched in the ribs, to fall flat on their face in the mud. These women aren't the travelers. They're the pit stops.

The idea that something bad has happened to me, coupled with the certainty that nothing will be done about it, shakes my very core. Even with Carly here, I know the two of us represent little more threat together than we do separately. We're at the mercy of this place. I have the overwhelming urge to flee, but I know that if I do, I will wrap up the whole country of Bolivia in this one bad day and tuck it away forever in some forgetting drawer of my mind.

I didn't realize how difficult backpacking could be. In Bolivia, especially, my romantic notion of traveling the world was constantly getting shipwrecked against the day-to-day reality of it. I had witnessed beauty and kindness here, but I was often overwhelmed, totally out of my element. Carly had prior experience traveling in South America. She was a born adventurer who determined early on that she had no use for fear, whereas I was scared a lot of the time. But I didn't want to let that emotion stop me anymore, not in my travels or in my life. No, I determined, tomorrow I would put one foot in front of the other and keep moving forward.

# [ 19 ]

*Our heroine and her trusty guide battle the great and mighty*
*Death Road, which is much feared by peoples other than the*
*native inhabitants of the equally great and mighty Bolivia.*
*Descends into a drug-induced slumber and*
*emerges with an epiphany.*

The next day we are off bright and early to bike the Death Road, both of us happy to leave La Paz behind. Although Carly does not display every emotion on her face, as I do, it turns out my misfortunes in La Paz have made her uneasy as well.

"Why didn't you say anything?" I'll ask her, surprised, when we discuss the incident some weeks later.

"I thought it was obvious. You'd had such a terrible time of it. Of course I didn't want to be there, either."

I probably would have felt a little less isolated if she had voiced this concern in La Paz, but it's not her style to spell things out. I was beginning to realize that Carly's stoicism is the way she copes, like mine is letting my thoughts and feelings all hang out like a beer belly.

We find ourselves in a van with a German pair, a French couple, and a Spanish girl. It is a quiet group. We stare sleepily out the windows, no one making a move to purchase anything when we pull up to a stretch of open stalls where apple-cheeked women hawk bottled water, fresh bread, and wool sweaters. The wind whips around them, pinning wisps of their long black hair to their foreheads.

By the time we stop to unload the gear, we are at nearly five thousand meters (15,000 feet), and it is absolutely freezing. It's also raining. We're given bright orange rain jackets and matching pants and paired with bikes. Mine is huge; the seat is so high that I have to hop up to get on. I take a little practice ride and quickly realize my brakes don't work.

"*Ayuda!*" I screech.

The guide looks at me as though I'm rather clever for figuring out this minor malfunction before we started downhill. I grit my teeth as he pulls one of the chains over some spokes and pronounces the problem fixed.

I make Carly promise to wait for me if I get too far behind, but once the wind is at her back, her word is swept away with it, mocking me from behind. Though her brakes are fine, Carly's gears don't work properly, so she's stuck at one speed: the fastest. The road is wet and windy and paved only for the first hour of our journey. The rain heaves itself at us, and within minutes we are drenched from head to foot. Heavy fog clings to the Andes. I grasp the handlebars with numb fingers and ride my brakes down the spiraling mountains. I want to close my eyes and let go, let someone else take over. But it's just me, and the terrifying death trap seems to go on forever. All I hear is blood pulsing in my ears. After twenty minutes, we stop to collect ourselves and detach our clenched blue fingers from the frozen handlebars. They're curled like an arthritic woman's around a walker. Everyone is smiling and laughing. I intend to throw a hearty chuckle into the mix, but somewhere between my brain and my mouth, it transforms into a heavy sigh, giving away my unhappiness.

It's clear immediately that I am the slowest rider in our group. As I approach the others at one of the many places where they stop to let me catch up, I hear one of the Germans who brought his own bike say in English loud enough for me to hear: "She is very, very slow, *ja*?"

Besides being generally embarrassed over my performance, I am aware of being the only American in the group. If I give up, not only am I the *girl* who gave up, but I'm the *American* who couldn't hack it. In my mind, they will immediately associate nationality and competence.

Often during our journey, we have to pull off to the side of the road to let huge trucks squeeze by, two or three passengers riding high atop them. We stand right at the edge of the cliff, our heels against the abyss, and my head spins from altitude and fear.

Last night before I fell asleep, I imagined myself gliding downhill in the bright sun of a Bolivian morning, the wind carrying me across the mountains. I didn't anticipate the rain and mud and the fact that I'm not E.T. Two hours into the bike ride, I have had it, no matter how determined I was the night before.

"I feel sick," I tell Carly. "I think it's the altitude."

"That's no good, mate."

She knows I'm faking it and so do I and we both pretend we don't.

Ten minutes later, I am in the minivan following behind the riders. This is the one thing I told Carly I absolutely refused to do: traverse the Death Road in an actual vehicle. Now here I am beside the toothy driver, carrying on a sulky conversation in my half-baked Spanish, irked at Carly for making us do this in the first place.

Later, she will generously strike this wimpiness from the record of our travels. When other backpackers ask if we've done the Death Road, she'll say, "Yup, we went, and it was fantastic. You should definitely do it." Meanwhile, I will look distractedly in the other direction, pretending to examine some interesting piece of wall in the distance.

When we miraculously reach Coroico, I swear there are angels singing. At a mere fifteen hundred meters above sea level, I feel the expanding sensation of oxygen flowing back into my starved lungs. Nestled in the Andes, Coroico is a popular vacation spot for middle-class Bolivians, though only in this country would folks willingly cross something called the Death Road for a little R & R. As usual, we are greeted by men advertising accommodations. They carry laminated photos of their respective hotels in large binders, each bargaining with the others so effectively that we have only to look on and wait for the lowest available price. It winds up being twenty bolivianos a night, about the equivalent of three U.S. dollars.

"Do not tell this to the other guests," our salesman warns us. "This is a special price. Only for you. Okay?" We nod conspiratorially.

Hotel Esmeralda resembles a Swiss ski lodge. It's at the top of a steep hill that we rattle up in his red jeep. When our escort drops us in the lobby and reveals our bargain rate to a woman folding laundry, she looks first at him and then at us with open dismay. He shrugs, and she motions for us to follow her down the hall, refusing to make eye contact. In our room, I open the white shutters onto a perfect postcard view of the Andes. An unobstructed panorama of snowcapped mountains stretches in all directions. We stick our faces out the window and inhale deeply. I feel the stress of La Paz and the trauma of our recent bike ride recede as if it happened weeks and not hours ago.

"Carly," I sigh happily.

"I know," she says.

It's not just that Carly and I often have different concepts of fun (see: Death Road). Traveling with someone isn't always easy in general. We were "in each other's pockets," as Carly put it. So any number of individual preferences and personality clashes were magnified, and we'd been together in close quarters so long that we also knew precisely how to get under each other's skin. Luckily, we shared a fundamental desire to see the world. So whenever we took in a new, spectacular piece of it, like at this moment, we let everything else go and embraced the awesomeness together. We were always ready to start fresh in a new place and with each other.

Our shared reverence is interrupted by a floating British accent. We follow it down to a very pale girl in a very pink bikini and a hairy guy floating on his back in the pool.

"I don't know what the big deal is," she says loudly. "It's just a bunch of ruins, yeah?"

"I think so," he agrees. "I mean, we're on holiday, and I'd rather sit by the pool and get pissed."

She nods thoughtfully, then slowly shakes her head again in disbelief. "In the pictures, it just looks like a bunch of bloody ruins. I can't even pronounce it. Maccho Pichi?"

Carly rolls her eyes at what is for her an abominable way to discuss the place she has already decided will be the highlight of our trip a few weeks from now.

"Ugh," I groan in agreement. These are the loud, ignorant kinds of tourists we try hardest to avoid. It's an irony of our present situation. Although traveling ideally makes the traveler more tolerant of other cultures, one sometimes isn't so tolerant of fellow vagabonds, especially when she believes, like Carly and I do, that they are somehow disrupting her own "authentic" experience.

"Let's get some wine," I say, closing the shutters and blocking out the voices.

Since I now fully appreciate the feat of transporting it, I am not too disappointed that the wine is twice as expensive here as it was in La Paz. We buy two bottles and some fresh bread and make our way back to the hotel. When we get there, pink-bikini girl has joined her friends on the patio, where they are all guzzling beer—except for the back-floater, who is grasping a massive bottle of vodka with both hands. I'm tired and really don't feel like making small talk. I can tell from Carly's quickened pace that neither does she, so we politely decline their offers to join the party, not knowing that we will all be together again soon.

Two white hammocks sway unoccupied at the bottom of a small hill behind the pool. We pour our wine into tiny white plastic cups and settle into the netting.

"Let's stay another day," I say.

"Okay," she immediately agrees.

Partly, I think Carly says yes because she worries I will have a stroke if forced back onto the Death Road so soon (we'll have to traverse more of it to reach the Amazon), but I know she, too, likes the quiet pace of Coroico. Through the trees, car lights still flicker along the route to La Paz. We learned today that a new, safer road is being built parallel to the Death Road; I hope it will have a more optimistic name. Bolivia is so surprising: dusty desert, endless salt flats, jagged mountains, and the sweaty Amazon all occupy the same vast landscape. Tonight I'm glad we're here.


Two days later, peaceful Coroico seems a world away as we race along a supposedly less dangerous stretch of road in a bus. My forehead is plastered against the greasy glass as I strain to see beneath the bus, to confirm that the wheels are connected to the road and we are not, as it appears, suspended in midair. I squash my face harder into the window, painfully flattening out my nose while I crane my neck at various angles. But I glimpse only the outer slice of one black wheel hugging the edge of a drop hundreds of feet from the ground; the muddy path is tucked neatly out of sight below the belly of the bus. Next to me, Carly ignores my manic investigation. She leans back against the seat and puts one flip-flopped foot across her knee. Behind cheap aviator sunglasses, her eyes close. She has gotten thinner since we arrived in South America two months ago—we both have. But Carly's body

is a muscular, compact thin, whereas I look more waify and ane-
mic. She wears knee-length tan shorts and a long-sleeved blue
cotton shirt. Her blond hair is pulled back into a short ponytail,
her Discman earphones dangle like a futuristic necklace.

I lean over her lap to get a better look at some of the other passengers and accidentally step on her exposed toes. "Sorry, Carlz!"
I whisper.

She reluctantly opens her eyes. "What's the drama?" Loosely
translated, this is Australian for "Why are you acting like such a
complete idiot and stomping on my foot?"

"We have a problem," I say, and gesture wildly toward the
window.

It has become abundantly clear over the past few months that
Carly and I have vastly different definitions of a problem. For
her, the word is employed only after something bad happens, as
in "Charlie had a bit of a problem last week when that shark bit
off his leg." I personally feel that experiencing actual misfortune
is a mere technicality. The real problem began with the idea of
the shark lurking in the water, something it would have occurred
to me to worry about long before I actually paddled out into the
ocean. In my opinion, a problem is the promise of disasters to
come, two seconds or two years from now. And considering its
treacherous landscape, foreign languages, unpredictable transportation, and total disregard for fixed prices of goods and services, Bolivia itself is, for me at least, pretty much one big problem.

"Don't stress," Carly says, and offers me a relaxed smile. "It's
no worries."

Now, unlike the word "problem," the expression "no worries"
tumbles off her tongue with alarming ease. After living in Australia, I've come to understand that this phrase doesn't always
mean there isn't anything to worry about—it's more like a sug-
gestion that you will be much happier if you go about your business believing everything is okay. Call it positive thinking or
unflagging confidence or maybe a Zenlike notion all Australians

share that the mysterious workings of the universe are completely out of our control, so why bother getting all worked up?
Or, I don't know, maybe surviving twenty-two years in a country
home to an unfathomable number and variety of creatures that
can kill you has instilled in Carly a profound nihilism. Whether
it's personal or cultural or what, I don't have it, so the fact that
we are barreling along at fifty miles an hour on a one-lane, two-
directional glorified horse trail suspended high in the air in a bus
that should have been scrapped for parts in the 1970s, driven by
a guy who I am reasonably sure is intoxicated doesn't trouble
Carly. Or if it does, she doesn't let on. It's infuriating.

"I think we should get everyone over to the other side of the
bus," I say, but the look on Carly's face stops me from further ex-
plaining my theories of weight distribution. Luckily, a movie is
starting on a small screen above the driver's head. I turn away
from her and pretend to be engrossed in the opening credits. The
film is in Spanish and begins with a lengthy car chase. Vehicles
crash and roll all over the road, spilling their contents and then
catching fire for a few seconds before exploding.

"I cannot believe they are showing this," I mutter.

Many of the Bolivians are engrossed in the film, and the rest
ignore it in favor of dozing against the headrests, outstretched
legs in the aisles. No one else looks worried about the seventeen
hours of treacherous driving before we (hopefully) reach Rurrenabaque, our jumping-off point for the Amazon. In fact, I realize that I have never seen a nervous Bolivian passenger on any of
the various jeeps/buses/trains/boats I have ridden through rain/
hail/snow. But all that is about to change.

"Look out the window," I urge Carly. My voice is shaking.
"What are we doing on this bus?" I ask a little too loudly. The Bolivian couple next to us shift uneasily in their seats and glance in
my direction. "What is anyone doing on this bus?" I press my
head against the window, taking long, dramatic gulps of air. I can

feel Carly's eyes boring through the back of my head. I feel, and must look, a bit deranged.

"Do you want to change seats?" she offers.

"No way," I say.

As ridiculous as it is, the only thing I have control over at this point is being able to see out the window of this suicide machine, and I am not giving that up, no matter how insane it makes me.

"If it upsets you to look, don't look." She puts her earphones in and nods to the beat of the music.

"As soon as this lunatic stops, I am getting off." She rolls her eyes. I try to reason with her. "The driver is going too fast, Carly."

"He's driven this road hundreds of times."

This is how Carly manages unpleasantness—as calmly as possible. She closes her eyes, puts on music, tells herself the wild-eyed bus driver is capable, then zones out. My panicked need to assess the situation is not helping her, just like her attempts at oblivion are further agitating me.

I look for escape routes and then, in one final attempt to get her to understand the gravity, I whisper, "We. Are. Going. To. Die."

"Okay, so we're going to die," she snaps. "Just don't think about it."

Is that seriously an answer?

Carly closes her eyes again, blocking me out.

Suddenly, I hate her, her insistence on being the bravest and baddest, on doing everything the most dangerous way on principle. I hate that she's such a know-it-all and that she thinks her Spanish is better than mine. I hate that she's always clarifying to people we meet, "Well, *she's* American. *I'm* Australian," as if I'm supposed to apologize for where I was born. I even hate her face, her superior, upturned button nose.

What murderous thoughts must she be having of me in that moment? No doubt that I am painfully melodramatic, that I'm annoyingly riddled with insecurities and anxieties. She probably thinks she made a mistake, that there is only so much you can do for a girl who claims she wants to see the world, then isn't willing to acknowledge what it takes to do that. She hates my face, too, I bet, my beady brown eyes and my chapped lips that I gnaw on when I'm nervous.

I stare out the window and down into the ravine. I cannot see the bottom because it is a tangle of green, the jungle growing in and among itself. It looks soft and welcoming. Maybe we will tumble, tumble, tumble slowly but never bang against the hidden floor. The green leaves will catch us.

But no. There is a bus behind us now, hurrying us through the mud. We swerve faster and faster around blind corners. I clutch the edge of my seat and dig my nails in to keep from crying. All of a sudden there are white lights and an oncoming truck racing toward us. All three drivers slam on their brakes, and we are thrown forward in our seats. Everyone is screaming. Our front wheel dangles over the edge of the cliff, and all we need is one tap from the madman behind us to send us the rest of the way. He stops just short of our back bumper. No one moves. When I turn to Carly, she has already wiped the fear from her eyes. She grins at me.

"I'm getting off," I tell her through clenched teeth, as if this is all her fault. I step into the aisle.

Annoyance flickers across her face. "Yeah," she says, closing her eyes again. "And then what? We're in the middle of nowhere."

She's right, of course. The only thing I can do is sit back down, defeated, pop my last sleeping pill (the one I was saving to numb the plane ride home), and drift into a drugged sleep for the next twelve hours.


When I wake up, I am surprisingly clearheaded. A simple epiphany rings in my brain: I do not have to be Carly. I realize my hesitance over meeting up with her in South America was partly that it would inevitably lead to activities that would scare the pants off me but not her. Yet I've never given myself credit for doing those things in the first place or acknowledged that they are more difficult for me than for Carly—that she has inched outside her comfort zone while I've skydived out of mine. All I've felt up until this moment is guilt for not living up to the challenges as well as Carly always does. Hers has become another expectant voice in my head, like my parents'. Her values differ greatly, of course, but the imperatives are still there. My instinct is, as with my parents, to please her, but although I love to travel, I am not a die-hard adventurer, and that's okay. Alternatively, I'm not ready to settle down in the predictable existence my parents have plotted. I'm somewhere in between. And only I can figure out how to make this balance work.

For now, I realize, it's unfair to blame Carly when things go wrong or are scary. I chose to be here, in part to test myself, and this involves inherent risks I cannot hold Carly accountable for. Who you are when you are tested might not be pretty, but it's always real.

# [ 20 ]

*Our heroine and her trusty guide brave the heart of darkness,*
*or at least the very edges of it. Insects of massive proportions*
*and thirst are encountered, along with many strange and*
*curious creatures. The author learns the only thing*
*to fear is fear itself. And snakes.*

Rurrenabaque sits at the edge of the Amazon basin, with a population of fifteen thousand. It's a more difficult, remote entry point into the Amazon than from Brazil, so it's less developed and less overrun with travelers, too.

We pay twenty bolivianos for a cell-like room without a private bath, though the water is currently off due to the massive floods that prevented any buses after ours from making it here today. We're so wiped from the tense trip—Carly didn't sleep at all, and I'm still groggy from the sleeping pill—that when no one knocks with sheets for our twin beds, as promised, we simply spread our sarongs across them and pass out for the next four hours.

After our lengthy nap, we set off into town to book a jungle tour. Scores of tour operators line the main street, and we spend the afternoon comparing and haggling. Everything in Bolivia is negotiable, but if a salesperson has the opportunity to rip you off, he will. It's the way it goes here, nothing personal, but it can be annoying finding out that someone else paid significantly less for the same good or service. It just doesn't seem fair, and Carly and I bristle at the discrepancies. At the same time, we're never quite comfortable with the process of bargaining. On one hand, we want to be like the locals—and the locals haggle. But we know even on our measly budgets, we're privileged, comparatively, and is it conscionable to spend ten minutes convincing a vendor to give us something for one U.S. dollar less than the asking price? In the end, we opt for a four-day jungle tour that costs the equivalent of twenty-five U.S. dollars per day with gear, meals, and transport included. It's not exactly the disappearing act of many weeks Carly hoped for, but it's a start.

That night we chow down on the cheapest, most delicious meal. Although Rurrenabaque boasts a handful of tourist restaurants serving familiar fare like burritos and pizzas, we have decided to follow a line of locals around the corner to a tucked-away side street. We find it difficult to communicate here because almost everyone speaks Quechan or Aymara, so our limited Spanish is of little use, but when we reach the front of the line, nothing can be lost in translation. One meal is on offer: succulent pieces of moist chicken torn from a rotating spit and accompanied by greasy banana fries, all for a grand total of under one U.S. dollar. We pull up a piece of sidewalk next to the others with their unwrapped meals on their knees and dig our fingers into the oily dinner.

Although we desperately need a good night's sleep, we are out of luck because it's El Día del Padre, Father's Day. This is not the brunch-and-golf-themed-gifts variety of the holiday. Here the ritual seems to be drink, karaoke, fight—in that order. Our room shares a flimsy wall with a raucous karaoke bar whose entrance is plastered with glossy posters of pouty blond women with bare breasts and heads thrown back in ecstasy as they croon into a microphone because, really, what woman doesn't come to Bolivia to sing topless? It's so noisy next door that we might as well be in there with them. I check my ticking travel clock first at twelve-thirty A.M., then three. The last time I look, it's five-thirty in the morning. Two of the singers are arguing loudly in the street out-side our window. Carly claims it's because one of them butchered the other's favorite song, but their words are so slurred, I can't translate anything.

At six-thirty I drag myself out of bed and into an icy shower. On our way to the tour operator's office, we pass a street parade. Boys in camouflage uniforms cradling rifles stride by. They are the new army recruits, and this is their first day of service. One blows Carly a kiss, his face serious and sincere.

In typical Bolivian fashion, we are on our way three hours after our scheduled time. We board a motorized canoe and wind down the muddy waters of the Río Beni into the Amazon. Our tour companions turn out to be the annoying Brits from Coroico who had an even hairier bus ride because they not only had to convince their driver to slow down but also politely request that he quit taking swigs from his flask.

"*Eso no importa,*" he assured them. "*Estoy con dios,*" which means "I'm with God," apparently leaving only those who were not with something to worry about.

We're put out that they're here, after we've braved the Death Road to get to this faraway spot. We don't think they belong, though we don't question whether we ourselves should be in this remote area untouched by tourism until recently. As hard as we've tried to be respectful, eager travelers—and to distance ourselves from those who are not—no doubt the tour guide mo-toring our canoe has no need for such distinctions among his customers.

Despite our initial snobbery, we grow to like most of the Brits, which is its own tidy lesson about jumping to conclusions. The only obnoxious one is the belly floater, a truck driver named Dan. He's traveled everywhere but seems to have gained nothing other than anecdotal evidence for his theory on why everyone else is inferior to the English. He drinks from sunrise past sundown, a red plastic cup filled with vodka his permanent appendage.

A middle-aged British couple is also part of our group. Are Kevin and Anne married? you want to know.

"She's no wife of mine!" Kevin bellows good-naturedly when I ask. He seems pleased with himself, as though he has managed something rather miraculous, and Anne doesn't appear fazed in the slightest by the outburst. But they've been together going on a decade and they look alike, as some couples tend to after time. Both are tall and lanky. Their hair is the same dusty-brown shade. And they wear matching hiking boots, pants, and shirts.

Carly and I nickname them the Wild Thornberrys because they remind us so much of that comically inquisitive cartoon family. Each time our guide, Melvin, points out some new plant, Kevin and Anne bend over and press their noses against it. They interrogate the stranger with deep, pensive inhalations.

"Smell that, Anne?" Kevin will say each time.

"Ohhhhh, yeeeees!" Anne will respond enthusiastically.

"What does this plant do?" Kevin always wants to know. Then he will mention how this particular foliage reminds him of some herb they came across in South Africa or maybe a tree they once encountered in Guatemala.

Kevin and Anne are extremely well traveled. Right before this tour, they were working with traumatized monkeys in another part of Bolivia. Before that, at a wildlife refuge in Peru, a puma tore a deep gash in Kevin's left leg, a rather gaping wound that he rubs ointment on a few times a day. It was Kevin's job to walk the injured puma as part of a rehab program, when he got startled and attacked one day.

"I hold no grudge against the old boy," he tells us. "No, no, I don't think he meant any harm."

In between their excursions, Anne is an aromatherapist and

Kevin works in construction. Given their jobs, as with the younger Brits (a truck driver and a few teachers and bartenders), I am surprised they can travel for so long, but it's all about priorities for these two. Plus, it doesn't hurt to be making pounds and spending bolivianos.

Our guide Diego's uniform is a pair of camouflage pants with a machete tucked in his waistband and a sleeveless red Adidas shirt. A wood cross dangles from his neck. His exposed arms seem immune to the bug bites that plague me and Carly. As he shows us around the campsite, he has only to extend a finger into the surrounding bush in order to point out each of the inhabitants that lie in wait. He teaches us about a species of ant whose bite inflicts twenty-four hours of misery, a nasty little creature that would give even his Australian brother the bull ant a run for his money. Diego details a variety of toxic plants. He sniffs out tracks of a tapir—a piglike animal with a short, prehensile snout. Diego is a master of jungle ingenuity who spins twigs into an elaborate water-bottle carrier when he notices I need one. Best of all, he finds me and Carly massive vines from which to swing through the trees like Tarzan.

Our basic campsite consists of a few picnic tables, a fire pit, and an enclosed structure with several rows of bunk beds, each pair draped in mosquito nets. The bathroom is a hole in the ground enclosed in four splintered wooden walls, open to the elements at the top. When it rains—and it rains a lot in the jungle—you rather efficiently have a shower and use the toilet simultaneously.

Our second day, Diego takes us fishing. The makeshift gear consists of a branch with a piece of twine and hook attached. Miraculously, I catch a catfish right away, a success that annoys Carly for several satisfying hours. She's not the only one with a competitive side.

"Do you want to eat it for lunch?" Diego asks.

"Don't mind if I do," I say proudly.

With that, he whacks it on the head with startling force, then stuffs it in a plastic bag.

Our fondness for Diego is tested by his constant attempts to make contact with our bodies, relentlessly offering a hand to escort us over any stray twig in our path, say, or randomly putting an arm around our shoulders. He often displays a frustrating macho bravado. For example, on the walk back from fishing, we pass directly below a wasps' nest. Diego marches past unscathed, but I'm second in line when the inhabitants notice our intrusion and set about declaring their displeasure by excitedly stinging my face and neck. I cry out in shock and pain, whereupon my knight in camo armor rushes to my aid, then proceeds to stand calmly beside me and look as though an important thought has just escaped him, while I continue swatting furiously at my face. After a few contemplative moments, he brandishes his machete and offers to avenge me.

"No!" I yelp. I've gotten blindly away from the wasps and am not eager to incite them further. "I'm okay."

Carly checks out the damage. It's minimal enough. In a final show of victory, Diego spits at the nest and gestures grandly for us to follow him back to camp.

The mosquitoes here are fat and nasty, bulging with blood. While at home, they magnanimously stick to feeding on exposed skin, here they have no problem chomping at you through clothing. Even when I wear layers, I feel the occasional sting just out of reach in the small of my back or behind my knee. My whole body is riddled with bites. After we get back to Rurrenabaque, the locals gasp, *"¡Dios mio!"* when they catch a glimpse of my ravaged skin, in this case Spanish for "Yo, your shit is seriously fucked up, lady, and we *live* here." Even though they are relatively immune to the bites, they have seen plenty of backpackers who aren't, and apparently, I take the mosquito-ridden cake.

Our third day in the jungle Carly and I head to the river. It's our only hope of washing away at least a little of the pungent odor that has begun to emanate from us. We make our way in shorts and bras down the small embankment where our canoe is docked, mosquitoes feasting in droves on our naked flesh. You can't call what we do swimming so much as clinging to the shore while the lower halves of our bodies are jerked downstream by a surprisingly strong current. When we emerge, a row of new bites marks the skin exposed above the waterline. Some of the bites are from sand flies, horrible little creatures whose marks leave a telltale spot of blood in the center like a target. They itch like chicken pox on crack.

In the jungle, we're all hopped up on malaria tablets. Even Carly (who to this day refuses to admit she took them) gratefully accepts a few extras I have in my pack after the agent who booked our spots on the tour made it sound as though the whole jungle is festering with the disease. Each of us is coping with the powerful drugs in different ways. Anne is a little dizzy. I have terrible insomnia, kicking around in bed until three or four A.M. while trying not to disrupt the tightly tucked-in mosquito net. Kevin loses his appetite. For Carly, colors are brighter. The greens of the jungle glow almost psychedelic; the river glimmers like the Pacific. And we all have unnervingly vivid dreams. I dream— a common enough one for stress cases like me—that I am in a play and don't know my lines. But the stakes are somehow higher, the audience bigger, the sense that I am really there more palpable. I wake in a cold sweat after dawn, the sounds of the jungle greeting a new day intermingled with Diego's thunderous, echoing farts.

After my sleeping-pill-induced epiphany, I've vowed to embrace all that backpacking in South America has to offer, even if it scares me, not because I want to be like Carly but because I want to test my own limits and also experience all that I can on my travels here. That is why I am currently venturing out into the

creepy-crawly jungle for a night walk. But I'm doing it my way—
properly attired. I do not want some heinous bug on me, or down
my socks, or in my ear even, so I cover myself from head to toe. I
tuck my pants into heavy socks. Diego lends me his rubber boots,
and I slip these over my sneakers after tipping them upside down
and shaking furiously. I wear a long-sleeved T-shirt. I tuck the
sleeves into a pair of alpaca gloves left over from our days in the
Andes. I wrap a scarf around my neck and mouth. I throw on a
hat, tying it below my chin like a bonnet. Have I mentioned it's
rather toasty in the jungle? When I emerge from the cabin
dressed to summit K2, everyone is waiting for me.

"What about your nose?" Carly says, and we all laugh, but I
consider it. Other than my eyes, it's the only piece of me left exposed. I have a quick malaria-pill-laced terror about a poisonous
spider scurrying down a web and landing gingerly on the tip of
my nose.

Our flashlights stream through the trees. Diego leads the way,
Carly behind him, me behind her, the Wild Thornberrys bringing up the rear. The Brits have begged off to start the vodka-fest
back at camp. Thwack. Thwack. Thwack. Diego brandishes his
machete, dismembering chunks of the jungle whether or not
they are in our way. The path is well trodden, maintained for
these kinds of night walks with backpackers. Even though the
accommodation is basic, the conditions au naturel, the tour companies that operate here are mostly established. Sure, the occasional female tourist gets molested by one of the guides, some
twenty-year-old smart-ass goes missing once in a while, an un-
lucky pair emerges with a wild-eyed case of malaria. These
mishaps are swiftly reported to the tourism board in town,
which maintains an enormous scoreboard listing each company's
rating in a variety of categories, wielding enough influence to
sink any particularly marred agency.

One of the ways our own tour company might find itself in
hot water is over the fact that a massive poisonous snake has just

brushed by Carly's left boot. Diego notices it first. He jumps, backs into Carly, and starts pushing us, Carly into me, me into the Wild Thornberrys. If a black adder sinks its venomous jaws into you, you have twenty minutes to contemplate life on this earth before you leave it.

We pause in a clearing. Diego is panting. He is saying something about not knowing the snake "lived there." Kevin wants to go back to have a look, but Anne cautions, "Don't listen to him, girls. He's not very good with snakes." Whatever that means.

"That's plenty of jungle for me for one night," I say, my voice muffled by my scarf.

For once Carly agrees with me. She is looking around, nervously glancing at her foot every few seconds, no doubt imagining vicious snake fangs dangling from her ankle.


Our return to Rurrenabaque from the jungle is a test of patience and endurance. I've convinced Carly we should fly back to La Paz, but when we show up for our scheduled flight, we're told our seats have been given away. Apparently, we were required to confirm our booking twenty-four hours in advance, a small detail our booking agent forgot to mention. We must finagle our way past rebooking fees (a cynic might suggest this is *why* our agent neglected to relay the minor detail) to get a seat on tomorrow's flight, and we settle in to spend another day in Rurrenabaque. Back at the hotel, we pay five extra bolivianos for a room with a private shared bathroom that doesn't abut the karaoke bar.

The next morning our flight is canceled because of more flooding, and we spend the entire day waiting around at the airport before that key piece of information is offered. The day after that, the airline office is positive our flight will be canceled again, so they put us on the one other flight leaving that afternoon. We arrive excited at the airport, no more than a sludgy strip of field. We sit there for many more hours. Our original flight takes off, but the new flight is eventually canceled.

By now the locals have started to recognize us. They wave with confused looks at seeing us pass by yet again. On our third day stuck in Rurre, my sandals inexplicably fall apart, as though the heavens themselves do not want us to leave. When I go to the market to buy some new ones, the hunched saleswoman asks my size.

"*Ocho,*" I tell her, not sure how this translates into Bolivian sizes.

She takes my bare foot in her rough hands. "*¡No le creo!*" she says over and over again. "*¡No le creo!*" (I don't believe it!) I'm not sure whether she doesn't believe my analysis or the actual size of my foot, though the latter seems more likely since she is turning it from side to side as though evaluating a suspect gem. She catches a glimpse of my fly-bitten calf.

"*¡Dios mio!*" she exclaims. She points in horror at the bites. Yes, yes, I nod. She fans herself a little, as if my busted-up, big-footed self is simply too much for her.

We spend a portion of every lost day in Rurrenabaque with the cake man, who pedals around town, his delicious homemade treats stuffed with Brazilian nuts and topped with cinnamon icing. The cake man is a native Floridian, former jockey, and current local eccentric going on five years now. Sweets are hardly his only interests. He's also more than happy to provide us with pamphlets outlining his philosophies on microchip implantation and global government conspiracies. He so desperately wants us to understand the true path to Christianity. Most nights we wander over to an elderly woman's stoop, where she is selling simple but delectable fried rice topped with a fried egg, passing the plates through her open kitchen window to customers.

On our fourth morning stuck in Rurrenabaque, we decide to take charge of our destiny. Bolivia is forcing me to be more flexible, to go with the unpredictable flow. So instead of spending another day moping around the airport, we book a four-day trip into the Pampas, the Bolivian wetlands, a wonderland of wildlife. There we fish for piranhas, swim with pink dolphins who nip at our toes, and prowl for anacondas. Okay, I do not prowl for anacondas because it strikes me as rather insane, but Carly does. From our campground, aptly called Mosquito #3, we hear the howler monkeys yodel at one another. After delicious soups and fried bread, the cook tosses leftover chicken heads to the resident caiman who gamely crawls ashore. Our guide points out the capybara (like an oversize guinea pig) shuffling through the grass a few feet away.

The jungle was Carly's speed. The Australian adventurer in her isn't bothered by the muggy heat or put off by the venomous insects and snakes. She wants to return and delve even further into that mostly uncharted territory. But the Pampas is much more my style. It's more temperate, and the twenty-four-hour ants are replaced with more familiar marine and wildlife. Other than the kamikaze mossies, as Carly calls the man-eating mosquitoes who literally hurl themselves against the windows of our cabin each night, unable to control their bloodthirst for the beer-soaked foreigners inside, I'm totally enthralled with the wetlands.

On our way back to Rurrenabaque, we pull our canoe up to the shoreline to feed bits of banana to big-eared yellow squirrel monkeys that emerge from the bushes to greet us. I extend my hand toward them, and they grip my fingers to balance themselves while they nibble at the food resting in my palm. It is a moment of pure travel pleasure. Carly already knew she was nowhere near finished having adventures, and right then I knew I wasn't, either. This is what I wanted for myself, for there to be more days with the possibility of getting to hand-feed wild monkeys in the future, not fewer of them. This was my real world.

*Our heroine and her trusty guide reach Peru, where the*
*islands float and the mud slides. A bearded stranger enters*
*their midst, followed by a dreaded illness.*
*The adventurers depart for Chile.*

My first impression of Peru is that it surprisingly resembles the
Irish countryside, with similar ancient stone walls zigzagging
across the green land. But Puno, the Peruvian town at the lip of
Lake Titicaca that will serve as our base for an expedition out to
the floating islands, is an unattractive locale. It's full of tacky
tourist shops and shadowy alleys. The run-down plaza is overrun
with angry protesters caught up in the bus strikes that have
taken hold of the country.

What Puno does have going for it is food. After a monotonous
diet of empanadas and white bread the past few weeks, we
splurge on a fancy restaurant our first night there. The word
"fancy" is highly relative, of course. The foundation of my outfits
these days is a pair of sandstone-colored fisherman pants Carly
brought me from Thailand. They are no more than a one-size-
fits-all piece of cotton pulled on, then tied loosely at the waist
with the top piece of fabric rolled over. Carly has a pair in blue,

and we match them with whatever shirt has been washed most recently. But in Puno we dress in our finery—wrinkled but clean jeans and sweaters. We wash our hair and even put on a touch of makeup. I awkwardly wield the mascara wand, blinking involuntarily as I coat my lashes.

At the restaurant, we savor gooey calzones accompanied by copious, cheap pisco sours—a regional drink made with pisco (a type of brandy), simple syrup, egg white, lemon or lime, and a splash of bitters. It's served in a small, squat glass with a green body and a frothy white head: Peru's version of Guinness.

Our ugly Puno hotel room with stained curtains and bars on the windows costs us ten soles (around five U.S. dollars), but it has a private bathroom. In the morning, we discover it also has bedbugs. Tiny bites run the length of our thighs. Carly wakes to her own futile scratching and then shakes me out of bed. Downstairs, we express our extreme dismay to the owner, a sweating beach ball of a man who insisted on keeping our passports overnight as ID.

"Bring us our passports," Carly demands. "And we want at least a twenty percent discount off the rooms." I cower nearby, trying not to scratch my irritated legs.

"No, no, no," says the owner. He salivates angry Spanish at us. "Full price."

"You're dreaming," Carly says.

Their faces grow redder and redder, as if it's a contest. Then the man moves out from behind the desk to block the lobby door. Carly and I stand side by side, a tiny wall compared to his impenetrable fortress.

"Let us out," I whisper.

"Full price, no discount."

While Carly and the giant brute who has trapped us face off, I have a momentary out-of-body experience where I float above the fray and look down at us foolishly trying to assert ourselves.

The fact is, we need our passports. We need to get out of here. And we need to appease a greasy three-hundred-pound sentinel in order to accomplish these things. Our personal philosophies of fairness no longer signify, and we'll have to get over the delusion that they do. I look at Carly, try to convey all this telepathically in the scrunching of my eyebrows. She scratches furiously at her thighs.

"Fine, okay," she finally gives in.

We slam the money on the counter. Like a thousand rancid pisco sours, the hefty owner's pungent stench assaults my nostrils as we push by him.

For most, a house represents stability. Your home is the place you return to, a solid force amid life's fluctuations. For the Uros people of the Islas Flotantes (Floating Islands), however, it's a flexible structure that must be rebuilt constantly. This colony of islands that spring from the surface of Lake Titicaca are man-made structures initially built by the indigenous people of Peru forced to desert the mainland or become enslaved by the Incas. They fled to the open water and constructed a series of islands out of the *totora* reeds, which grow plentifully in the shallow areas of the lake. The reeds become soggy at the bottom, forcing the residents to perpetually insert replacements. Imagine your bed rotting beneath you while you sleep. There are currently about three hundred Uros/Aymara citizens who call the Floating Islands home.

We pass by young boys standing tall on reed boats they push through the shallow green waters. A small girl runs to the edge of her family's island to wave at us. When we stop on a designated tourist floating island, we're offered the tasteless *totora* reed as a snack, giving new meaning to the phrase "eating me out of house and home."

Our destination is Isla Amantani, a circular anchored island amid its more fluid neighbors a three-hour boat ride from Puno, where the terraced hillsides grow abundant maize, wheat, and potatoes. Ancient Incan ruins dot the highest points of the island, some 4,200 meters up. We're spending the night with a local family.

The women who greet us all have long black braided hair covered by a waist-length black shawl intricately embroidered around the edges. Different-colored skirts are paired with stiff white shirts decorated in more delicate embroidery. Our host, Benita, looks somewhere in her thirties, but it's difficult to tell; the harsh climate ages people prematurely. She's fit and small: her head barely reaches my shoulder. After we follow the winding, rocky path up to her house, she shows us to our room, small and sparse and painted a cozy pink with two beds and an unlit candle on the dresser. We leave our things, then make our way to the kitchen, where Benita is already busy preparing the afternoon meal. Her one-year-old daughter crawling along the dirt floor examines us shyly as we approach. Our curiosity is more overt. The kitchen is tiny and unventilated, with ceilings so low our short host is half hunched over. She's stirring five or six pots emitting various steams and aromas, adeptly preparing an intricate soup. We watch her cook until our eyes tear up so much from the stifling smoke that we're forced outside into the cold, though we know Benita spends most of the day in there.

Dinner is friendly and awkward. An older man who we assume is Benita's husband comes to the table, as do a teenage boy and another, younger boy. We offer our stilted Spanish but soon realize we aren't being understood after the patriarch simply answers "*Sí*" to all our questions. The islanders speak the indigenous language and seem to know even less Spanish than we do; eventually, we all give up and sit in silence, sipping our soup, huddled together for warmth. The main course is eggs with rice and tomatoes. Meat is an expensive commodity, so most meals are vegetarian, which suits Carly and me fine, since we eat only chicken and fish anyway.

After dinner, Benita appears in our room with traditional island outfits. We have eaten two enormous, carb-laden meals today, one at four P.M. and another at seven P.M., so it is an effort for her to tie three layers of skirts around our distended bellies. Next comes one of those intricately patterned white blouses. The whole ensemble is secured with a thick corset-tight belt.

"I think I might puke," Carly says.

"Just pretend you're dressing for a Victorian ball," I whisper through clenched teeth.

Benita drops heavy black shawls on our heads to keep us warm. It's so cold that we pull on pants to protect our last remaining bits of exposed flesh. The completed look is, well, bulky. Benita steps back to survey her work. She nods once, satisfied, then ushers us out the door and up the hill to the dance being held in our honor, along with the other ten or so guests on the island that night.

At the top of a stone staircase, there is no respite, as we are expected to dance excitedly for the next three hours. The male guests have fared better in terms of outfits. They wear loose-fitting ponchos and the local-style hats with pom-poms swinging from them. But the other women are suffering as much as Carly and I as we are whirled around and around the spinning room, emitting high-pitched hysterical laughs at ourselves. The body-constricting clothes, coupled with the lung-constricting altitude, make me wonder if this is what a heart attack feels like.

Carly and I have been adamant about "roughing it" the entire trip. Backpacking has noble ideals: to see how the locals live, to interact with them, to be respectful and blend in as much as possible. Backpackers want to learn, we want to understand the worlds we have entered, not simply consume them. And I savor those values. We want to be travelers, not tourists, but on Amantani, when we are literally in the garb of another culture, it hits me that some of this is just "dressing up." Tomorrow Benita will go back to her routine, and we will move on at our leisure, and to pretend otherwise is to deny our advantages and our impact.

Isla Taquile, where we spend the next day, has the same terraced look as Amantani. The families here are the ultimate collective. They build one another's houses, sew one another's clothes, till the various plots of land in rotation. The clothes here represent the various statuses of the inhabitants. For instance, the male political leaders wear black hats, while married men wear red ones and single men wear white. Single girls wear brightly colored clothing, while married women are required to choose darker, more somber colors.

Before they can marry, young couples must live together for one year. If this trial arrangement reveals they're incompatible, they are free to call off the ceremony. When two people do marry, it's customary for the woman to cut her hair. From it, the man weaves a belt that encircles his waist from then on, the island equivalent of a wedding ring. I try to imagine what goes through the mind of a young Quechan woman sitting with her scissors. The guide does not tell us what the hair means to the young woman or the emotional impact of cutting it off. Is she proud of her impending status as a wife? Is she distraught over the sacrifice? Does she wonder how her new cut will change the shape of her face or if, when she looks in the mirror afterward, she will see herself as a different person? Maybe it is meant to prepare her for the significant changes marriage inevitably brings, unlike in America, where we turn ourselves into princesses for the day, then wonder at our disappointments when our lives do not resemble the fantasies we have created.

*   *   *

We spend twenty soles each on bus tickets from Puno to Cusco and learn again that the cheapest way is always the longest in South America. Our rattling two-story bus can barely keep a steady pace on flat roads and seems to be almost rolling backward when forced to tackle a hill. It is driven by an impatient man who blasts his horn every ten seconds or so, as though our time is constantly being wasted, though when he attempts to pull ahead of someone, the bus emits an angry, high-pitched wheezing. At a checkpoint, we're pulled from the bus, and everyone's bags but ours, the only gringas, are searched.

Our lovely little Cusco hotel is a step up from where we have been staying, but it is a long six blocks from the main plaza so we're still only paying about what you shell out for a Sunday *Times* back home. Our room has hot water, and the bathroom is so clean it's disorienting. We haven't bathed in three days, but our top priority is food. We're famished after a light, early breakfast and the long bus journey.

"Here's what we'll do," I say to Carly. "We'll eat a gigantic meal, take hot showers, then go straight to bed."

"Amazing," she moans.

We test the mattresses, run our hands along the soft, clean sheets. The joy and appreciation of these simple pleasures has become crisper since we started backpacking. I feel the needs of my body sharply in ways I never have before.

Cusco's center is a well-landscaped plaza dominated by an ornate Gothic-style cathedral that took over a hundred years to build. It was completed in the mid-1600s when the Spanish were conquering much of South America. Today Cusco is aggressively tourist-focused. Outside all the restaurants, hostesses shout out the evening's specials. Club promoters circle the crowds with drink-promotion coupons. And unsettling herds of children beg in the streets. I hand over some coins the first few times, but there are so many small outstretched hands that soon Carly and I begin denying the requests and continue on our way.

"*Lo siento*," I apologize.

"*No más*," Carly says.

I'm embarrassed by how quickly I find them frustrating and wish we could walk unimpeded. These kids have learned English expletives, and they are ready to hurl them at you the moment you turn your back on them. "Fuck you, lady," shouts a little girl no older than seven. "Fuck you, go back to your own country. Leave my country alone and go back to your own country, shit lady."

Almost everywhere we visit in Bolivia and Peru seems conflicted about the Western travelers who descend on the remotest pieces of their land, grudgingly accepting our money, but these Cusco kids force our deepest reckoning with our culpability as travelers. Maybe it's because they are so young and so furious, or because they scream at us in English, our own inescapable language. Especially unnerving is that they are out until all hours of the morning, shouting at clubgoers drunkenly departing the plaza at two, three, four in the morning if no one purchases their animal finger puppets.

"Just go home," Carly pleads with a girl one night. "It's late. You should go home to your family."

The girl responds by flipping her the bird.

There are dozens and dozens of tour companies ready to take you to Machu Picchu, the main reason we're all here in Cusco. The trip will be our most expensive tourist activity, mainly due to the fact that the British own the one railroad that leads to the attraction; the charge is more equivalent to pounds than to soles. We booked our tour back in Puno with Miguel, a lovely, unusually tall Peruvian decked out in a flashy cowboy hat and a big brass belt buckle who was a relief to deal with because his English was impeccable and he emanated honesty. Miguel booked us our perfect little hotel in Cusco and arranged for a woman holding a sign with our names on it to pick us up at the bus station, as if we were celebrities. It's Miguel who told us about the different tour companies and how certain ones give locals like Benita a fair share of the profits for hosting, while other companies part with virtually none of their earnings. And now we are happy not to have to wade through the sea of entrepreneurs that line the cobblestone streets and instead concentrate our energies on finding dinner.

Some days in South America we are worn out, and this is one of them. We're sick of haggling. We're totally over being harassed by men who think that lasciviously licking their lips and commenting on our bodies is their inherent right. We're very tired of bread. And empanadas. And broken buses. And waiting around. And getting ripped off because we are foreigners. Most days travel is thrilling: it's new and exciting and challenging, and you want to take it all on. But some days, as in any place you happen to be, you're tired and blue. Cusco is different from the parts of Bolivia and Peru we've encountered so far. It's filled with tourists and European- and Australian-run businesses. Cafés here serve pancakes for breakfast, of all miracles. We've gone pretty far off the well-trodden path these past few weeks, sometimes encountering few other backpackers, so Cusco feels like a relief we didn't know we needed. We're craving familiar food, something that will remind us of home or, in this case, apparently, Ireland.

The pub we alight upon is as befuddling as our sparkling hotel bathroom. Everyone inside is white and speaks English. They have Guinness on tap, and three big screens glow with a variety of soccer games. We haven't watched TV in months, so the sight of the bright, blaring screens only adds to the overall strangeness.

"Where are we?" Carly asks.

"Galway," I say.

We find an empty table and unload the four gin and tonics

we've just ordered, compliments of the two-for-one special. Behind us, a waitress floats by with an enormous tray of heaping nachos. My hungry eyes follow the food to its destination, three scruffy guys—though it's a more cultivated roughness than the half-starved, barely showering, no-clean-clothes scruffiness Carly and I are currently practicing. One of them has a bushy blond beard and squinty blue eyes, as if we're not in a poorly lit pub but rather some sun-beaten desert. Around his neck is a small white bone carving curled in an intricate, indecipherable pattern. I am struck by the contrast of his burly-man appearance with the delicate way he wields his knife and fork when the nachos arrive, carefully carving up the messy meal. My attraction to him hits me with freight-train impact, but then I hear the accent.

"They're Australians," I tell Carly with a disappointed sigh.

Although after my time there, my affection for Australia and Australians runs deep, the few romantic encounters I had with their men did not go well at all. I found them either brash and macho, like overzealous frat boys, or intense and clingy, like the strange café customer I once went out with who tried to hold my hand all through dinner and started discussing a trip he wanted us to take together before the tiramisu even arrived. Did I mention he wore a T-shirt with a giant panda on it? So I've resigned myself to some intrinsic incompatibility between myself and Australian men, even though the ones I knew there but wasn't attracted to were superb companions.

"No, mate," Carly responds. "They're Kiwis."

"What's the difference?"

"Everything," she says, raising her eyebrows sagely.

That's when bearded blue eyes walks up to our table.

"G'day," he says, "I'm Martyn. You girls want to join us?"

"Sounds great," I say. "We've just come out of the jungle." I don't know why I blurt out this unasked-for detail, whether because I'm nervous or subtly trying to explain our unwashed appearance.

"Well, then. You two are quite the adventurers, yeah?" He grins at me, and my heart flutters wildly inside my chest.

The next morning Carly and I are meant to be up at five A.M. and on the train at six, headed to Machu Picchu. But we only arrived back at the hotel around three A.M. after relocating with the Kiwis from the Irish pub to a club, where Martyn and I danced for hours under the hypnotic disco lights. When we parted, he kissed me chastely on the left cheek and asked when he could see me again. Carly and I haven't had a raucous night out since back in Australia, for alcohol and altitude do not a good match make, and we apparently made up for this by drinking our body weight in gin and tonics. We both have pounding headaches, our limbs are wobbly, and Carly's stomach is emitting a worrying gurgle.

"I don't think I can do it," she laments. "Can you take care of things? Reschedule our tickets for tomorrow, mate, please?"

"Of course! Leave it to me." I spring into action, gathering our passports and tickets, throwing some cold water on my face. I'm disgustingly hungover, too, but this has been our dynamic in South America, where we oscillate between being the one with the worst altitude headache, the worst upset stomach, the closest to her breaking point from not having a hot shower in days on end. Whoever is a little less worse for wear on that day takes over. And today it is my turn.

This was a new concept for Carly, who was used to taking care of herself on her travels and in general. On this trip, I had learned I was stronger than I initially thought, and Carly discovered that it didn't make her weak to rely on someone else once in a while. She didn't have to be an island. It wasn't simply about having one of us watch the packs so the other could wait in line to buy train tickets, or whatever other practicality, though that was an advantage; it was also good to be able to share our travel experience, to be in this together, hangovers included. I've also secretly been entertaining the idea of seeing Martyn again, so the idea of putting off Machu Picchu for a day isn't all that disappointing.

A word of caution: don't ever postpone your trip to Machu Picchu. It will not go well for you. It turns out we'll have to wait until Saturday to get new spots on the train and on the two-day hike we booked, nearly an entire week to see the ruins we've come so far for. At least there is a warm, clean bed with a day to sleep off our hangovers and the possibility of meeting up with Martyn later on.

In the afternoon, we head into town to book a hostel closer to the plaza. It's a grimy little abode with uneven floors at the end of "gringo alley"—a long row of restaurants, shops, and buskers selling handmade jewelry spread open on blankets they rush to scoop up whenever anyone gets a whiff of the authorities. Our room has two twin beds that squeak bloody murder every time you move a muscle. The walls have cracks and holes and are decorated with the strangest pair of paintings. Each depicts a naked female body with ample breasts, but the head is a man's, with sideburns and mustaches, the whiskers of an incoming beard. Our strange room has no private bathroom, though it does have a small barred balcony where we can sit and people-watch. The first day we are lounging on this balcony, two familiar voices float surreally up to us.

"Would you look at this, love?" says the man.

"What's this, now?" a woman replies.

"It's a handmade necklace. Let me hold it up to the light. Yes, yes, I thought so. This reminds me of the beads those old Indian women in Calcutta use. Do you remember that, love?"

Travel is a funny thing. Just when you expect never to see someone again, you run into him or her in an entirely new country on a day you weren't even supposed to be there.

Down below us, the Wild Thornberrys are characteristically

captivated by some vendor's wares. Before Kevin has the opportunity to examine the beads further, no doubt licking one or sticking it up his nose to test its medicinal properties, we race down to them.

"Girls!" Anne cries. "How are you both?"

I half expect Kevin to examine us and conclude, "Ah, yes, love, these two look just like the ones from that jungle in Bolivia, remember?"


It is also from this vantage point that I watch Martyn make his way toward me the next couple of days and nights. Sometimes he's with his friends and we all go out to eat. Other times he wanders up alone and we spend our time sharing the earphones of his CD player and drinking wine on the balcony. One night he stays over and we cuddle chastely, since the bed squeals every time we move and Carly is not shy about telling us to shut up.

"He really likes you," Carly says the next morning.

"I'm not sure," I hedge, because my feelings for him are so much stronger than I've ever experienced that I don't want to jinx it. I know I could very well be just some chick he hangs out with on the road for a few days.

"He went *shopping* with you instead of motorbiking," she says, amazed or disgusted, I can't quite tell.

It's true. The day after we met, I emailed Martyn to say my Machu Picchu trip was off and I was heading to the markets. He showed up at the hostel within the hour, mumbling something about needing a new pair of pants. His two friends had rented motorbikes for the day but Martyn had begged off, sending Carly scampering out to see if she could join them before they took off.

Martyn and I spent the day browsing and flirting and buying hats that will be ridiculously out of place once we leave South America. When I returned to the hostel, I was flushed and smitten; Carly looked the same way after having spent the afternoon racing around Cusco's countryside with the Kiwis.

Although I miss him disproportionately to the amount of time we've spent together, I'm glad that Martyn leaves for Machu Picchu the day he does because it's the same day Carly and I get so sick we think we're dying. We have eaten the local food throughout our trip with nothing more than the occasional irritated stomach. We've carefully avoided raw vegetables and any suspect water sources, but these precautions aside, we've congratulated ourselves heartily on our willingness to sample the local cuisine and our obviously strong constitutions. So the irony of becoming ill in the most touristy town in South America is thick. We think the culprit was a fresh salad we splurged on at a restaurant down the street. We hadn't had lettuce in months, and it looked so clean and crisp, but who knows what did it? All I know is no culinary sin in the history of womankind ever deserved this degree of punishment.

We get ill within five minutes of each other. We've just left a late showing of the film *Psycho* that was playing at one of the many movie houses around town. There we overindulged on popcorn, soda, and chocolate bars, then wandered back to our hostel. Two blocks away, a sharp shooting pain rips through my stomach, buckling me.

"What's wrong?" Carly asks.

I grimace. "Not. Good."

"Okay, okay." She puts her hand on my back. "Let's get you to the hostel."

No sooner have we passed the lobby and are rounding the corner to mount the stairs than Carly puts a hand on her own stomach and inhales sharply. The uneven floors seem to rush at her, and she trips over herself. We race as quickly as the nausea will allow to the hostel's shared bathroom and proceed to emit sounds no other human being should ever have to witness. I stay in the bathroom for what feels like hours, dozing in and out of consciousness. Carly is back in the room when I stumble in. She's shivering and curled in a fetal position. I collapse groaning on my bed, and there we both stay, trapped in our own private hells, for the next twenty-four hours. We set each other off every hour or so, Carly's throwing up into the plastic bag beside her sending me scurrying back to the loathsome shared bathroom to do the same. Neither of us has the strength to help the other or even say anything comforting; we just toss and turn in our neighboring beds. When there is nothing left in our systems, we are too weak to move, too weak even to take a drink from the nearby water bottles. We need help, I think, but even the thought is exhausting.

My thoughts wander psychedelically from one subject to the next, though my brain is too tired to sustain anything more than fragments. I consider the hermaphrodites on the walls, who put them there and why. I think of Martyn. I have long cinematic visions of him trekking the Inca Trail, which in my mind is an ethereal Narnia-like tunnel into another world. I have never been so sick away from home. I have never been this sick in my life, sick to the degree that I seriously think we might waste away in this room. When I was ill as a child, my mother always made me chicken-and-stars soup and French toast and wrapped me in the coziest comforter to while away the day on the couch.

"I want my mom," I whisper into the dank room, tears streaming down my face.

"Me, too," Carly says.

But we are alone.

I think back to my freshman year at music school. Like clockwork before my lessons, I'd find myself in the bathroom, offering up my insides from the stress. I remember the freezing, endless winter my first semester. I'd lost weight since I started college in the fall, ten or even fifteen pounds off an already smallish frame, and was like a little old lady, perpetually shivering away.

My teacher, a violist in the Boston Symphony, was famous and

brilliant and incredibly intimidating and never said much during my lessons. Instead he perched mere inches from me in a
stiff-backed wooden chair, his callused fingers neatly laced in
his lap, and winced noticeably every time I played a note even
a hair out of tune. He considered his lessons no less than a
Carnegie Hall performance where he was audience, critic, and
instructor. His reputation for screaming at, then promptly kicking out, those students who didn't live up to his expectations
was legendary. I waited for this moment; deep down I secretly
hoped for it. But it never came. Other than the involuntary winc-
ing, his behavior toward me verged on kindness, and that was
how I knew I was absolutely hopeless. I was not even worth his
anger.

Finally, one day when the Boston snow was still piled high as
the tops of car tires and I'd just finished a blistering performance
of Hindemith's concerto, he asked bluntly, "What is going on
here? You appear to be getting worse."

It was true. All the deconstruction of my technique—posture,
bow hold, vibrato, and on and on—had made me self-conscious
to the point where every move I made was stilted and clumsy. On
top of that, I couldn't get my brain to halt its constant, harsh cri-
tique, and this brutal self-commentary had snuffed out my passion for playing, the wondrous feeling of abandon that used to
come so easily.

"I know," I replied. He stared hard at me. "I'm sorry."

"This is the thing," he said. "You must be one of two things at
this point in your career. You must be a prodigy, which you are
not. Not many are. Or you must be willing to work hard enough
to make up for not being a prodigy—so hard that you give up
everything else, all your other interests, relationships, desires.
Do you think of nothing else besides music? Are you willing to
sacrifice everything for it?"

I looked back up at him. I parted my lips to say yes, yes I was willing to do whatever it took, it was all I had ever wanted, it was the only thing I *was,* but for a split second no words came out.

"Too long," he said.

On the third day, Carly and I totter like an elderly couple the few steps it takes to reach the nearest market. We buy a bag of oranges, then retire back to the room to attempt the daunting task of eating them. I place a little orange in my lap—it's no more than a clementine, really—and stare at it. I wrap my fingers around it. Peel the orange, I tell myself, but the idea of digging in a nail to get out that first section is just so tiring. We both know we have to eat something. When we stood to dress ourselves for our outing, both of our stomachs were ghastly concave.

"There's nothing to you," I told Carly.

"I can see your ribs," she said back.

I thought of a girl I met in Argentina who was excited to be in South America because she had heard traveling there was the ultimate diet. "Parasites, here I come!" she squealed with excitement.

In the end, I bite straight into the orange, peel and all.

On Saturday we awake at four A.M., healed and energized by our impending train trip and two-day hike to Machu Picchu. A representative from our tour group piles into a taxi with us, and when we roll up to the station, I think how funny it is that one of the PeruRail employees is present to meet us.

"I'm sorry, no trains today," the representative informs us. "Mudslide."

He's nonchalant, but the destructive mudslide turns out to have wiped out a whole section of the rail line and killed five people in the small town at the base of the Inca Trail where all the tourists spend the night before or after their treks, Martyn included. That evening I get an email from him letting me know he's thankfully safe. It ends: *I'll walk through landslides and see you soon I hope.*

Cusco is a mess of people annoyed about their missed tours and trying to get tickets on a train that does not promise to leave any time in the next week. Carly and I decide it's time to move on altogether—me because I believe in signs and Carly because she is sick of being stuck in one place for this long. Martyn doesn't make it back the following night, so we plan to meet in Buenos Aires two weeks from now. It will be the end of both of our trips. He is off to London to live abroad for a few years, and I am heading back home to do who knows what.

We spend the rest of our time in Cusco trying to get back some of our money from the expensive Machu Picchu tour we're no longer taking. It would be a difficult enough task anywhere, but in Peru it seems insurmountable. Since Carly and I started traveling in South America, I've grown accustomed to letting her do the talking when we're in sticky situations like this. Or I pretend to be Canadian. What I've found is that Canadians are given the benefit of the doubt, whereas Americans are not. When demanding something from a Peruvian or Bolivian travel agent, he may ask where you are from. If you tell him you're American, he looks knowingly down at you, as though saying, "Of course you're causing trouble, then. That's what you people do. What—are you going to get a lawyer and sue me?" If you claim to be Canadian, however, he appears satisfyingly confused. Then he looks a little bit sad, as though he never intended to bring such a peaceful and rational person to the brink of insanity. You still won't get what you're asking for, but he'll let you yell at him a little bit longer as a courtesy, to get it out of your system and all.

But I'm sick of being the apologetic American trying to disprove stereotypes. The possible loss of both Machu Picchu and several hundred dollars is too much, so I do the only thing I can think of—I lie. I tell an elaborate fib to the tour operator, whereby I am the daughter of the American ambassador of tourism and Carly is the daughter of the Australian ambassador to Peru (I want it to seem believable, hence our not being daughters of exactly the same imaginary positions). We are in Peru on a tourism fact-finding mission, a kind of tourism ambassador internship, really, and boy, do we know people in high places. Does he think it's a good idea to upset the peaceful balance between our nations? Does he? He does not, so says the plain envelope he finally tucks in my palm with our cash nestled inside.

As exaggerated as it sounds, it is the first time I've ever truly asserted myself, used as I am to being the good girl, the one who avoids confrontation at any cost. I was used to navigating the icy space between my parents. I had found safety in their approval and, later, the praise of teachers and coaches and boys, anyone who would offer it to me. Now, however, I realize that if I'm going to take charge of my life, I have to start standing up for myself, and arguing with a Peruvian tour operator in broken Spanish seems as good a place to start as any.

# [ 22 ]

*Our heroine and her trusty guide reach Chile,*
*where they consider their impending separation*
*and a good many churches. Our heroine*
*searches the heavens for answers.*

We splurge on a forty-five-minute flight from Cusco to Arequipa,
a city near the bottom of Peru bursting with Spanish colonial-era
architecture wrought with striking alabaster-colored volcanic
rock. We spend the day rock climbing and rappelling in a canyon
outside the city center, accompanied by two skilled teen guides.
It takes us thirty-six hours by bus to reach La Serena, Chile, from
Arequipa. In that time, we descend from roads that zigzag
through the Andes into the Atacama desert, the driest in the
world. It extends 1,600 kilometers from the Pacific to the Andes.
In certain places not a single drop of rain has ever been recorded.
We head farther south down the narrow strip of land that is
Chile, and the scenery changes yet again at our destination. La
Serena is a sleepy little seaside town. It's the off-season here, just
the Serenians and a few backpackers on their way to somewhere
else. We're staying a block from the tiny main plaza in a place
run by the Chilean version of my grandmother. She is stout and

heavy, with the same drooping nose and chopping-block laugh. It wouldn't have surprised me one bit to hear her exclaim, "Oy vey!" Other elderly Chileans pepper the old hotel, but they have the air of fixtures. We appear to be the only guests.

La Serena is the city of churches. There are twenty-nine of them to see, if you're into that sort of thing, a few dominating ones and many tiny stone structures tucked away on side streets like secrets. In the plaza, a group of seniors gathers each after-noon to strum guitars and sing folk songs. There is a picturesque—though incongruous—Japanese garden, furnished with manicured lawns and wading swans, where we pass a blissful, lazy after-noon.

In La Serena, we exchange polite nods with trim Chileans we pass on the street, or are ignored altogether. I feel a distinct sense of relief at being back in the Chile/Argentina region of South America. It has been strengthening to face the challenges of trav-eling as a woman in Bolivia and Peru, but I cannot deny that I feel more at home in the other two countries. Carly, too, seems more relaxed, though I know she is as eager as ever to test herself with new trials. Our trip together is almost over. Since we met in Ireland, we've always had a plan to reunite, but now, for the first time, it's unclear when we will see each other again after I leave Buenos Aires in two weeks.

"I'm going to miss you," I tell her.

She laughs. "I'm still here!"

"You know what I mean."

"Yeah," she says. "I'm going to miss you, too."

We've been living and traveling together for so long that I can't even imagine what it will be like to wake up and not have her in the next room or the neighboring bed. In many ways, we understand each other more than anyone else in our current lives. She has borne witness to the person I've become on the road, and I have done the same for her.

In La Serena, we visit the famous Chilean observatory I've

been so eager to see. At seven P.M., we board a van with a quiet British guy; two British girls who spend the entire drive agreeing with each other about how difficult Spanish is to learn; and a six-foot-tall Swedish girl who asks after eyeing the magnificent twinkling sky through the powerful telescopes, "I'm just seeing a lot of stars. Is that it?"

We drive through Vicuña, home of the poet Gabriel Mistral, then up a mountain where the Observatorio Cerro Mamalluca occupies a royal spot above the city. It's pitch black and the clear night is stuffed with stars, like the night I spent in the Australian Outback feeling like I was exactly where I wanted to be. Our guide takes us into a white-domed room where a gleaming thirty-centimeter telescope extends out through a gap in the ceiling. He shows us Jupiter and Saturn (you can actually see the rings), Orion, and the Southern Cross. He tells us about the new planet they photographed a few weeks ago and talks excitedly about what we'll be able to see in the future when our telescopes are able to zoom even farther into the galaxy.

I had a brief love affair with astronomy in college. During my freshman year, I took an introductory solar-system course taught by an animated professor. In a spherical room with stadium seating, he lectured on the development of astronomy as a discipline, the motion of the planets, the sun's effects on the earth—all the basics.

I loved our discussions of other planets' atmospheres and moons, how they compared to Earth's, but most of all, I loved black holes. I was fascinated by gravitational time dilation, in which time passes more slowly or quickly depending on an object's distance from the black hole. If there was one thing I thought I could be certain of, it was the breakdown of years into months, months into days, days into hours, the even rhythm of the clock ticking away the minutes and seconds. The way time became flexible in the presence of these entities completely blew my mind.

Because I liked it so much, I excelled in my studies, and my professor encouraged me to take higher-level courses, but I begged off. I felt a sense of danger inherent in this new interest in the vast spaces beyond when I was in the midst of a battle for extreme focus on my music. I worried that to branch out in new directions was further evidence of my inability to meet the demands of my chosen field, that to turn my eyes up to the sky instead of keeping them concentrated on my prize would be to realize there was more to the world than my tiny basement practice room and that there was more to me, too, that was as undiscovered as the universe. After all these travels, I find I no longer have that fear. Life feels full of opportunity and possibility—and maybe even adventure.

# [ 23 ]

*The two friends take their leave of each other.*

Crossing the border back into Argentina is a welcome return. We take another overnight bus to save cash, pausing in hazy Santiago, Chile, for a few hours before arriving in Mendoza, a city on the Argentinean side of the Andes. It's a relaxing spot, wide tree-lined streets filled with cafés offering outdoor seating under broad umbrellas. The main square, Plaza Independencia, provides a home for an artisans market during the afternoons. We stroll around the shaded walkways, checking out the various leather goods and handmade jewelry. At night various performers take the artists' places.

In Argentina, we're back in the world of hostels. The one in Mendoza costs us twelve pesos a night, about four U.S. dollars. In the evenings, a group of us pitch in a few pesos each so someone can run off and buy *asado* supplies. We pile up to the rooftop terrace and dish out salad and potatoes and meat. Massive amounts of wine and beer circulate, and so does the dense, rich ice cream that has become a staple of our diet since arriving in Mendoza. In the wee hours of the morning, anyone still awake squeezes into the tiny common room to smoke thin cigarettes and watch nineties movies starring Keanu Reeves.

Our plans were to head farther south in a day or two, to Bariloche on another dreaded overnight bus, but we're indecisive. Mendoza is such a peaceful little spot, and there are enough wineries and trekking in the area to keep us occupied. I'm inclined not to seek something better than the good life we're already experiencing, and for once Carly seems to feel the same way. We're quite pleased with ourselves, with all we have accomplished, and spending a week in Mendoza relaxing and recounting our adventures is an appealing idea.

The only thing that interrupts my tranquil state of mind is the fact that in two weeks I will be back in the U.S. A familiar anticipatory depression starts to cloud my vision, though Carly does her best to pull me out of it.

"If you keep thinking along those lines, you're not going to enjoy these last few weeks at all," she says matter-of-factly, and of course she is right. Still, I cannot entirely extract the excitement of our last weeks together—plus seeing Martyn again in another week, and Muriel, who is coming a few days after that to travel with Carly for three weeks—from the inevitable set of goodbyes that awaits me.

Now that the Internet connections are better, we've been checking email once a day, and mine is awash with questions from parents and friends. I have run out of money and have to suffer the humiliation of asking my mother to borrow four hundred dollars. That's all I have to my name, and the pressure to remedy this situation upon my return weighs on me. I don't feel any closer to being ready to start a career or even some random job.

"Did you see the sign at that shop?" I ask Carly one day when we're walking back to our hostel. "They're hiring an English teacher here."

Although Carly and I have known each other only a few years, I am totally transparent to her. We've lived and traveled together for months, and there is no place to hide any part of myself. By now our innermost thoughts are completely available to each other so she knows me well enough to realize that I'm imagining what it would be like to live in South America. "You could stay," she tells me.

It sounds easy when she says it, like it really is possible. Back home, my parents are waiting for me to start my "real life," which, now that I have a college degree, I'm pretty sure does not include wearing the same T-shirt every day. My friends are a year into their Manhattan careers; they live in tiny studios, dress in tailored suits, and charge their BlackBerries. I look down my jeans to my dirty flip-flops. Suddenly, I cannot think of anything more depressing than heels.

I could stay, I tell myself. People do it all the time. They just forget their old life and get a new one.

But going home is about more than starting a real life. I have to return and face all the questions I've left unanswered. To stay would be running away from the expectations awaiting me, not confronting them, like I need to. In travel, I have found a passion, and I know I will keep on seeing the world. But I have to go home and make some conscious choices about my perhaps less-traditional-than-my-parents-hoped-for place in the world.

Carly has begun considering her circumstances as well. She is extending her South America ticket instead of returning to Australia with Muriel. She feels like she fits in here with the people and the culture. The Wild Thornberrys' stories (minus Kevin's nasty puma incident) have worked on her these last few weeks, and she's toying with the idea of volunteering. She's going to settle in South America for a while, learn the language, and see what she can make happen. We have heard murmurings especially of Colombia from other backpackers, and the idea has been creeping into Carly's brain that that country might just be the next to conquer.

Travel is a complicated animal for both of us. We're running away from home on some level, and at the same time, we're sprinting toward what we want most—the fulfilling, unpredictable lives we've carved out for ourselves on the road—our versions of the real world that we love so much.

The wineries in Mendoza are flourishing, and there are no two more eager to witness their tremendous beauty and growth than Carly and me now that we've dropped to an altitude where the smallest sip of alcohol doesn't leave us with throbbing hangovers. The hostel books us a day tour of several different wineries, and when the van arrives to collect us, we are the youngest of the group by a good three decades. At the first stop, we stare down into a massive barrel holding millions of tiny handpicked red grapes ready for destemming and crushing. After the fermentation process, the concoction will descend into the bowels of the building to enormous wooden casks, protected from the elements by thick stone walls. Here it waits, sometimes for years. I think back to Jenny from Buenos Aires. I picture her gathering up her peasant skirt to step inside, her feet sinking down into the grapes like quicksand. I wonder whether she has made her way to this same winery, and where she is now.

At the end of each tour, we get free wine samples with olives and sun-dried tomatoes. We drink heavily from the glasses, getting tipsy enough to scandalize a few of the older members of our tour who are swirling and sniffing the wine, taking a swig, then spitting it back out as delicately as one can expectorate. Carly and I take no notice of their disapproval. We're in our own little happy world of sneaking more free samples and taking increasingly silly photos of ourselves in the cellar, where we pretend to glug straight from the casks. Our exchanges are full of in-jokes and completing each other's sentences. We're proud of ourselves and our experiences and determined to enjoy ourselves now that we have survived them more or less gracefully. We buy a few of the cheapest bottles. Back in Mendoza, we gather together some massive hunks of cheese and proceed to gorge ourselves on the combination for many blissful hours.

We leave our hostel to ascend into the Andes for a few days. Our first activity is a four-hour horseback ride meandering through the mountains to get a glimpse of the enormous black condors swooping through the cloudy skies. They come close enough to let us see their priestlike ensemble, black bodies with white tufts of feathers ringing their necks. My horse, Marcello, is chocolate brown with a cream strip between his eyes. He's fond of being the leader of our pack, but we're not allowed to overtake the guide, a constant point of contention for Carly, who wants to race ahead of us all. I amble along with a chatty Frenchman, Aurelian, who wishes please to know if I am related to the very famous French Dr. Friedman who was the first in the country to develop test-tube babies. When I say I am not, he pats me on the back. "Okay, okay," he says, as though comforting me.

At night we stay at a little hostel twenty-five hundred meters up in the mountains, nothing but snow-covered peaks in all directions. Aurelian stays for dinner, then heads back to Mendoza for the night, leaving Carly and me as the only guests. We wrap ourselves up in front of the stone fireplace and drink one hot chocolate after another. The steaming glasses are delivered to us filled three quarters with whole milk and a big chunk of half-melted chocolate. We assume the drinks are included in our fee, but at the end of our stay, we get a bill for the eight we consumed within forty-eight hours, mostly in front of the perpetually burning fire with old reruns of *Friends* playing on the small TV.

In the morning, we wake to snow. Inches have fallen while we slept, and the whole place seems buried away like Brigadoon. Because of the direction of my travels, I've missed winter back home and haven't seen snow in over a year. For Carly, it's been much longer, so we head out to kick around in it. It's not the kind of heavy, sticky snow good for making snowmen, but Carly manages a miniature one complete with a button nose. She steps back to admire her work and is congratulating herself on her ingenuity when a dog emerges from out of nowhere like an apparition, trots over to the snowman, and pees directly on it.

"He's ruining my masterpiece," she grumbles. "Oi, dog!"

"Maybe he's just turning it into performance art," I joke.

Back in Mendoza we decide to go paragliding. Carly loans me the ninety pesos to come with her, since I've budgeted my final days down to the last penny with no wiggle room.

Paragliding feels nothing like skydiving or bungee jumping. Whereas both of those activities were accompanied by the adrenaline of free fall, paragliding is floating through the sky. We glide like condors attached to our blue half-moon parachutes. The guides strapped behind us control our movements while we stare down at the slowly approaching land. Even the first race off the cliff, where we must catch the wind precisely, is in surreal slow motion. When our sneakers leave the ground, the wind catches us and carries us up for a few seconds like a parent lifting a toddler to embrace her. For thirty minutes we make our lazy way to the ground. Thirty minutes soaring, riding wind currents that lift us higher and lower. At the bottom, people are lying on their backs in the flatbeds of parked trucks. Most of them are paragliders, but some obviously just like to watch the bodies float down to earth for entertainment, or maybe to see the look of someone who has just experienced the awesome sensation of flying for the first time.

\* \* \*

I leave for Buenos Aires by myself. Carly wants to stay for a few days to take a paragliding course so she can fly alone, but I have plans with Martyn. Even though Carly and I will each see each other soon, this smaller parting registers the larger one to come. I charge the ultimate luxury to my credit card, a seat on a bus whose plush seats recline all the way back, and sleep almost the entire way to Buenos Aires.

I don't see much of the city this time, at least not during the day. I do see lots of my hotel room, where Martyn and I set up house, the contents of our backpacks strewn across every available surface. He and his friends have rented rooms in a hotel instead of a hostel, fancier and more expensive accommodation than anywhere Carly and I have stayed in our three months in South America. The room Martyn and I share even has a quaint balcony that overlooks a tiny shop where teens gather after school lets out, smoking and gossiping like teens anywhere. In the bathroom, our toothbrushes sit side by side. I purchased a painting in Cuzco that I hang on the wall, desperate to make it feel like a homey apartment the two of us share. We are in love, in the very beginning part of it, when you don't ever want to separate your body from the other person's.

Since the story of Martyn and me could fill another book entirely, and because this is not a love story and I do not wish it to be, let me simply summarize our week in Buenos Aires. We fit. When he curls up behind me, his knees lock perfectly behind mine, his arms offer exactly the right amount of embrace—somewhere between protection and ownership, desire and comfort. Our physical match is met by an emotional and intellectual one. With Martyn, I hold forth some of the philosophies I've been honing since beginning my travels in Ireland almost two years ago, about universal health care and the travel practices of American youth, about my country and the way I was indoctrinated to believe that America was number one in everything, but actually people in other countries have what we have—and sometimes better—about my obligations as a daughter, about the ways that I have put my faith in all the wrong things and now I am hopelessly lost but at the same time realizing that's okay so maybe that means I'm not lost at all, just searching.

"I'm afraid I'll lose this freedom when I go home," I confess.

"Your life is your own," he says, exactly what I need to hear.

Martyn is twenty-seven, five years older, and more comfortable in his own skin than anyone I have ever met. While I'm prone to being tied up in existential knots, he is entirely at ease in the present moment. He is a vortex of confidence, straight talk, and irresistible charm. I want to hold on and never let go. To him I am a passionate twenty-two-year-old, exuberant and searching and in love with this travel version of myself. Maybe that's why we met when we did, when I had come so far on my own. When we say goodbye, neither of us talks about the future, afraid we might not have one after Buenos Aires.


Carly arrives three days before my flight back to the U.S. Muriel is there, too, in time to see me off. The two of them are headed back up to Peru, where Carly is planning to try her luck a second time at Machu Picchu. The three of us stand outside the open doors of the airport shuttle, dusk descending on the city, and try unsuccessfully not to cry.

"Oh, Rach," Muriel sighs. "What will you and Carly do without each other?"

I honestly don't know. In all of my travels, she is the common thread. I knew initially that I needed her more than she needed me. She had arrived at precisely the right moment, when I was floundering and longed for someone to show me there was another way to live my life. But somewhere in South America, I stopped needing her as a guide, and we became equals. That's how we are leaving each other—and as best friends.

In the end, we don't say goodbye at all.

"Let's make a pact," I say. "We'll meet every five years in a new city."

"If not before then," Carly says.

"If not before then."

We throw our arms around each other and blubber into each other's hair. I flash on an image of us in Paris when we're ninety, sipping cappuccinos in the sun—old, arthritic women who have seen every corner of the world.

I have only three pesos in my pocket and no way to get more when the agent at the airport announces the departure tax is close to twenty U.S. dollars.

"I don't have it," I tell him.

"You must pay this tax," he says. "Or you cannot leave."

"I can't," I insist. "I have no money." I have nothing, I think, no money, no possessions to speak of, nothing concrete to show for myself. Yet other than the departure tax, I've got everything I need. The agent and I stare at each other.

"Please?" I try again.

"Next!" he yells.

"How much do you need?" This question comes from the pretty Argentinean woman behind me, clutching her small son by the hand. The man repeats the figure, and before I can protest, she has handed him a few scrunched bills. "Shame on you," she tells the agent. "Can't you see this young girl is just trying to get home?"

# [ 24 ]

*Our heroine returns home, where many*
*unanswered questions await her.*

I arrive in New York City during rush hour. I'm staying at Erica's tonight and having dinner with her, Tara, and Jen in a few hours. The city is a live organism: jackhammer accents, manic jostling, the odors of fried meat mixing with sweaty, hurrying bodies. A sea of people march in every direction, chattering to one another or into cell phones, punctuated by the constant beeping of car horns. I tuck myself out of the way to catch my breath and lean my backpack against the side of a high-rise. A trail of suits and skirts flows in and out of the building. Suddenly, I feel self-conscious about my handmade Andean sweater and ratty fisherman pants, my cheap flip-flops.

"Excuse me?" says the one person in Manhattan even more dazed than I am. She's brandishing an enormous map. "Can you tell me where Lincoln Center is?" Being addressed on the street in English is disorienting, like Spanish was those first few weeks. I have to think my answer before saying it aloud.

"That way." I point confidently to my left. The South American trait of claiming you know the answer to a question no matter what has apparently rubbed off on me, since I'm only half certain Lincoln Center is in fact in that direction. I've only been to NYC a few times. I barely know where I am myself.

I find my way to Erica's aunt's apartment, where she has been living the past few months until she finds her own place. Erica is at work but has arranged for the doorman to let me into the beautiful one-bedroom in a geriatric neighborhood on Seventy-fourth and Madison. It's sparsely decorated, like a hotel room, or like an apartment someone resides in only a few days a month (as Erica's Connecticut aunt does) or who works so much she's hardly ever home—as Er does.

The far wall of the living room is a row of tall windows stacked above an inviting bench piled high with decorative pillows. This is where I ensconce myself for the next few hours, blissfully watching the people on the streets below without having to hear any of the city's noise, like a silent film.

In the afternoon, I take a long, hot shower. The city grime between my toes streaks down into the drain. Erica's body wash is from some boutique store I've never heard of. The brand is a blossoming blue flower, and it smells like lemon. I lather myself up three times, then let the steaming water slowly wash it away. I take a nap in Erica's enormous, soft bed. Even after showering, I feel as though I'm not clean enough for the immaculate apartment, so I stay atop the covers instead of wriggling beneath them.

When Erica arrives home around seven, I'm munching Triscuits over the sink, trying not to get any crumbs on my one semi-clean shirt or in the spotless apartment. She is dressed in a charcoal skirt and jacket. Her long curly hair is tucked back in a straightened ponytail. When she slips off her black heels, I notice the faded Prada label.

"Friend!" she shouts. We hug fiercely. She's always been slender, but now she's model-thin, all sharp angles. "Tell me everything about the last nine months," she says.

We sit on the couch, and I tell her about Carly and the Dawsons and Martyn. I tell her about the Outback and bedbugs in Peru. I tell her about Hans and his fear of knots. Every few minutes she checks her blinking BlackBerry, sends a text, then puts it back on the glass coffee table.

"What about you? How is your job?" I ask.

"Awful," she says, smiling. "I work all the time. I leave at seven and usually get home at midnight. Once every few weeks, we have some stupid project due and I have to stay there all night. I haven't slept over five hours in the last six months. I barely have time to eat."

She does seem jittery, like a person who doesn't get enough sleep and food. And she seems distracted.

"What are you going to do?" I ask.

"Wait until I get promoted and then leave."

"How long will that take?"

"Maybe six months, maybe a year." She shrugs, sends another text.

"Where are we going tonight?"

"To a little Italian place in the West Village."

"What should I wear?" I ask her, knowing that what I have on is pretty much my only option.

"It's New York casual," she tells me, sends another text. I feel like I've landed on another planet.

Tara and Jen are waiting for us at the restaurant. They've secured a round table by the window and ordered us a bottle of Australian Shiraz to celebrate my return. More hugs, more catching up. Tara loves her job teaching at the 92nd Street Y. "Cutest kiddies ever," she summarizes. Jen's job in finance isn't quite as demanding as Erica's, and she doesn't hate it quite as much, but she doesn't exude any sort of happiness while talking about it. "It's a living, you know?" she says.

I tell more stories. I describe the adorable squirrel monkeys that ate out of my hand in Bolivia, my raucous jeep tour to the salt flats, the magnificent *totora*-reed floating islands. I cannot stop talking about my travels, bubbling over with enthusiasm and epiphanies, even after my friends have run out of steam for polite "uh-huhs" and their eyes have glazed over or they are staring drowsily at their wineglasses. In the last nine months, we've moved in completely opposite directions, and I'm wondering if we have anything in common now other than our shared college years. We're catching up on the big events of our lives, but I've missed almost a year's worth of the small ones, which are what most female friendships need in order to survive. I wonder what Carly's doing at this moment.

After we've paid the bill, we stand around for a few clunky minutes outside the restaurant.

"So what's next?" Jen asks.

"Not sure, really," I say. "I'm going to see my mom for a few days and consider my options."

"My friend is looking for a roommate if you want to come to the city," Tara offers.

"Come to the city!" Erica cries. "It will be so fun!"

"Maybe," I say. "Who knows?"

"Either way, let's def get together soon, okay?" Jen says.

"Definitely," I reply, though I have no clue where I'll be "soon," and the exchange is rather halfhearted on both ends.

Jen and Tara air-kiss me on both cheeks. "Love you, girl," Tara shouts as they are walking away.


In the morning I take the train upstate. The town is the same; that much can be counted on. There's Sno Top, the popular local ice-cream stand, which will open in a few months once the warm weather arrives. Next to it is the swan pond, behind that the local library. Farther down the road at the intersection, you can turn right to go to the video or liquor store, left if you want to get a beer at the dive bar or have a meal at the only Chinese restaurant around. Across the way is Pavone's, the pizza place where I killed time with my friends when I was a teenager.

I grew up a few streets past the video and liquor stores. Turn left up a steep hill until you reach the very top, where my old house used to sit hidden behind trees. Our labyrinthine drive-way was never paved, and I'd walk up and down it in my bare feet, convinced I could harden them to the point where pain would no longer exist. I was so proud of my callused heels—of their strength and functionality. I pictured myself walking across hot coals amid awestruck audiences.

I was ten years old when my mother began to work furiously on her garden, which up until then consisted solely of a few neglected azaleas. My mother proved to have the proverbial green thumb. Everything she touched in the backyard bloomed with enthusiasm, and we were awash in cherry tomatoes, green peppers, and squash. My father mostly stayed indoors, writing and grading. All that came to life in my father's study was his first book. Neither appeared overly impressed with the other's efforts.

When I turned thirteen, I asked my friends to write on my bedroom walls. Dylan's lyrics and Plath's poetry mingled with the intense and garbled insights of teenagers. Sometimes, while examining the work at night, I discovered lines I'd never witnessed being scrawled. While my parents bred plants and words, I grew miniature epiphanies on those scrapbook walls.

When I returned home from college for the first time, I found the written revelations housed in that room painted over in a sterile creamy white. My mother informed me she was selling the house. "Too many memories," she said, as though that was a bad thing. The last time I saw my old house was two years ago. The new family had put up a basketball hoop and paved over the driveway. I knew the backyard no longer belonged to my mother's tomato plants. They had cut down all the trees out front where I used to camp out and pretend I'd run away.

The few times I returned to my mother's new house during college breaks, I was inevitably drawn to the closet in the guest room, which housed my photo albums, old gushy letters to pen pals, various children's books, stuffed animals, and shirts I will never wear again (both because they no longer fit but also because sporting the quote OLD COMPOSERS NEVER DIE, THEY JUST DE-COMPOSE is no longer as cool as it once was). Always under the guise of *finally* cleaning out this portal to my past, I would begin the slow process of rooting through my things, having forgotten three quarters of what was in there. Everything I touched was attached to a memory, and I went whizzing from one year of my life to the next. Here was the sweatshirt my dad bought me from the local college where he used to teach, there stood the *Nutcracker* collection from our old mother-daughter tradition of attending the ballet each winter. Eventually, typically when I was cross-legged on a bed that was completely covered in old pictures, journals, and the nostalgia party to which all my raggedy stuffed animals had been invited, I grew first exhausted from the emotional shuttling back and forth in time, then overwhelmed by my options to: 1) put it all away again, 2) throw it away (sometimes I manage to toss out an old Tiffany cassette or two, but never much more), or 3) go through the rest of the now disheveled closet. Most times I decide to stuff it all back in. Halfway through this task, I'd get bored and collapse on the couch to watch *Dirty Dancing* in one of the patchwork hippie dresses I used to wear to Phish concerts in high school. I always left my mother's house with the closet in disarray, items haphazardly stuffed back inside, but when I arrived for my next visit, the closet had been put back together, photo albums neatly stacked on the appropriate labeled shelf, old prom dresses hung up in order of appearance.

Upon returning to my mother's house after traveling, I instinctively move toward the closet. I open the door. An old shoe box with the word "teacups" in my grandmother's handwriting stares back at me. But I don't remove anything. I don't even reach inside. For once it simply looks like a closet full of stuff I don't remember owning.

After nearly a week of sleeping away the days, my parents and I engage in a series of conversations about my future, my mother's in person and my father's over the phone. My father is secretly relieved I'm home. A Ph.D. in English might be just the ticket now. "It's in your blood," he says ominously.

My mother isn't so sure. "Maybe you should talk to Ed's kids," she says. Her husband's two grown children work in corporate advertising. "Tanya is working on the Philip Morris campaign right now, and you should see the perks she gets!" she tells me.

"Philip Morris, as in the cigarette company?" I ask her.

"Well, yes."

"You want me to work for a cigarette company?"

"I didn't say that, Rachel," she says, her lips tightening. "I'm just trying to help. You have to do something."

I open my viola case. I haven't touched the instrument in over a year. It's the longest I've ever gone without playing it since I picked it up when I was eight. I bring it to my shoulder, put it under my chin. I draw out a long note. I play one of Bach's cello suites, letting my bow roll over the strings. I'm rusty, not precisely in tune. But I feel something stir inside me. Some ray of passion is still burning. I thought I had extinguished it that year in music school, but here it is again.

With my parents, I commit to nothing but another helping of French toast. I mumble incoherently about how I want my life to be different. When I can't take it anymore, I drive out to my sister's in Rhode Island. We dig our toes into the sand and stare into the ocean together, and I am grateful she doesn't ever ask me what my plans are.

I'm still in possession of that graduate-school acceptance letter to Trinity. One day I bring it to the beach with me. I ball it up inside my left hand and dive into the freezing Atlantic. When I emerge, blue ink drips like alien blood through my fingers and streaks down my forearm. Guess I've made at least one definitive decision about my life.

One night I'm up late watching TV on my sister's beat-up couch when *The Wizard of Oz* comes on. It's been digitally remastered, so now the ruby slippers are incandescent red. *The Wizard of Oz* is the first film I ever saw. Other kids were terrified of the flying monkeys. They covered their eyes or ducked below the sticky cinema seats. But these creatures had no hold over me. No, what sent me into my father's arms was the scene where Dorothy's house gets caught up in the tornado. How would Dorothy ever find her way home if her house has disappeared? I demanded to know. Her entire family would move away without her; they'd forget her. And I never believed the ending, in which she clicks her heels three times and says, "There's no place like home," then is transported back to her pre-Oz world. Even then I sensed that nothing would ever be the same, and this made me terribly sad. More perplexing was that the film wanted us to believe Dorothy's experiences in Oz were a fantasy. I asked myself then, as now: Could it all really have been just a dream?

What seems strange is how little going to Ireland was about traveling. Ireland equaled far, far away, not the beginning of some profound journey. In saying that, I realize that a part of me must also have been implanted somewhere along the way with the kind of curiosity inherent in people who ultimately stuff all their worldly possessions into a backpack and disappear for months at a time. What happens when we lose the things that anchor us? What if, instead of grasping at something to hold on to, we pull up our roots and walk away? Instead of trying to find the way back, we walk deeper and deeper into the woods, willing ourselves to get lost. In this place where nothing is recognizable, not the people or the language or the food, we are truly on our own. Eventually, we find ourselves unencumbered by the past or the future. Here is a fleeting glimpse of our truest self, our self in the present moment. After that, maybe we can finally go home—or maybe not.

Before, some places just seemed too far, too difficult to reach, but once you start traveling, you never want to stop. You want to hear other people's stories, see where they live, eat their food. You realize—and of course it's a cliché, but like many clichés, it's true—the way we are all interconnected. Like music, that porous reality I could enter into even in my darkest moments. Back home, this other reality has been waiting for me: the job, the apartment, the bills, the permanent address. It feels heavy. Even the thought of it weighs me down. I'm not ready for that. It can wait. For me, at least. It's hard being home. I cling to the hard-won discoveries about myself that I've made these last months, but it's easy to get distracted. The old voices of expectation are there, waiting. Only I can decide whether or not to listen. I have to keep reminding myself over and over what I want. Carly was right. Ever my wise guide, she told me I was looking for adventure, and, well, even if I wasn't, it found me.

What I found on the road was a tiny piece of myself, the one I kept unknowingly shuttered for so long in order to play the many roles I thought were mine. It was no cyclone, but these past few years I had survived my own personal disasters and realized I was strong enough. I was on the other side. In this new place, I could hear the whispering voice inside my head growing louder, *my* voice—not those of my parents or teachers or Carly or Muriel, even—telling me to live my life without fear or worry or doubt that nothing was going according to plan, as though such a plan ever existed in the first place.

# [ Epilogue ]

I never saw Carly Dawson again.

Just kidding. I saw her a few months ago, when I visited her in Colombia. She's living there now, doing what she does best: traveling, volunteering, and occasionally risking her life. She ended up staying in Buenos Aires for two years after we parted ways in South America. Since our travels together, she has set foot in dozens of new cities. She's been a bus driver, an ESL teacher, a telemarketer, and a master crocheter. During those same years, my own passport has filled up enough to have to send away for extra pages. I've lived in London; I've trekked through Thailand; I've snorkeled in Fiji. It turns out Martyn and I did have a future, though it was a long and windy one—as often happens when you fall in love with someone from a different country. It eventually led to a raucous wedding in New Zealand, a closet-sized apartment in Manhattan, and a very fat beagle named Tyler.

# Acknowledgments

First I must thank the wild and lovely Carly, without whom my life would be infinitely less heart-stopping. Thank you for helping me with this book and for being my friend. Thanks to my husband, Martyn, who encouraged me throughout this process, and reminded me that just because I'm a writer doesn't mean I should wear pajamas all day. Thanks to my own parents, and also to Delia and Sandy, my second set of parents, and to Muriel and Pete, my Australian parents. And thanks to Erica, who is always there when I need her, as are all my wonderful friends.

I'm insanely lucky to have my agent, Jane Dystel, who is always on my side, and answers emails faster than I can type them. I'm forever grateful to Miriam Goderich, who gave me a chance. Danielle Perez was a warm and intelligent editor, and Marisa Vigilante has been a dream to work with. My appreciation goes out to Beth Thomas, Beth Pearson, and Jane von Mehren—and to all those at Random House who made this book happen.

There are too many others to thank, and if this were the Oscars the music would have started by now: James Goodman, Mauro Altamura, Scott Bowman, Leslie Mitchner, Carol Sasson, Gordon Moore, Patricia DeAngelis, Margie Nichols, Pat Bentley, Diane Cook. Lastly, thanks to all those travelers who appear in the book. I hope you're still out there on the road somewhere.

PHOTO: © TOM JUDGE

RACHEL FRIEDMAN has worked, lived, and/or traveled in more than twenty countries. Her writing has been published in *The Arizona Republic, Syracuse New Times, Get Lost Magazine,* and Brave New Traveler, among others. A graduate of the University of Pennsylvania and the creative nonfiction program at Rutgers-Newark, she teaches literature at John Jay College of Criminal Justice. She is married to a New Zealander she met in an Irish bar in Peru. They reside in Manhattan...for now.

## About the Type

The text of this book was set in a digitized version of Figural, a typeface originally designed in 1940 by the Czech calligrapher and book designer Oldřich Menhart. It is an expressionistic face, echoing the forms of rough, pen-made letters.